Intimate Disconnections

Intimate Disconnections

Divorce and the Romance of Independence in Contemporary Japan

ALLISON ALEXY

The University of Chicago Press

Chicago and London

The University of Chicago Press, Chicago 60637
The University of Chicago Press, Ltd., London
© 2020 by The University of Chicago
Published 2020
Printed in the United States of America

29 28 27 26 25 24 23 22 21 20   1 2 3 4 5

ISBN-13: 978-0-226-69965-3 (cloth)
ISBN-13: 978-0-226-70095-3 (paper)
ISBN-13: 978-0-226-70100-4 (e-book)
DOI: https://doi.org/10.7208/chicago/9780226701004.001.0001

Library of Congress Cataloging-in-Publication Data

Names: Alexy, Allison, author.
Title: Intimate disconnections : divorce and the romance of independence in
    contemporary Japan / Allison Alexy.
Description: Chicago : University of Chicago Press, 2020. |
    Includes bibliographical references and index.
Identifiers: LCCN 2019045142 | ISBN 9780226699653 (cloth) |
    ISBN 9780226700953 (paperback) | ISBN 9780226701004 (ebook)
Subjects: LCSH: Divorce—Japan. | Marriage—Japan.
Classification: LCC HQ937.A549 2020 | DDC 306.89—dc23
LC record available at https://lccn.loc.gov/2019045142

♾ This paper meets the requirements of ANSI/NISO Z39.48-1992 (Permanence of Paper).

For my mother, Alice Gorham

Contents

A Note on Names

All names and identifying details included in this book have been made pseudonymous and have been written in the Japanese order with family names first. In the Japanese language, there are many degrees of familiarity demonstrated by the name you use for someone. Adding -*sama* to a name, for example, demonstrates your belief that the other person deserves a lot of respect. To a lesser degree, adding -*san* is often the polite thing to do and is a respectful way to refer to people with whom you have a professional relationship. Usually, -san is added to a person's family name. Although calling someone Tanaka-san could be glossed as Mr. Tanaka, Mrs. Tanaka, or Ms. Tanaka, it does not seem nearly as distancing in Japanese as it does in English, and instead just sounds polite. In more intimate relationships, names often get truncated—Makiko becoming Maki or Ma, for example—and gendered suffixes can be added. Thus if I am very close friends with a woman named Tanaka Makiko, I might call her Maki-chan or Ma-chan, whereas a stranger would use Tanaka-san or maybe Tanaka-sama.

Following these conventions, although I have changed all names in the book, I represent different kinds of names as a way giving the reader a sense of relationships. Each name is a negotiation that demonstrates the quality of our relationship, and I have maintained these variations in the pseudonyms I am using. Thus, I refer to some people using -san, some by first names, some by nicknames. There is nothing systematic, but the complexity reflects the reality of our relationships. Many people referred to me as Ally, Ally-chan, or Ally-san, which conveniently capture the sounds of both my first and last names.

Anxiety and Freedom

In February 2006, I stepped into an elevator with a middle-aged Japanese man. I had never met him before and we had no connection but, presumably noticing that I did not look Japanese, he struck up a conversation by politely asking why I was in Tokyo. When I explained I was researching divorce and contemporary family change, he responded with a bit of nervous laughter and then said, "*All* the men I know are scared. *We're all scared.*" With little prompting from me, this man volunteered his fear of divorce or, more specifically, his anxiety that his wife would divorce him against his will. He shared these very personal worries even before he introduced himself. Yamaguchi-san's willingness to discuss these fears with a stranger was matched by his assuredness that he wasn't the only one feeling anxious. As scared as Yamaguchi-san was of getting divorced, he was sure other men were in similar positions because divorce was a threat hanging over many of them. As we walked to the nearest train station, he elaborated on his reasons for worrying that his wife might leave him, including their separate hobbies and friend groups, as well as his career that kept him frequently out of their home. Those reasons were no less real for being so common, but divorce was also in the air. A recent legal change stood to provide divorcing wives more financial stability than ever granted before. This seismic shift had made Yamaguchi-san, and other married men like him, suddenly more anxious that their wives would abandon them.

At the same time, other people felt distinctly different emotions in imagining divorce. A middle-aged woman, Nagako-san giggled as she told me about her plans to divorce her husband. She was gleeful at the thought. As a housewife in her midfifties who had supported her husband's career for more than twenty years, Nagako-san embodied stereotypes of gendered labor division in Japanese postwar society. She started narrating a litany of her husband's serious faults a few minutes after I met her. She had been unhappy in the marriage for years but finding email evidence that he had been having a long-term affair was the final straw—or *almost* the final straw. At our first meeting, in a support group organized around family issues, Nagako-san had not yet made legal moves to divorce her husband but was visibly enjoying her plans to do so. In contrast to Yamaguchi-san, for whom divorce portended only looming solitude, Nagako-san veritably exploded with joy imagining all the possibilities divorce could manifest for her. As she described it, divorce symbolized a vital step toward freedom and happiness.

Although divorce has been legal in Japan for centuries, and the divorce rate has risen unsteadily throughout the postwar period, early in the twenty-first century divorce in Japan rapidly became a newly visible and viable option in ways it had never been before. People who had never before thought seriously about divorce were fantasizing about leaving their spouses. Some moved past fantasizing to explicit planning and took concrete steps to end marriages. Others were anxious they might get suddenly abandoned. Such fears and fantasies were reflected in popular media, which were awash in discourse about divorce. Television dramas that centered around divorce garnered surprisingly high ratings especially with older viewers, and newspapers and weekly magazines published "how to" guides about requesting divorces or navigating the legal process, as well as "how not to" advice about improving a marriage (Saitō 2005). Daily talk shows offered quizzes to measure marital strength and often tailored answers by gender and age, suggesting certain actions, for instance, that older men might take to improve their marriages. Guidebooks gave generalized advice, such as in *Divorce Makes Some People Happy but Others Miserable* and *Definitely No Regrets: The Easy Guide to Divorce* (Yanagihara and Ōtsuka 2013; Okano 2001). But publishers also targeted smaller segments of readership with advice books titled *Parents and Children after Divorce, My Husband is a Stranger,* and *The Best Divorce Strategies for Men* (Himuro 2005; Okano 2008; Tsuyuki 2010). The government and local municipalities published new websites advising men and, especially, women about their legal rights after divorce. People who sought therapeutic counseling found many more options than had been available ten or twenty years before, and anyone interested could now easily find on- or offline counseling sessions, support groups, or therapists. With all of this activity, divorce had become a more viable option in mainstream consciousness, and many people were thinking, planning, worrying, and fantasizing about it. Although it was slightly unusual for Yamaguchi-san to strike up a conversation about divorce with a stranger in an elevator, that kind of spontaneous attention to the topic was not as extreme as it might seem, given that debating the risks and hopes surrounding divorce had become a mainstay of popular, private, and governmental discourse.

This book examines divorce as a moment of personal and familial transition, situated within a broader context in which previous norms, social contracts, and implicit guarantees are no longer secure but might nonetheless remain attractive to some people. As people fantasize about divorce or attempt to save a marriage, they debate and discuss how best to create and sustain healthy relationships with other people, as well as the risks and possibilities that disconnection brings. In these discussions, almost every term is ripe for debate, from what exactly makes a marriage "good" to the foreseeable and unforeseeable risks that come with divorce, including the effects it might have on children. On a personal level, the idea of divorce often prompts serious reflection about the specific characteristics of relationships that cause harm, provide security, create opportunity, or simply feel good. This book traces how people are trying to figure out what they want—in a marriage, in family relationships, in life—at the same time as they struggle with manifesting those needs and desires in relationships with other people. At individual, familial, and national levels, in the early 2000s divorce prompted serious conversations about the value of relationships and the risks and security they bring to the people involved in them. How could people feel confident deciding which relationships should end?

Intimate Disconnections argues that when considering divorce, Japanese men and women often struggle to reconcile tensions they perceive between intimacy, connection, and dependence. As people try to decide what reasons justify ending a marriage, connection and dependence become defining yet unstable measures by which to judge the quality, security, and success of intimate relationships. These framing terms reflect the intersection of ideologies surrounding romantic love, Japanese cultural models for relationality, and the increasing popularity of neoliberal ethics privileging individuality and personal responsibility. In these models, Japanese men and women find recommendations about what makes intimate relationships strong, how to repair problematic marriages, or, potentially, when to leave an unsatisfying spouse. But they also find contradictions and dilemmas, particularly surrounding the types of subjectivities best suited for partnerships and the divergent methods necessary to strengthen a marriage as opposed to a family.

As men and women consider divorce, or work to avoid it, they face questions about the risks and possibilities intimate relationships bring: How can people be intimate without becoming suffocatingly close? How should one build meaningful, loving, or supportive relationships when older models for behavior no longer feel feasible? What styles of intimacy most benefit the people in a marriage, families more generally, or the nation as a whole? When does disconnection become a salvation or rescue, and when is it just evidence of selfishness? Or, to put it in more human terms, what do you do when you just can't take it anymore?

The End of Permanence

Throughout Japan's postwar period, heterosexual marriage has been a powerfully normative social force, marking married people as responsible social adults (*shakaijin*, literally "social person"). The vast majority of people got married, and being in a heterosexual marriage demonstrated a person's "normalcy" (Dasgupta 2005; McLelland 2005). In the early twenty-first century, however, both the centrality of heterosexual marriages and the particular forms those relationships should take are being implicitly and explicitly called into question. Many public debates and private conversations compare contemporary relationships with the relational ideals of older generations, describing newer practices, preferences, or recommendations in explicit comparison with what used to be normal. When commentators articulate tips to save marriages, or metrics by which to judge the quality of a relationship, frequently they are idealizing intimate behaviors diametrically opposed to patterns popular just a generation before. Those patterns' predominance in postwar Japan made them seem effectively permanent, which only exacerbates the anxious rhetoric circulating about divorce as its frequency mounts.

The increase in public and media attention to divorce was coupled with, but not only a response to, an increasing divorce rate. The divorce rate in Japan increased from 1.02 divorces per 1,000 people in 1947 to 1.81 in 2015, with a peak of 2.30 in 2002 (MHLW 2017). Since the early 1990s especially, divorce has become an increasingly common experience, and in absolute terms the number of people experiencing divorce increased from approximately 157,000 in 1990 to over 226,000 in 2015, with a high of almost 290,000 divorces registered in 2002 (ibid.).

But the ubiquity of popular anxieties and fantasies about divorce cannot be fully explained by the increase in the divorce rate or actual numbers of divorces. Divorce—as an idea, threat, or fantasy—signifies far more than numerical data on actual divorces can convey. As suggested by Yamaguchi-san's confession in the elevator and Nagako-san's gleeful planning, many more people were thinking about divorce than were actually experiencing it, and thinking about divorce led people to reconsider what kinds of intimate relationships were ideal, desirable, and possible.

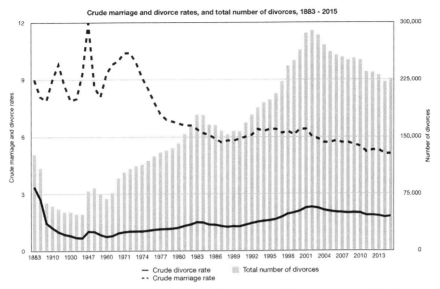

FIGURE 1. Crude marriage and divorce rates, and total number of divorces, 1883–2015. "Crude" rates calculate the number of marriages or divorces, respectively, per 1,000 adult persons in the population. For details of how these figures were calculated, see MHLW 2017, tables 6.1 and 6.2.

In particular, anxieties and fantasies coalesced around what is known as "later-life divorce" (*jukunen rikon*), divorce between spouses who are near retirement age or older. Later-life divorce captured the public imagination because a change to the law made it newly possible for divorced women to claim up to half of their former husband's national pension (Alexy 2007; Itō 2006). With this legal change, which was passed in 2004 but went into effect in 2007, the government granted marginal financial support to older women who wanted to leave their husbands. Although the actual amount of that support did not supply enough to live on, the unprecedented legal change constituted a powerful symbol prompting many women to consider divorce.

On evening television dramas or daytime talk shows, later-life divorce was offered as evidence of both female empowerment and changing ideals for marriage and intimacy. In a turnabout from earlier representations of husbands as bread-winning patriarchs, men were now depicted as powerless, incompetent losers dependent on their wives and subject to their whims. Standards for a good husband, ideal wife, and perfect marriage—while still debatable and different for every person—had shifted. As many older men pointed out to me, they were suddenly being threatened with divorce for behaving precisely as had been hailed as ideal a few decades before. In the 1970s and 1980s, common images of an ideal marriage represented husbands and wives as a pair tightly linked through economic dependencies but nevertheless largely disconnected from each other in everyday life. Husbands and wives, in these models, had very separate spheres of responsibilities and work—husbands in paid labor and wives in charge of the household and children—and very rarely socialized together. The newer ideals for marriage and intimacy in the early twenty-first century instead suggested that the best marriages are those in which spouses become more tightly linked through emotional connections. In this model for intimacy, the best marriages are those in which spouses are also best friends, bound by love and support for each other rather than financial dependencies.

Public and private conversations focused on later-life divorce were, in fact, concerned with much more general questions about the ideal forms of intimacy, how intimate relationships impact the people within them, and the personal and national stakes of such relationships. Later-life divorce had captured much media attention because it was shocking to imagine a generation of grandparents—the very same people who had built Japan's "miraculous" postwar economic recovery—deciding that they could no longer stand to be married to each other. The statistical incidence of later-life divorce has not yet matched the levels anticipated by this media and private attention. Most Japanese people get divorced between the ages of thirty and thirty-four, and divorces involving husbands over the age of sixty-five accounted for less than 3 percent of all divorces in 2015. But later-life divorce nevertheless attested unequivocally to changing intimate norms, giving people an easy shorthand with which to discuss how previously normative styles of intimacy appeared ever more risky or damaging.

Defining Intimacy

Within recent decades, scholarly attention to "intimacy" has boomed, particularly in the social sciences and humanities. Referring to a wide range of beliefs and practices, from friendships to parent-child relationships to sexual activity, "intimacy" stands at the center of an amorphous but growing body of academic attention. Although popular understandings suggest intimacy as a state of emotional closeness, or as something that is very personal or private, academic definitions challenge and complicate a simplistic equation of intimacy with closeness. An intimate relationship, Zelizer argues, is not merely close but also clearly marked as such; it is close in demonstrable, recognizable ways with "particularized knowledge received and attention provided" (Zelizer 2010, 268). She labels two types of connected and overlapping intimacy—first, the transfer of personal information and, second, wide-ranging long-term relations, both of which can contain different "kinds" of intimacy: "physical, informational, emotional" (Zelizer 2005, 16). Boris and Parreñas (2010, 2) similarly suggest that intimacy might come either from "bodily or emotional closeness or personal familiarity" or "close observation of another and knowledge of personal information," which need not be simultaneous. Moreover Berlant (2000) and Mendoza (2016, 10) convincingly argue that intimacy is never only as private as it might feel. Political and governmental attention, not to mention moral panics, regularly focus on intimate lives and practices, from same-sex marriage to abortion rights or citizenship acquired through family membership. Despite its feeling, intimacy is never *only* private and operates "intertwined with material social relations and public fantasies" (Frank 2002, xxviii). Therefore although intimacy is often assumed to be only private, in practice it exists at the center of public consciousness (Faier 2009, 14; Ryang 2006; Wilson 2004, 11). Building from this scholarship, I define intimate relationships to be those (1) marked by particular emotional, physical, or informational closeness, or aspirations for such; (2) taking place within realms commonly understood to be "private," although I recognize the constructed nature of such a category; and (3) often, but not necessarily, framed through bonds of love and/or sexual desire and contact.

In Japanese discourse and scholarship, intimacy stands within a cluster of terms, and the most direct translations from English are not necessarily the terms at the center of contemporary Japanese discussions. In the contemporary moment there is a similar range of vocabulary used to talk about romantic love, including *ren'ai*, *ai*, and *rabu*, the latter of which is a loan word from English (Shibamoto Smith 1999; 2004). Although *ren'ai* can, at times, sound a bit more formal and conservative, there is regular debate about which terms are best used to describe different forms and styles of love, and people regularly switch between these terms when they're discussing romance. As people debate the ideal forms of intimacy, they tend to focus terminology used to describe spouses, for instance the implications surrounding a common term for "husband" (*danna*), which literally means "master."

Romance and Styles of Intimacy

When I first started this project, I expected that divorced and divorcing people would likely feel sad, lonely, abandoned, or depressed. Although I certainly met people who shared such feelings—and indeed, I learned that almost everyone cycles in and out of such feelings on a regular basis—I never expected to have so many conversations about romance and love. Contrary to all my expectations, many divorced people really wanted to talk about romantic love, including the kinds of romance they sought, the best methods to get it, and how their understandings of "good" romance shifted over their lives. Following the interests and suggestions of my interlocutors, I was pushed to make room in my project to theorize divorce in relation to romantic love. In many ways, I shouldn't have been surprised by a link between breakups and ideologies of love and romantic intimacy. After all, if divorce is the result of a marriage no longer measuring up to someone's ideal, romance can be one of the yardsticks used for such an evaluation.

Although the particulars of what counts as romance are frequently shifting and remain under debate, scholars have positioned romance as a key platform through which to understand social bonds in various cultural contexts. In particular, they have focused on the rising popularity of companionate marriage, also called love marriage, which Hirsch (2003, 9) characterizes as a "new form of marriage focused on the affective elements of the relationship." Rather than being founded on family obligations, reproduction, or a sense of duty, these relationships are based on a sense of "partnership" or emotional intimacy as well as "friendship and sexual satisfaction" (Smith 2009, 163; Simmons 1979, 54).[1] People frequently link their "love marriages" with self-consciously modern sensibilities—suggesting that being a modern person requires loving in this form—and companionate romance is often represented as "the epitome of progressive individualism" (Masquelier 2009, 226; Smith 2008, 232). Thomas and Cole (2009, 5) suggest that "claims to love are also claims to modernity" and Gregg (2006, 158) describes companionate marriages as "a core ideology of modernity." For instance, some Mexican men and women insist that, compared with their parents' generation, contemporary relationships are "better—supposedly freer from constraint, more pleasurable and satisfying, perhaps even in some way more prestigious" (Hirsch 2003, 13; see also Schaeffer 2013, 17). Despite these common assertions that certain styles of intimacy are more modern, Wardlow and Hirsch (2006, 14) make clear that companionate ideals bring "gains and losses, both for men and for women." Scholars find that even in so-called modern marriages, "ties to kin and community remain strong" (Smith 2009, 163), suggesting that discursive shifts might not be matched in practice or, more importantly, that the struggle to be and feel modern in an intimate relationship brings potential risks to one's identity, community standing, or physical health (Collier 1997; Hirsch 2003; Smith 2006). Thus scholarship on romance traces popular belief in particular intimate forms and practices as instantiations of modern identities, themselves supposedly enacting new forms of freedom, at the same time it critically positions such intimacies in structures of power and inequality. Although many people imagine romantic love as an instantiation of personal choice and modernity, scholars complicate those popular beliefs by challenging any simple equation of romance with freedom.

People are constantly deciding not just *that* they want to share intimacy, but *how* that intimacy should be performed and experienced. Although differences in styles of intimacy comprise common points of contention in contemporary Japan, they should not be read as merely the absence or presence of affection. For instance, couples can be verbally or physically affectionate, holding hands, kissing, or whispering sweet nothings when there are other people around. Such displays might also mortify other couples who instead limit those intimate practices to private spaces. Further along this continuum, we can imagine couples who believe intimacy is best demonstrated through actions rather than words, and who might feel uncomfortable or silly saying "I love you" even in private. All of these couples could very well be deeply loving and intimate, while performing this intimacy in varying ways. They have different *styles of intimacy*. Although one couple might look more or less intimate to an outsider, in practice, judging this quality accurately proves difficult. Moreover, it's very possible for spouses to disagree about how to demonstrate their affection for each other and for that disagreement to cause tension in the relationship.

In Japan after the turn of the twenty-first century, shifting styles of intimacy were central to discussions about how to improve marriages or avoid divorce. As people considered what a marriage needs to be strong, or what counts as a legitimate reason to get divorced, they often debated conflicting styles of intimacy. When later-life divorce entered the public consciousness, it shocked people partially because it represented a denunciation of the styles of intimacy normative throughout Japan's postwar recovery—styles of intimacy, moreover, that had directly *enabled* that national recovery. In the period since that recovery moment, denouncing styles of intimacy as outdated, problematic, or risky signals more than merely asserting personal preferences. In these patterns, we see how intimate choices, which always *feel* personal, also reflect and exacerbate broader social, political, and economic transformations.

Kinship in an Age of Insecurity

Debates in contemporary Japan about the stakes of intimate relationships now include recommendations reflecting the increasing popularity of neoliberal ethics, as they shade from government policy to economic restructuring and into personal relationships. First created and popularized by economists and philosophers, neoliberalism is an ideology privileging individualism and

the benefits of economic markets set up to support individual wealth. Concretized in 1947 by the Mont Perelin Society, neoliberalism was designed as
a reaction to classic liberalism, which had recommended laissez-faire non-
intervention to allow a "free" market. In contrast, the neoliberals suggested
that "markets are not natural phenomena that emerge when institutional ob-
stacles are removed" and instead must be actively cultivated by state policy
pushing privatization, extensive deregulation, and tolerance for high levels
of unemployment (Cahill and Konings 2017, 19). Neoliberal standards push
governments to advocate private rather than public ownership and individual rather than collective responsibility, all within the rhetoric of freedom,
choice, and individualism. In practice, these policies increase precarity for
most workers, at the same time as they hold those same workers accountable
for the risks they now face: being laid off in a neoliberal regime is your fault
for failing to stay employable (Gershon 2017; Lane 2011). Rather than provide
welfare for citizens in need, neoliberal states emphasize literal self-help as the
solution for anyone unable to keep up with social change. At its most positive,
neoliberal governance encourages citizen-workers to take personal responsibility for all that happens to them and to enjoy this as a form of freedom
(Gregg 2011, 3). At its most negative, neoliberal governance dramatically reduces public support, increases social and economic inequalities, and blames
anyone who isn't able to keep up.

Within the extensive scholarship on the topic, neoliberalism has become
a popular, if slippery, category of analysis. Although some find the category
too broad or undefined to be helpful, many anthropologists have examined
the means or results of neoliberal policies and governance (Ganti 2014, 100).
Johnson (2011) situates the American government's response to Hurricane Katrina as a perfect storm of neoliberal policies intersecting with race and class
disparities to strip already impoverished communities of all support. By jus-
tifying abandonment as the ethically correct response to people who cannot
help themselves, neoliberal ethics reinforce certain people and certain types
of selves as the least deserving. Similarly, when the (nominally socialist) Chinese government privatized industries and laid off workers, it did so through
leveraging the rhetoric of self-reliance. Rather than offering workers new positions, or the state support offered previously, the government instead provided therapeutic counseling designed to teach people to be independent individuals responsible for their own success. By framing this individualism as
"self-reliance" (zi li), the government was radically repurposing the same term
from its Maoist revolutionary associations with collective bonds (Yang 2015,
68). In conjunction with rhetorics of personal responsibility, neoliberalism
suggests that successful people cultivate selves that are atomized or entrepre-

neurial. "The ideal neoliberal self, after all, is the one that can adapt quickly to changing circumstances, anticipate future market demands, and transform skills and capabilities accordingly" (Gershon 2018, 176). Tracing how neoliberalism reconfigures "people's relationships to others, their sense of membership in a public, and the conditions of their self-knowledge," scholars have extended analysis from financial policies to epistemological dilemmas caused by neoliberal ethics applied in contexts beyond the market (Greenhouse 2010, 2; Ong 2006).

Ethnographers argue that neoliberal ethics infuse romantic relationships, particularly when those relationships include explicit financial exchanges, as in sex work. Bernstein (2007) traces how male workers in Silicon Valley seek ongoing intimacy with sex workers, some of whom advertise a "girlfriend experience." These men actively prefer paid relationships precisely because payment defines the intimacy so as to obviate extended obligations. Unlike with "real" girlfriends, relationships built on paid exchanges do not provoke mutual obligations; buying time means that clients can have a "girlfriend" only when they want one, sidestepping the emotional labor necessary to sustain other relationships (ibid. 120). In Japan, neoliberal models for intimacy, commerce, and citizenship saturate relationships between male sex workers who labor as "hosts" in clubs catering to female clients (Takeyama 2016). Rather than selling overtly sexual contact, hosts sell attention, flirtation, and fun to older female clients. Facing the intersecting hostilities of sexism and ageism, female clients pay astronomical sums to buy male attention that had been freely available when they were younger. Host clubs promise to manifest neoliberal dreams for both male sex workers, who seek masculinity through labor and competition, and their female clients, who seek to recover femininity through "lovability" (ibid., 10).

At the same time that neoliberalism privileges individualism, neoliberal policies have paradoxically pushed individuals to become more reliant on their families. Despite neoliberal emphasis on independence as a marker of a mature self, anthropologists clearly demonstrate that neoliberal policies often push people into tighter reliance on their families. For instance, Han (2012) examines how Chile's national privatization created a generation overwhelmed by debt who therefore turned to kinship networks for support. Analyzing how International Monetary Fund policy caused tremendous dislocations in gender, familial, and labor systems, Song (2009) concludes that the South Korean government used the 1997 debt crisis to designate heterosexual, male laborers as more "deserving" of welfare, thereby leaving all others in more dire straits. In these ways, "neoliberals persistently exhort individuals to take responsibility for their own fate, and yet the imperative of *personal responsibility* slides ineluctably into that of *family responsibility* when it comes to managing the inevitable problems of economic dependence" (Cooper 2017, 71, emphasis in the original). Contrary to its rhetoric, neoliberalism in practice often requires and amplifies particular family interdependencies. Blindness to the fundamental imbrication of families in economic markets reflects the constructed divides between public and private, masculine exterior and feminine interior, exploitative capitalism and revitalizing kinship (Eng 2010, 8; Fernandes 2018, 4; Zelizer 2005). This book uses the Japanese case to explore how neoliberalism manifests as one set of ethics people use to navigate familial relationships at a moment when social contracts, particularly those that held families together, are shifting and dissolving.

In Japan, neoliberal policies first came into being in the late 1990s and early 2000s. Since the bursting of the postwar bubble, the economy had been at or near recessionary levels, no matter the policy attempts at recovery (Alexander 2002). Secure employment opportunities that had previously been available to some male workers—so-called "lifetime employment" that effectively guaranteed a stable and predictable income from hiring to retirement—gradually disappeared. In addition to substantial economic restructuring, and the privatizing of previously public utilities, labor laws were changed to allow employers to replace relatively well-paying permanent positions with "contract" or "dispatch" positions, in which workers were paid substantially less for the same tasks.[2] Arai (2016, 35) characterizes the concurrent dissolution of social contracts and popularization of neoliberal rhetorics, saying: "Well-known and expected systems of support in schools and work were rolled back following the collapse of the bubble economy of the 1980s. Simultaneously, the language of strength and independence, self-responsibility and skills, was rolled out."

Advocating structural readjustments as the best solution for economic stagnation, Prime Minister Koizumi Jun'ichirō popularized rhetoric celebrating individual self-reliance, making clear the government's abdication of responsibility for citizens' welfare, well-being, and happiness (Takeda 2008, 154). Using terminology similar to that used in other cultural contexts, Japanese politicians and media began emphasizing self-responsibility, independence, individualism, and tolerance for risk as attributes of good citizens and mature adults. Miyazaki (2010, 239) describes this new rhetoric as "the pervasive celebration by the government as well as by the media of the neoliberal ideal of 'strong individuals' (*tsuyoi kojin*) ready to take risks (*risuku*) while taking responsibilities for their own risk-taking action (*jiko sekinin*)." Like neoliberal Chinese rhetoric focused on "self-reliance" mentioned above, Japanese neoliberal terminology glorified actions people could and should perform for themselves—hence, "independence" (*jiritsu*), "self-responsibility" (*jiko sekinin*), "being true to oneself" (*jibunrashisa*), and "self-restraint" (*jishuku*).[3] Advice books and other media represent such attributes as necessary for success and happiness in the current moment (Hook and Takeda 2007; Mathews 2017, 237; Miyazaki 2013).[4]

This new emphasis on individualism was matched by popular rhetoric describing Japan as a society problematically without "connections" (*muen shakai*; literally, bondless or disconnected society). In contrast with discourse lauding the potential for freedom through individualism and being true to one's self, this term suggested the stressful and unsettling results of neoliberal policies. People who were once tied to extended families, secure employment, or a supportive education system might now float in precarious isolation. Ethnographers have focused on the impacts of neoliberalism in Japan from different perspectives, including working-class men who seek social mobility through sex work (Takeyama 2016), citizens facing precarity as the result of environmental disasters (Allison 2013; Takahashi 2018), and the problems confronting young people as they try to find work (Brinton 2010; Cook 2016; Toivonen and Imoto 2013). Roquet (2016, 13) emphasizes the bait-and-switch embedded within neoliberal possibilities, saying "neoliberal biopolitics pairs personal 'freedoms' with intensifying demands for self-discipline and self-restraint (*jishuku*)." To be freed from restrictions or requirements can be both positive and negative, releasing people from restrictive social norms but removing structures of support, allowing new possibilities but shutting down pathways to success and security.

Starting in the early 2000s, government policies concentrated on Japanese families as a primary target of neoliberal ideologies. In recommendations about how to recover from decades of recession, the Koizumi administration described families, and particularly the women in them, as ripe for structural adjustment. Dismissing standard employment patterns in which breadwinning husbands pair with wives who work part-time in addition to covering all domestic needs, Koizumi recommended women as a "potential reservoir of labor" (Takeda 2008, 160). Such a recommendation ignored both women's tremendous (unpaid) domestic labor as well as the economic benefits of having a flexible (underpaid) labor force readily available. Specifically, a 2002 white paper recommended the government remove or restructure tax benefits that provide financial incentives for married women to work only part time (ibid., 157). Here we see one manifestation of neoliberal ethics of "self-responsibility" as translated into familial relationships: the marital partnership, previously lauded by the government as a vital element of economic growth, was now disparaged as women were encouraged to pull their own weight through paid labor. By this logic, being a housewife—even one who works part-time, as most do—was no longer a responsible way to contribute to society.

At the start of this project, I wasn't interested in neoliberalism and certainly wasn't looking for evidence of it in the data I collected. Only years after the original fieldwork did I start to notice patterns linking a new emphasis on independence with dissolutions of previously inviolable social contracts. Perhaps readers might now think that neoliberalism is almost overdetermined in a project exploring how people leave marriages during a moment of social and economic upheaval, but that was far from the case. In fact, when I first became aware of neoliberalism as a category ripe for social analysis, I was frustrated because it felt like a term scholars were using in almost any project, using it as a declarative answer rather than a provocative and genuine question. At the time, the term felt both over- and underinclusive, as a "lazy way" to "group together any number of heterogeneous things" (Cahill and Konings 2017, 5; see also Fernandes 2018, 7; Ganti 2014, 90). I understand now that my reaction likely had as much to do with patterns surrounding any disciplinary buzzword, but suffice to say I was highly skeptical of neoliberalism both as a set of practices being used to privatize wealth and also as a heuristic for analyzing social worlds. My skepticism might have slowed this analysis somewhat but also brought my situation closer to that of my interlocutors. Many people with whom I spoke found real confusion and contradiction in recommendations to apply neoliberal ethics in their family relationships. Even if they found ideas of self-responsibility or independence compelling in some contexts, few people found them easy to apply in relationships with spouses, parents, children, or members of their extended family. Moreover, these same people pushed back against the neoliberal suggestion that independence and self-reliance were necessarily positive attributes. For anyone who felt constrained by family norms, new rhetoric privileging freedom and flexibility could bring welcome relief and new possibilities. But for others such separations can also feel like abandonment, the evaporation of loving ties previously imagined as permanent. Figuring out *if*, let alone *how*, neoliberalism might be relevant to intimate relationships became an overwhelming task.

Theorizing Relationality through Dependence and Connection

When Prime Minister Koizumi suggested housewives were unproductively dependent members of society, his choice of language registered an irony he surely didn't intend. Many women and mothers in Japan are associated with dependencies—but as the figures on whom others depend. Koizumi's rhetoric represented an inversion of how the term was used by Doi Takeo, a prominent psychologist, who identified dependence (*amae*) as an elemental Japanese emotion vital to sociality (Borovoy 2012, 264; Doi 1973). In his theory, all humans desire dependency on others, but Japanese society particularly emphasizes this tendency as a key part of socialization. Unlike the neoliberal rhetoric Koizumi espoused, children and other family members being dependent on wives and mothers has been normal, normalized, and idealized in Japan. Moreover, facilitating relationships that include *amae* is often marked as a sign of both intimacy and maturity.

This book's theoretical contribution explores how neoliberal ethics shape relationships built on companionate ideals within a cultural context space allowing for, if not idealizing, dependency as a key element of intimacy. On the surface, these different ideologies of relationality seem to contradict each other. If neoliberal logics suggest people should craft themselves as entrepreneurial free agents, and that possessing dependence or enabling it in others opens up dangerous risks, companionate romance suggests almost the opposite. Compared to a marriage built on duty, companionate love recommends interdependence through shared emotions, ostensibly equal exchange, and deep honesty, an interweaving that suggests loving selves should be closely together in particular ways. Japanese rhetoric of *amae* suggests a similar closeness but also that real love can be cultivated in situations of intentional inequality, with one person dependent on their partner. As I show throughout this book, these multiple ideologies of and for intimacy saturate contemporary Japanese society, becoming options from which people cautiously pick and choose as they imagine the relationships they want, negotiate actual relationships with the other people involved, and try to end relationships they deem problematic.

The book's subtitle—the romance of independence—refers to the potentially contradictory pulls from multiple ideologies shaping relationality in contemporary Japan. On the one hand, some Japanese men and women see romantic potential in relationships that enable independent, rather than dependent, partnership. In this thinking, when partners can be independent of each other, however they define that shifting and contested term, it enables better, stronger, and more secure romantic attachments. Thus personal independence facilitates relational romance. On the other hand, these relational choices are being made in a social context with new emphasis on independence, self-responsibility, and actively avoiding structures of dependence. In this broader sense, beyond specific attention to intimate relationships, independence itself takes on a captivating aura and can seem to some people to be a categorical good. Rather than a clear transition—from liberalism to neoliberalism, from dependence to independence, from duty to desire—*Intimate Disconnections* traces the unsteady shifts people make between different relational ideologies.

As they imagine what makes relationships strong, men and women also shift between discourse about intimacy and the practice of intimacy. From talking with friends about their marriage, to watching a popular television show depict divorce, or taking a quiz in a weekly magazine that purports to diagnose marital risk, men and women experience any intimate relationship within a cloud of discourse and representation (Swidler 2001). Because this book focuses on the practice of intimate disconnections—*how* marriages end through divorce—it also includes media and popular discourse as pertains to people's own relational practices. By that I mean that rather than prioritizing analysis of Japanese media representations of intimacy, this book situates people and their choices at the center. Discourse about intimacy and intimate practices are never fully separate, but I focus on the former as it impacts the latter.[5]

Divorce as Symbol and Statistic

In Japan and elsewhere, divorce can be a vibrant symbol of personal failure, family disintegration, and threats to vital networks of connection. But it is also used to represent women's empowerment, as a shorthand measure for women's capacity to legally assert rights, refuse and rebuild kinship ties, and financially support themselves.[6] In practice, any divorce likely walks the line between these two extremes, but even as a "highly individuated process" the deeply personal choice to end a marriage often exists in relation to divorce's symbolic value (Coltrane and Adams 2003, 370).

In Japan, moral panics surround divorce, grouping it with other "family problems" (*kazoku mondai*) such as later marriage, fewer marriages overall, and children struggling with psychological problems (Alexy and Cook 2019; Arai 2016; White 2002). In the course of my research, single, married, and divorced people were likely to describe divorce generally as an obviously modern crutch and point to it as evidence of the destructive stress modern lives put on family ties. Indeed almost everyone I spoke to in the course of this project imagined the contemporary divorce rate as unquestionably higher than it had ever been, and therefore evidence that Japan's families, and perhaps Japanese society, were coming apart. To these people, the divorce rate symbolized contemporary families' perceived demise in relation to a hallowed traditional past. My interlocutors are not alone in these assumptions, and divorce is frequently framed as a uniquely modern problem (Giddens 1992; Vaughn 1990).

In fact, though, these common perceptions are simply incorrect and the current divorce rate pales in comparison with Japan's historical peak, which occurred in 1883. At that moment, as the Meiji government restructured the nation, marriage and divorce practices were wildly divergent between Japan's regions. Social and family norms suggested that couples should use "trial marriages" to test the fit of their match, through either informal unions or marriages that could easily be dissolved free of stigma (Fuess 2004; Kawashima and Steiner 1960). Fuess found that "most Japanese [people] are neither aware of nor care about their ancestors' frequent divorces" (2004, 6), and in the course of my research I found that practically no one imagined divorce as a regular occurrence in Japan's history. The substantial gap between common perceptions of divorce as a uniquely modern problem signaling the erosion of traditional family norms, and the historical reality of divorce as an unremarkable practice used by many families, demonstrates that divorce often becomes a potent symbol floating free of its historical and statistical referents.

Yet statistics help to chart a number of broad trends surrounding divorce in Japan, some of which complicate common assumptions. On average, in 2015, divorces ended marriages of between five and nine years, which reflected a slow increase from previous years. In the same year, most divorces involved women aged thirty to thirty-four, and men who were slightly older, mirroring the common age gap between spouses when they marry. Approximately 60 percent of divorces are between parents with minor children, a figure that has stayed fairly steady since the 1950s, although there are now more children, in absolute terms, with divorced parents. There is no joint custody in Japan, and children's custody after divorce represents one of the most substantial shifts: in 1950 48.7 percent of custody was granted to fathers, but by 2015, that figure was only 12.1 percent (MHLW 2017). I explore the factors prompting this shift and its implications in chapter 4.

The statistics describing divorce fit within broader demographic trends that continue to reshape families and the national community. Most prominent and influential are the simultaneously falling birthrate and rapidly aging population. Following the postwar baby boom, Japan's total fertility rate has been slowly falling below the "replacement level" of 2.1 children born to each woman. Despite increasingly frantic government attempts to persuade people to have more children—with tax rebates, new preschools, and rewards for companies who offer paternity leave, among other policies—the fertility rate is now 1.45, without signs of increase (MHLW 2017; Ogawa 2003; Osawa 2005; Roberts 2002; Takeda 2004). These trends represent tremendous challenges for Japan because by 2065, 38.4 percent of the population is predicted to be over the age of 65 (NIPSSR 2017a). Barring a major change to Japan's restrictive immigration policies, the working population of Japan won't be able to afford to support the elderly (Campbell and Ikegami 2000; Świtek 2016).

The rapidly aging population is now coupled with a wide range of family changes, of which the likelihood of divorce is just one. Compared to the immediate postwar period and as recently as the 1980s, Japanese people are now much more likely to be living alone (Ronald and Hirayama 2009). At the same time, unmarried segments of the population have increased for both men and women (S. Fukuda 2009). People are waiting longer to marry, and in 2015 the mean age for women's first marriage was 29.4, while men's was 31.1 (MHLW 2017). The increasing number of "never married" people, and the rising average age at first marriage, include both those who explicitly reject marriage and those who might very much want to get married but haven't found the right person or an acceptable situation (Dales and Yamamoto 2019; Miles 2019; Nakano 2011). At the same time, the term "sexlessness" entered common vocabulary, describing married couples who lack a formerly expected intimacy (Moriki 2017).

Despite the plethora of demographic changes visible in contemporary families, one figure has remained strikingly steady with weighty implications: throughout the postwar period, less than 2 percent of children have been born to unmarried parents. This figure reflects the effects of birth control decisions, accessible abortion, and "shotgun" weddings that ensure a mother is married when her child is born, if not when conceived. But it also demonstrates the staying power of a very strong social norm linking marriage with childbirth, which continues even as other family norms shift (Hertog 2009; Raymo and Iwasawa 2008). This strong preference for children to be born to married parents, in conjunction with the rising age at first marriage, combine to drive the birth rate even lower. Within these demographic patterns, the symbolic associations surrounding divorce—what it means and signifies—in contemporary Japan locate it not only within "family problems" or, more neutrally, "family changes" but also within a broader awareness of threats and possibilities embedded within more generalized disconnections.

Gender and the Dynamics of Leaving

Before the early 1990s, in Japan divorce was generally something men requested and women worked to avoid, and men's requests were commonly explained as attempts to begin other marriages. Narrative fiction, legal cases, media representations, and ethnography from that period reflect common assumptions that divorce was often initiated by men. In 1983, when a popular television show, *Friday's Wives* (*Kinyōbi no tsumatachi e*), represented divorce, it depicted a pig-headed husband abandoning his family to begin a new relationship, with little thought toward the difficulties his stay-at-home wife would face as she tried to support herself and their daughter. Akin to the 1987 American show *thirtysomething*, *Friday's Wives* was a huge hit that gained popularity because it represented "real" problems that middle-class couples were facing (Kitazawa 2012, 163). Centering upon a small group of friends who lived in the same bedtown neighborhood in Yokohama, the characters dealt with infidelities, work stress, and women's anxiety about keeping careers or having children. The divorce occurs when a husband suddenly falls in love with a young model he meets at a car show. Although clearly melodramatic, this representation of divorce conforms to common perceptions at the time of how divorce could and would happen. In it, divorce testified to male desire and agency, as an option only reluctantly accepted by a wife who was desperate to stay married—even if in title only.

Older divorced people with whom I conducted research articulated experiences aligned with such patterns. For instance, Sato-san, a grandmother in her eighties, described her husband's request for a divorce back in 1975. They were married and living in Matsuyama, Shikoku, when he began an affair with another woman. Requesting a divorce from Sato-san, he intended to marry this other woman so that he could declare the children they had legally "legitimate" (*chakushutsu*). Concerned about the potential stigma that could harm her own children and herself, Sato-san simply refused the divorce and never signed the forms. As I explain in chapter 3, the legal process most typically requires both spouses to agree to a divorce, so by refusing Sato-san was able to prevent the divorce her husband wanted. She was very worried that, if she allowed the divorce, their children would have a more difficult time getting married because no one would want to be linked with them. Therefore, she stayed legally married to her husband, although he moved out of their house and in with his other family. Luckily for Sato-san, she managed to hide this separation and both her son and daughter married happily. After their weddings, she allowed them to tell their new spouses and in-laws the truth of her marriage, and in 1994, almost twenty years after he first requested it, she felt secure enough to agree to the divorce her husband requested. She was sixty-six years old. In these two examples we see patterns typical of divorce in the postwar before the early 1990s: men initiated divorce, often to legalize relationships begun with other women, and women refused it, aware of the stigma divorce would bring to themselves, their children, and other family members.

By the early 2000s, mentioning divorce as a male initiative regularly elicited nostalgic giggles in the support groups I joined. In 2005, when I began conducting research, everyone seemed thoroughly certain that divorce was something that women sought and of which men were terrified: a diametric gender shift so neat I first doubted it. Although I met men who initiated divorces, and legal demographics make it hard to determine who first requests a separation, in this case the popular perception reflects broad trends. Contemporary television shows about divorce almost uniformly represent a wife leaving: *Haruka of the Wind* tells the story of two sisters raised by their earthy, rural father, after their career-driven mother abandons the family (NHK 2005); *Me and Her and Her Life Path* focuses on a single father raising his daughter after his wife leaves them both to find herself through art (Fuji TV 2004); *Later-Life Divorce* portrays a couple in their sixties torn apart when the wife asks for a divorce on the very day her husband retires (Asahi TV 2005). Although these female characters vary in their selfish inattention to their children and their focus on careers, they encompass popular perceptions of divorce in the current moment. In these representations, women make choices and men struggle desperately to decrease the likelihood they will be left, which seldom helps. Unusually, in these shows, fathers hold legal custody of their children at much higher rates than the statistical average of 20 percent, a pattern I understand to reflect the melodramatic possibilities of counterexamples.

In this book, gender is both an emic and etic category of analysis. From popular ideas that women are more likely to end marriages to gendered differences in wealth after divorce, naturalized differences between men and women play a constant role in considering, discussing, and critiquing divorce in Japan. For that reason, I lace gender analysis throughout the book, rather than make it a specific focus in any single chapter. Indeed, this enables me to better situate gender intersectionally, in relation to other identifications that matter, such as class, generation, and region. My analysis takes seriously the popular discourse that divorce produces empowered women and hapless men, but I complicate such a clear divide, finding instead shifting understandings of success, security, and the benefits of intimate relationships.

An Anthropology of Divorce

Divorce can feel like a wonderful relief, a long-desired freedom won after a difficult fight. So, too, can it feel debilitatingly lonely, the manifestation of a personal failure and the foreclosure of a long-imagined future. Indeed, any given divorce often oscillates between these two extremes at different moments: salvation on some days and appalling loss on others. Additionally, divorce operates at the level of multivocal symbol, for individual people, families, and communities, at the same time that inflexible legal requirements delimit it. It can exemplify selfish behavior, undesirable gender shifts, or the "disintegration" of family bonds and, by extension, an entire nation. Yet it can also denote an empowering independence, salvation, or escape. This book engages divorce at all these levels: analyzing how people imagine, enact, and transcend marital endings at precisely the moment when divorce seems over-determined as a symbol of feminine power and deteriorating social ties.

Cultural anthropology's long-standing disciplinary interest in kinship in-cludes a marked lacuna around divorce. From the field's early attention to structures of descent to the Schneiderian shift and more recent focus on fami-lies we choose or reproductive technologies, anthropological research has long centered on kinship. No longer the sine qua non it once was, kinship neverthe-less continues to be recognizable as a central focus within cultural anthropol-ogy (McKinnon and Cannell 2013; Strathern 2005). However, despite this broad and extended attention to kinship, relatively few anthropologists have explored divorce (notable exceptions include Hirsch 1998; Holden 2016; Hutchinson 1990; Simpson 1998). How families and conjugal units fragment—through choice, force, or law—has interested anthropologists less than other aspects of family lives. In American and Japanese scholarship, most research on divorce has been conducted by sociologists, and my project draws on their insights.

This book highlights the revelatory potency of divorce as an anthropo-logical object of analysis. Although divorce, like marriage or kinship more generally, manifests in culturally specific forms, attention to it enables analysis of key intersections between personal, legal, social, and economic structures. As people divorce, they disentangle and reconfigure kin relations, economic flows, and legal and social identities in ways that simultaneously expose cul-tural norms, ideals, and ideologies—along with their limitations and poten-tials. For example, divorce brings to the fore debates about the structures of "ideal" families precisely as enacting such possibilities becomes newly fore-closed. Moreover, these negotiations often take place at moments of height-ened stress and within broader discourse about personal, familial, or national transitions. Contrary to common perceptions, in this book I do not under-stand divorce to be only about failures or endings, but also about vital and contested beginnings of newly emergent styles of sociality and kinship. The emotion and contentiousness surrounding divorce make it a pivotal site for ex-amining affective intersections of personal, political, and public relationships.

Locating Divorce Methodologically

Because divorce is such a personal, private, and potentially stigmatizing ex-perience, many people in and outside of Japan were initially incredulous that any anthropological research could be done about it. Almost everywhere I went, people were curious about how I was planning to do any research at all. "Do people really want to talk to you?" was one typical question I got in many different situations, followed quickly by, "How do you meet them?" Although people rarely referred to them as such, my research methods were of immediate interest to almost anyone who heard about my project, and, before they asked about my preliminary conclusions or my personal history, they wanted to know how I was doing what I was doing.

Throughout my research, the *how* of my project was entwined with being asked to explain myself. Because of how I look, most people correctly assume that I am not Japanese. When I walked into a party with friends, or struck up a conversation with someone at a bar, or sat down in a support group, it was extremely natural and obvious for other people to ask me "Why are you here?" My obviousness—which often felt like awkwardness, both physical and linguistic—not only made me an object of curiosity for some people but also enabled me to start talking about my research in conversations in which it might not have otherwise come up. Why I was there, I told anyone who asked, was to learn about divorce and families in contemporary Japan, and this unusual and unexpected topic was often enough to get people talking. Divorced people weren't the only ones who had opinions about the state of marriages and family problems and, as one happily married housewife laughingly told me, "Every married person has thought about divorce!" My research demonstrates how right she is, while also suggesting the broad gaps between thinking about divorce and acting upon it.

The primary fieldwork for this project occurred in Japan from September 2005 to September 2006, with follow-up work conducted in 2009 and 2011. I rented a room from a widowed woman who lived within the Tokyo city limits, but I worked to expand my research beyond the stereotypical images of urban middle-class Japan. I had many contacts in and made frequent trips to Yokohama, Chiba, and Saitama. Chiba prefecture provided my second fieldsite, where I spent time with an extended family and their friends. This family had lived in the same small town for generations and because both parents remained there after their divorce, their daily lives were circumscribed both by small town gossip and by attempts to avoid seeing each other unexpectedly. Similar concerns occurred in my third fieldsite, Matsuyama city on Shikoku Island. As residents told me, the largest city on the smallest of Japan's four main islands is very different from Tokyo, and family expectations and divorce experiences are also understood to reflect this distance from urban Japan.

Throughout my time in Japan, I tried to make my life as typical as I could. I lived on the west side of Tokyo in a house so close to the neighbors' that, through open windows, I could hear them splashing in the bath. Like most of the people I knew, I spent a good portion of each day on trains, returning home many nights exhausted and ready to watch cheesy television with my roommate. I regularly commuted into the distant suburbs and let friends crash at my house when they had missed their last train. I joined friends for meals, went with them to see movies, or invited them to hear another friend perform at an open mic. My thumbs started to hurt from texting on my cell phone, and I let my time get sucked away by social media exchanges.

My daily life was also unusually concentrated on divorce. Much of the television I watched was about divorce. I was particularly excited to find new comic books about divorce. I got my hair cut by a professional stylist who was a divorced woman. Because people knew why I was in Japan, they were more likely to bring up divorce-related topics in casual conversation, which meant I was much more likely to talk about divorce. And I was always carrying a notebook to jot down quotes or ideas. Commenting on the unnatural focus of my life, a few different people labeled me a "divorce geek" (*rikon otaku*), using a word that suggests a person obsessively, and probably unhealthily, consumed by one thing. People's identification of me with divorce became so strong that they would literally gesture toward me when they said the word "divorce" in conversation, in a motion similar to what they might use to link me with "American."

Through these motions of identification, I encountered what I came to call ambient divorce stories. Knowing what I studied, or hearing it for the first time, led people to tell me long stories about divorces they heard about or witnessed. In these stories I wasn't getting first-person accounts, but from friends or strangers I would hear about their cousin's divorce, their bartender's divorce, or their coworker's divorce. As I very usefully became known as "the divorce girl," these ambient divorce stories helpfully followed me like a cloud. "Oh, Ally," one friend said when I ran into him at a coffee shop, "I got my hair cut last week and my barber is in the middle of a divorce. I thought of you. Do you want to hear the details? It's pretty awful." My attempts at a "normal" life were regularly punctuated by these pockets of divorce, some of which I sought out and some of which seemed to find me. In this way, my daily life resonated with the lives some people lead after they have been divorced; although I tried to live a normal life, at times I would be broadsided by divorce, put myself in a group organized around divorce, or literally gestured toward when divorce became the topic of conversation. In these situations and others, divorce could surface abruptly or fade into the background, could be the reason for a gathering or a secret that wasn't appropriate to share.

I conducted research by talking casually with people, joining five different support groups that focused on divorce and family problems, consuming media that considered similar topics, and recording interviews with seventy-two people who were married, divorced, or divorcing; whose parents or grand-parents had divorced; or who were counselors or lawyers paid to assist divorce proceedings. I spent much time with married and divorced friends, volunteered with NGOs concerned with family topics, participated in online listservs about "family problems," and joined their offline parties. I gathered as many media representations as possible, setting an alarm to get up in time to watch *Haruka of the Wind*, an NHK drama about a young woman with divorced parents broadcast daily at 8:15 a.m. In addition to the media I found on my own, I asked for recommendations and thus read guidebooks that divorced men and women found especially helpful, as well as other books they liked. For instance, two middle-aged men—one happily married and the other divorced and remarried—wanted to read social psychology, so I found myself in a small reading group discussing *The Art of Loving* (Fromm 1956).[7] Like most ethnographers, I was a willing participant in almost anything and thus bounced between casual conversations with a friend and her (married) boyfriend, support group meetings organized around particular themes, and "afterparties" (*nijikai*) that followed those events with many more hours of eating, drinking, and talking.

Despite the relative lack of popularity for formal "talk therapy" in Japan, for many people becoming divorced includes a tremendous amount of talk. For the vast majority of men and women with whom I did research, talk was a vital element of becoming divorced. In particular contexts, people absolutely wanted to talk about a great variety of things, from their opinions about how the historical stem-family system (*ie seido*) impacted contemporary Japanese families, to the anger they still held about their former spouse, to how their in-laws reacted when told about an impending divorce. My awareness of talk as a key instantiation of divorce comes partially from my location in support groups that were, quite often, centered on talking. Yet the research in this book reflects more than these organized, if relatively informal, venues for talk. In addition to participating in various types of support groups, I recorded interviews with people who were willing, and hung out with lots of people in many different contexts. Very open-ended and often far-reaching, recorded conversations typically began with me asking broad questions about personal experiences—"How did you decide to get married?" "Why did you get divorced?"—and also their perceptions about contemporary social patterns. Especially toward the end of these conversations, after I explicitly invited any questions about me, the talk usually became less one-sided and I was happy to answer people's questions about my motivations to conduct
          ·h a project. People were interested in my personal experiences with dating

and divorce, any tentative conclusions I'd reached so far in my research, and descriptions of how American culture might or might not be different from Japanese culture.

Throughout these various interactions in myriad contexts, I never deluded myself that I was getting pure unvarnished truth. I wasn't confirming the events of any relationship with both spouses, investigating what "really happened," or fact-checking like a detective or divorce lawyer.[8] Instead, I was interested in what people wanted to tell me, the details they used to signal a justifiable or unreasonable divorce, and how they told the stories they wanted to tell. I present the data I gathered in this book with a tripartite caveat: not only are these narratives often one-sided, and shared only by people who were literally willing to talk about their divorce, but they also tend to be *retrospective reimaginings* of moments in the (sometimes distant) past.[9] By this I mean that as they told me about their relationship and divorce, men and women were reframing their narration, or how they characterized key people, to accommodate information they only found out later. When divorced people started to tell me about how they'd gotten married years before, they were likely to plant narrative seeds foreshadowing the directions the relationships would take. For instance, one woman highlighted nagging worries she had felt the night before her wedding that, when they turned out to be justified, contributed to her divorce years later. I don't doubt that she had these worries, but I also understand that her narrative positionality likely contributed to the way she told the story of her marriage and divorce. Looking back on her marriage now, she understands how it ended; had she instead been asked to tell the story of her marriage one year into it, we can imagine her narration taking a different tone.

When people craft narratives, especially narratives about intimate relationships and divorce, they create logical coherence that might not have been present in the moment. Such narratives are influenced as much by the moment in which they're told as the events they describe. For instance, in her classic analysis of divorce in the United States, Vaughn (1990) identifies the substantial differences between descriptions offered by someone who leaves a relationship and someone who is left: the leaver often characterizes the relationship as fundamentally flawed from the beginning, while the person who is left suggests that everything was good (or good enough) until their partner suddenly changed their mind (see also Hopper 1993a). Narratives and explanations depend on the context in which they are articulated, and while such flexibility and fluidity does not invalidate data gathered through conversations about divorce, I worked to capture and analyze speech at the same time as I found other ways of locating divorce ethnographically. I talked with many people but also did my best to live alongside them, gathering observations about divorce as it fit into the other elements of their lives.

Because this book explores legal divorce in Japan, it exclusively focuses on heterosexual relationships. Although many gay, lesbian, and queer people in Japan have built lasting and loving families for themselves, as of the time of this writing, same-sex marriage remains legally foreclosed.[10] In response to that formal discrimination, many same-sex couples have created legal relationships by having one partner legally adopt the other, thereby generating some, but not all, of the rights and privileges that come to legal family members (Maree 2004). Although such adoptions might seem unusual to foreign audiences, in Japan adoption of adults has long been used to extend family lines that would otherwise end; so when same-sex partners become linked to each other through adoption, the mechanism is highly recognizable and not itself stigmatized (Bachnik 1983, 163; Goldfarb 2016, 49). Aware that a project focused only on legal divorce in Japan would be fundamentally heteronormative, during the course of my fieldwork I also spent time with advocacy groups focused on promoting queer rights and same-sex marriage. My intention was to both understand more about the relationships legal divorce couldn't capture and to more broadly situate people's simultaneous desire for, and critiques of, Japanese family norms. Ultimately, those examples did not fit into the analysis presented in this book (cf. Alexy 2008, 129–34). I welcome future research focused on how Japanese same-sex couples break up, particularly because laws provide even less assistance than for straight couples. At the same time, I hope this difference will soon be rendered moot when everyone in Japan has the legal right to marry if they wish.

In this fieldwork, at different times and in different contexts, the characteristics that mattered about me shifted between three clusters: first, that I was a relatively young, white, American woman; second, that my parents are divorced; and third, that I was also dating and watching my close friends move in and out of romantic relationships. The first two were the ideas most prominently articulated by other people, although the third is what I felt most acutely. For instance, in multiple support group meetings, as participants imagined how their divorce would impact their children, they asked me direct questions about my own experiences and then discussed how cultural differences might impact their children's reactions.

The importance of my non-Japaneseness was made clear when Yamada-san, a divorced woman living in a very small town hours from Tokyo, prefaced some further disclosure with, "I'm only telling you this because you're a foreigner." When I brought the conversation back to that point later, she said that she imagines my research would be very hard for a Japanese person to do because she, at least, was worried that another Japanese person would judge her more harshly. For this woman, and I suspect for other people, my non-Japaneseness indexed a lack of critical judgment—or, more pejoratively, a welcome cluelessness—that made people more inclined to share potentially stigmatized experiences with me. In this, they were correct. Very quickly into my fieldwork, I realized that given the sheer quantity of stories I was hearing and people I was meeting, I had no interest in or energy for judging what I heard and instead focused on understanding anything someone wanted to tell me, what they cared about, and why.[11] This book tries to represent these data such that you might simultaneously be able to recognize both recurring motifs and palpable diversity in what I heard, saw, and learned.

Mae: Divorce Made Visible

My ethnographic pursuit of divorce, and the ways divorce could become visible in unexpected moments, was made clear one night I spent dancing—or, more accurately, sitting in a dance club—at the edge of the Roppongi area of Tokyo. I had gone out with a good friend, Mae, a thirty-seven-year-old woman who had been divorced two years before. We had known each other for three years and had originally been introduced by a mutual friend who patronized the salon where she worked. Mae was incredibly chatty with her customers and talked about personal topics, so our mutual friend learned about her divorce. Knowing my research topic, this man introduced us both, and we began hanging out on a regular basis, becoming friends.

A few weeks before I found myself wedged onto a tiny bar stool at 3 a.m., Mae had texted saying she had some big news that she wanted to tell me. When we met for coffee and snacks, I asked if she was thinking of moving to Thailand, something she'd been contemplating for a few years. "No, no," she said, "but I've decided I need to start a new project to find a boyfriend!" Although she had gone out on a few dates since her divorce two years before, Mae hadn't dated anyone seriously but very much wanted to. As she explained it to me, she didn't want to be married again, but she was feeling very lonely and wanted someone to touch her. It wasn't sex that she missed, but she wanted to be hugged, to be touched on a regular basis, and to have someone who would care about how she was feeling. She wanted to start a new "boyfriend search" with my help and thought some dancing might be a good way to begin. Figuring that a night of dancing wouldn't help me with my research, but nevertheless wanting to help Mae, I agreed, mentally writing off the night and following morning for any productive research.

Thus many hours after my regular bedtime, and after the last trains had stopped running, I found myself making small talk with other late-night dancers. After picking the day and location, Mae seemed less interested in actually participating in the meat market we were witnessing, and I wasn't about to push her. Instead of whatever proactive boyfriend searching I'd imagined we be doing—I had been making pith helmet jokes as we walked to the club—we sat, watching people and talking.

My low expectations about how much the night out would advance my research were proven utterly wrong when a man approached our table. His opening line really surprised me: "So," he asked, "are you two really friends?" Having never heard that particular pick-up line before, I asked what he meant. He elaborated, saying, "Well, you almost never see a Japanese woman and a foreign (*gaijin*) woman together. There are lots of Japanese women and foreign men, or pairs of Japanese women, but I've never seen a couple like you." Mae laughed and assured him that we were "really" friends, but he wouldn't let it drop. *How*, he wanted to know, were we friends? With a sideways glance at me, and getting increasingly flirty, Mae delivered her punch line: "Well, I'm divorced and she studies divorce!" When she used variations of this line throughout the night, it never failed to provoke a reaction, most usually a shocked "eh!?" After his surprise, this man was quick enough to say, "But you look so young! How can you be divorced?" Through the course of the night that I thought would be a waste of my research time, Mae's pithy explanation for our friendship provoked conversations about divorce with different men. Unexpectedly, I faced a dilemma: I wanted to give her space enough to meet a potential new boyfriend, but also wanted to hear how these men would react to her announcement, whatever they might say about divorce, and if this would be enough to drive them away. From what I could tell, it wasn't so stigmatizing as to immediately end an interaction.

When the club wound down in the early morning and we headed to the station to wait for the first train, Mae was still without a boyfriend but said she'd had a good time. "After all," she said, "I was more interested in going out and having a good time and was pretty sure I couldn't find a boyfriend in one night." Contrary to all my expectations, the evening turned out to be more productive for me than for her. Because many people were interested in asking why a white woman and Japanese woman were hanging out together, and because Mae usually answered this question with the punch line that she continued to perfect over the evening, interactions unexpectedly came to focus on divorce.

I provide this vignette to highlight the unexpected manner in which ethnographic data could be gathered, with opportunities for conducting research on a sensitive topic like divorce sometimes arising as a consequence of my conspicuous presence. More often than not, my positionality opened spaces for interpersonal exchanges between a range of people who might otherwise feel unwilling to discuss their personal experiences. Hence, paradoxically, my obvious differences regularly bolstered an intimacy that enriched my analysis of Japanese divorce.

Organization of this Book

No divorce is a single event. Instead, divorces expand and extend over time, shifting from a private thought to a spousal conversation, a legal status to a rearrangement of parental identities, with new freedoms that come with literal and emotional costs. This book is organized to capture snapshots of divorce across these moments, to provide perspective unlikely to be available to individuals at any particular moment in the process. In three sets of pairs, the chapters move the reader from predivorce considerations about how to diagnose and repair bad marriages (chapters 1 and 2) to middivorce legal processes and custody arrangements (chapters 3 and 4) and finally postdivorce financial, emotional, and social implications (chapters 5 and 6).

Throughout these chapters, I intersperse analysis with extended profiles of people at different stages in the divorce process, representing their perspectives, strategies, and frustrations, to illustrate my genuine respect for people's own invaluable interpretations and analysis. Rather than seamlessly integrate these profiles into the content of each chapter, I decided to label them clearly with each person's (pseudonymous) name, hoping that such a designation might make it easier for readers to remember "characters" and compare their choices across the book.[12] To further this goal, appendix A includes a chart summarizing characteristics of the people included in these profiles. Appendix B includes all quotes in the original Japanese language. Unless otherwise specified, all translations are my own. Although any representation is necessarily partial, I hope this format might bring a more realistic sense of wholeness and complexity to these people as they navigate challenging transitions.

PART 1—THE BEGINNING OF THE END

Chapter 1, "Japan's Intimate Political Economy," analyzes how marital norms and intimate possibilities have shifted in response to a restructured labor market. The *salaryman*—a white-collar, self-sacrificing workaholic—was once a popular symbol for Japan's postwar economic muscle but more recently has become an icon of all that is wrong with Japanese marriages. Stereotypical salarymen worked hard from early morning until late at night and relied on their wives for all domestic needs. In this model for intimacy, although spouses were tightly reliant on each other, they shared few interests or emotional connections. In the recessionary decades since the Japanese economic bubble burst, the salaryman's primacy has been increasingly challenged in both economic and intimate realms. Downsizing companies are less likely to hire full-time workers and instead prefer contract workers who can easily be laid off. Simultaneously, the Japanese divorce rate's increase is driven by people ending marriages that conform to the intimate ideals popular a generation before. Marital guidebooks and support groups implore spouses to retire those models for domestic intimacy, and people of all ages idealize intimacies based on emotional connections and shared activities. During Japan's postwar recovery, the intimate political economy dramatically shaped expectations and opportunities within heterosexual marriages; now it shapes how people decide to divorce.

Chapter 2, "Two Tips to Avoid Divorce," describes common tips to avoid divorce in order to analyze the characteristics of marriages that are no longer deemed healthy, good, or attractive. It is framed around two tips that seem simple but nevertheless radically challenge family norms. First, spouses are recommended not to call each other "mother" or "father," a naming practice extremely common in Japan. Second, husbands especially are entreated to begin articulating their appreciation, affection, and, most importantly, love for their wives. Voicing these feelings—saying "I love you" out loud—is touted as a simple solution to marital problems. Contextualizing this advice within broader calls for improved "communication" in marriages, I analyze these tips as substantial, but contested, revisions of ideal marital forms. Clashing with the marital patterns described in the previous chapter, these suggestions urge spouses to be atypically open with each other, nudging them to walk a fine line between detachment and overdependence. I use ethnographic examples of people trying to negotiate this delicate balance to argue that despite these tips' popularity, enacting them proves arduous.

PART 2—LEGAL DISSOLUTIONS

Chapter 3, "Constructing Mutuality," examines the legal processes of divorce in Japan to characterize the negotiations and conflicts that occur as people try to agree to divorce. To get legally divorced, both spouses sign a two-page form and submit it to a government office. These divorces are legally labeled "mutual" (kyōgi). When a divorcing couple signs and stamps the form, they acknowledge both that they want to be divorced and that they have already agreed to terms. Thus the vast majority of divorces in Japan appear to be uninvolved with the legal system. However, many protracted negotiations occur as a spouse who wants to divorce attempts to convince the other to agree to it, often by promising material property or forgoing any financial demands. Such negotiations occur in divorces that are eventually legally registered "mutual." I expose what this legal terminology obscures to argue that divorces appearing to occur with no influence from family law are in fact fundamentally shaped by legal categories and ideologies.

Chapter 4, "Families Together and Apart," explores how changing ideals of parenting, and in particular fathering, are impacting relationships between parents and children after divorce. All dynamics of postdivorce kinship begin from the legal fact that there is no joint custody in Japan. Throughout the postwar, rates of custody being granted to mothers have steadily increased and currently stand at about 80 percent. Moreover sole legal custody is coupled with a strong cultural belief that a "clean break" can benefit children because it is psychologically less damaging to have no contact with one parent than to shuttle between two households. However there is a growing movement, organized mostly by noncustodial fathers, to "reform" Japanese family law and popularize a joint custody option. This chapter focuses on both people who experienced a "clean break" divorce and those who are increasingly calling that disconnection into question. I argue that although there are no requirements for shared custody, a substantial minority of families sustain de facto joint custody. Demonstrating contested, shifting ideals of familial bonds, these attempts to share custody highlight desires to redress the disconnection divorce produces and to create connected families, even when they bring risks.

PART 3—LIVING AS AN X

Chapter 5, "The Costs of Divorce," begins by analyzing the stigma implicit in the common slang term that describes divorced people as those with "one X" or "one strike" (*batsu ichi*). In the last twenty years, the long-standing stigma around divorce in Japan has become tightly wrapped with poverty. As in other cultural contexts, divorce often decreases the standards of living of women in particular. In Japan, amidst popular awareness of increasing economic inequalities, divorce exacerbates and extends poverty in highly gendered patterns. In this chapter, I focus on the lives of women to provide a portrait of lived realities following divorce. Many of these women actively sought divorce and remain happy with that decision, although their lives after divorce can tumble quickly into poverty or walk a precarious line near it. I argue that contrary to popular images of divorce as evidence of women's ascendance and men's enervation, the lived realities of divorce leave women worse off by many measures.

In chapter 6, "Bonds of Disconnection," I analyze and refute popular assumptions that divorce isolates so completely that it leaves people desperately alone. Amidst popular discourse about the new lack of "social bonds" (*muen shakai*), divorce seems to be the most obvious instantiation of these trends: people intentionally breaking bonds they had previously held. While divorce can bring loneliness and disconnection, it also enables new bonds that would have been otherwise impossible or inconceivable. Rather than merely isolating individuals, divorce catalyzes "bonds of disconnection," opportunities for new types of connection and relationships emerging precisely because of previous separations. In therapeutic spaces, among groups of friends unified by similar experiences, and in recreational contexts, divorce brings people together and enables them to create enduring social ties. The chapter is organized around a series of extended profiles intended to give the reader a broader sense of how divorce shapes people's daily lives.

In the conclusion, "Endings and New Beginnings," I situate the book's ethnographic descriptions within my broader claims about the struggles surrounding selfhood, relationality, and intimacy in contemporary Japan. Reminding readers of the diversity of experiences analyzed and the range of people represented, I return to the book's main themes to highlight the ways in which independence and connection persist as especially fraught in the current moment. I reiterate the possible benefits and pitfalls of divorce, dismissing any simplistic notions of social collapse, family degradation, or unmitigated female triumph.

PART I

The Beginning of the End

Japan's Intimate Political Economy

Ando Mariko had been dating her boyfriend for four years when he first asked her to get married. They had met in college, when they both attended an elite university, and after graduation began jobs in the Tokyo financial sector. Although they didn't work in the same company, they had similar jobs and experienced the requirements that come with such positions—lots of stressful work, long hours, evenings and nights socializing with coworkers and clients. As they approached their midtwenties, Mariko's boyfriend thought it was time for them to get married. She wasn't against it, exactly, but she did take time to think about what she would want from a marriage. She finally agreed to get married if her boyfriend would consent to two requests. First, she wanted to be able to live close to her mother, to help with support as she got older. Second, she wanted to be able to keep working. Throughout the postwar period, the unmarked expectation has been for Japanese women to leave full-time paid work either when they get married or at the birth of their first child. Although the majority of women eventually return to the labor market, usually after children are in school, at that point they are likely to hold part-time or underpaid positions. Mariko liked her job and had worked very hard to get it, and she wasn't interested in quitting. Her boyfriend agreed to both requests and they got married in 2000, when they were both twenty-five years old.

Despite Mariko's forthright attempt to build a style of intimacy that would fit her needs and plans, it didn't take long for serious problems to manifest in her relationship. Although her husband kept his promises and had no problem with her staying at her job, he also had firm expectations about the division of labor within their new home.[1] It became readily apparent that he expected her to be responsible for all the housework, from cleaning to laundry to preparing meals. She tried to get his help but, at best, he'd agree and not follow through; at worst, he'd refuse and make her feel bad for not being able to do what he felt she was supposed to do. Because she was still working a demanding job, Mariko found herself devoting her entire weekends to frantically accomplishing household duties. In between cleaning and doing laundry, she made and froze a week's worth of meals, so that she and her husband would have something home-cooked when they came home exhausted. She kept up this blistering schedule for about a year before she had an epiphany: her husband hadn't *lied* when he agreed to let her keep working after they got married. He'd meant it. But he'd also assumed that her paid work wouldn't reduce her responsibilities for the housework. When she had articulated her desire to keep working, he understood that as permission to *add* paid labor to the roster of household tasks that he imagined as automatically her responsibility. They split a couple years after marriage, and Mariko says they're still friendly enough. Her key insight, which she imparted to me in a tone reflective of a hard-won life lesson, was: don't marry a housewife's son. No matter what such a man says, he will always expect his wife to act like a housewife.

Mariko left her marriage not only because her husband was unwilling to share domestic responsibilities. She divorced her husband because his behavior—and the unstated requirements he held for her—reflected a very recognizable type of marriage she didn't want and had intentionally worked to avoid. For much of the postwar era, normative models suggested that a breadwinning husband and stay-at-home wife create the strongest marriage and most successful family. Stereotypically, men worked hard from early morning until late at night and relied on their wives for domestic needs. In this model for intimacy, although spouses were tightly reliant on each other for some needs, they were less likely to share interests or emotional connections and therefore conformed to what I call *disconnected dependence*. Spouses in marriages built on such ideals were fundamentally linked through "practical" matters such as shared finances, at the same time that they self-consciously separated their hobbies, friendship groups, and emotional lives. But in the recessionary decades since the Japanese economic bubble burst in the early 1990s, the male breadwinner's primacy has been challenged in both economic and intimate realms. Downsizing companies now shirk hiring full-time workers in favor of legions of contract workers who can easily be laid off. Simultaneously, marital guidebooks and support groups implore spouses to retire the disconnected dependence model for domestic intimacy, and people of all ages envision intimacies instead based on emotional connections and shared activities. Styles of intimacy that were idealized a few decades before are now being held up as predictors of divorce.

Throughout the course of my research, many people with whom I spoke assumed a clear, if simplistic, relationship between divorce, gender, and labor: when a woman gets a job that pays her enough, she will leave her marriage. More than a few men were incredulous that I was doing anything other than interviewing women about how much money they made. For these men, and others who shared their perspective, divorce happens when women can finally afford to support themselves and therefore no longer want to be married. This chapter takes seriously these energetic assertions that economics and divorce are obviously linked. I agree that they are linked but not because, as implied by economic determinism, money unconsciously motivates people's decisions in intimate realms or because financial need is the only thing binding women to heterosexual marriage.

Instead, I argue, men and women diagnose marital problems and decide to divorce partially in response to models for intimacy that are themselves constructed through labor patterns, an interweaving I call Japan's intimate political economy. In this term, I connect employment structures, tax systems, and gendered hiring practices with the conditions of possibility for intimate relationships. Throughout the postwar period, the intimate political economy has created powerful norms suggesting certain overlaps between familial, intimate, and labor spheres are more natural, healthy, and beneficial for everyone involved. In the current moment, as men and women contemplate divorce or work to avoid it, they are more likely to contest and refuse these previously normative linkages. As demonstrated in the examples throughout this chapter, men and women perceive real risk—to marriages and families, but also to individuals—emanating from the ways spouses work. During Japan's postwar recovery, the intimate political economy dramatically shaped expectations and opportunities within heterosexual marriages; now it shapes how people decide to divorce.

Economic Miracles, Corporate Families, and Japan, Inc.

At the end of World War II, few people predicted that the Japanese economy would ever become one of the largest in the world. The defeated nation lay in ruins, not only from two atomic bombs but also from the extensive firebombing by Allied forces and the human and financial costs of decades of extensive colonial expansion (Dower 1999; Young 1998). But between 1950 and 1973, the Japanese economy doubled in size every seven years, and between 1946 and 1976, the economy increased fifty-five-fold (Blomström, Gangnes, and La Croix 2001, 2; Ikeda 2002; Johnson 1982, 6). By 1968, Japan had the second

largest economy in the world as measured by nominal gross domestic prod-
uct. This growth came to be labeled the Japanese economic "miracle" and,
precisely because it was so unexpected, significant scholarly and public attention focused on analyzing what made it possible. Japan's intimate political
economy was fundamental to this recovery and shaped standard labor practices and expectations.

At the level of policy, Japan's economic miracle was facilitated through a
so-called "Iron Triangle" linking large companies, ministerial bureaucracies,
and politicians through shared models for development and production. In
this system, politicians advocated policy created in conversation with business
leaders, which was then articulated by government bureaucrats as the standard to follow. Although any recommendations advocated by government
ministries were always technically optional, this arrangement created extremely
strong obligation, reciprocity, and debt between the three corners of this triangle. The tight partnership was eventually labeled "Japan, Inc.," implying that
the entire national economy was running as if it were a single conglomerate
(Abegglen 1970, 35; Johnson 1982). This extended collaboration between government ministries, corporations, and politicians created stringent economic
policies shaping the labor market as it transitioned from agricultural to industrial and eventually service economies. From the early 1960s until the early
1990s, this method for economic growth was so successful that Japan was, on
one hand, lauded as having "lessons" for the United States and, on the other,
represented as an existential threat to Western supremacy (Alexander 2002,
283; Vogel 1979).

Although the terminology "Japan, Inc." was first created to describe high-
level interactions, it translated into personal and familial realms as a commitment that regular people felt to the national project of growth. The miraculous national growth was manifesting in concrete improvements in people's
lives: Prime Minister Ikeda's "income doubling plan" began in 1960, and
within seven years average personal incomes had doubled (Moriguchi and
Ono 2006, 162; Rohlen 1974, 11). In the 1960s, 1970s, and 1980s, a range of Japanese citizens felt part of the larger project to return Japan to a global stage and
then to grow the economy at a miraculous pace: housewives felt their labor
was fundamental to national success; white-collar businessmen linked their
success with that of their employer; blue-collar workers held a strong sense of
how their labor contributed to national improvements; agricultural workers
were proudly aware of how their labor improved the nation.[2] In this national
project, we see a "mobilization of a large majority of the population to support
economic goals" (Johnson 1982, 307), what Cole evocatively calls a "community
of fate" (1979, 252).

Such commitments were reinforced through common rhetoric that characterized an employee's relationship to their employer as akin to a family bond. Reminiscent of Meiji-era political discourse linking all citizens as members of the same family (a topic I'll discuss more in chapter 3), this rhetoric suggests that employers, managers, and employees at all levels were on the same team working toward success (Tachibanaki 2005, 61). Although such collectivizing rhetoric might be attempted in other cultural contexts, during Japan's booming economy, it accurately described the shared goals and sense of community that many male, full-time workers felt (Sako 1997, 4). For instance, Rohlen (1974), conducting research in the 1960s and 1970s, found bank employees were sometimes organized through strict hierarchy and other times as a "harmonious" group of equals. Researching during the 1980s economic bubble, Kondo (1990, 161) suggests "company as family" was a pervasive idiom "shaping workers' lives and creating disciplined, loyal employees who strive to achieve group goals." In these ways, Japan's miraculous economy relied on rhetoric characterizing labor as creating a family-like bond, with the attendant burdens of loyalty and responsibility. More broadly, Japan's intimate political economy linked actual families with rhetorical families organized around labor.

Gendered Labor at the Core of a "Miracle"

Government and corporate policies facilitating Japan's economic recovery were built through, and in turn reinforced, a deeply gendered labor market. Laws, standard hiring practices, and common norms pushed men and women into very different types of labor, both of which were fundamental to Japan's economy. In general, men were most likely to have access to "regular" (*seishain*) positions, characterized by full-time work, the possibility of promotion, and at least an implicit promise for long-term employment. Although most commonly associated with middle-class men in white-collar positions, during the postwar economic recovery, these kinds of "regular" positions were available to men in different types of work from blue-collar manufacturing to business. Indeed, in contrast to popular images presenting postwar Japan as a "middle-class society" with minimal class differentiation, the labor market shifted between moments of greater and lesser income equality. For instance, in the late 1960s and early 1970s, a labor shortage minimized the differences between remuneration offered to regular employees of small companies and to those at larger firms (Tachibanaki 2005, 60). Earlier in the postwar era, and after the economic bubble burst, male employees earned substantially different salaries based on the size of their employer. Throughout the postwar period, women, particularly wives and mothers, were most likely to be hired into nonregular, flexible, and marginalized positions that were no less vital to the labor market but rhetorically minimized in popular discourse and scholarship. These gendered hiring patterns fundamentally shaped Japan's intimate political economy, linking employment with particular styles of intimacy.

Despite the diversity of employment possibilities, popular imagination in Japan and elsewhere often linked the postwar "miracle" economy with a particular character: the "salaryman." Although the English term might suggest any man who earns a salary, the meaning in Japanese is quite specific.[3] The quintessential salaryman is an overworked white-collar man in a relatively anonymous suit, with a conservative haircut and boring tie. He goes to work early in the morning and works long hours that are extended even further by mandatory socializing either with coworkers to build "team spirit" or with clients to improve business. He might get home very late at night, too late to see his children awake, only to wake up early the next morning to start the whole process again. Significant scholarly and ethnographic attention has been focused on the salaryman as a key social character in Japan's long "miracle" economic boom.[4] In the many comic books (*manga*) and films representing salarymen, their relatively privileged white-collar position belies the brutality of a daily grind keeping them from almost everything but work (Matanle, McCann, and Ashmore 2008; Skinner 1979). Although many people identified with the archetypal salaryman, wanted to become one, or wished the same for their sons, media commentary during the economic miracle highlighted the difficulties of the salaryman lifestyle, especially the long hours away from family and the daily requirements for work (Cook 2016, 3; Crawcour 1978, 245).

Such male laborers were only made possible by particular forms of domestic intimacy created through a gendered division of labor. Working long hours, augmented by obligatory late-night drinking, a salaryman rarely had time for anything else. For requirements of basic living—prepared food, clean clothes, paid bills—a breadwinner relied on his wife, who often accomplished all tasks surrounding the household and children. Decades of ethnographic research represents common gendered responsibilities for domestic spaces, family relationships, and childcare. Wives shouldered substantial domestic work ranging from buying food and preparing healthy meals to calculating and tracking a household budget and providing elaborate educational opportunities and support for their children (Allison 2000; Frühstück and Walthall 2011; Gordon 1997; Imamura 1987). The clarity of these responsibilities is visible in the ethnographic record but also in survey responses: in 1974, Ootake et al. (1980) found that husbands did less than 3 percent of their family's housework. By 1981, for instance, Japanese married couples reported husbands did less than twenty minutes of housework, including childcare, each day, a figure that rose slightly to 2.5 hours per week in 1994 (Ishii-Kuntz 1994, 33; Tsuya, Bumpass, and Choe 2000, 208; see also Fuwa 2004). Precisely because women's responsibilities were commonly understood to be vital to both the national economy and raising the next generation, housewives were given respect not always found in other cultural contexts, which translated into some collective political authority (LeBlanc 1999; Nakamatsu 1994, 100).

For decades, salarymen stood as a key symbol in the postwar Japanese political economy. Almost from the moment of the creation of the term "salaryman," men who fall into this category have been simultaneously envied for their regular salary, pitied for the requirements that come with their job, and constructed as a synecdoche of the nation—a pinnacle of masculine power in a nation constitutionally forbidden to raise a military.[5] The salaryman was such a common representation of Japanese men that when Roberson and Suzuki (2003) assembled a volume concerning Japanese masculinity, they subtitled it "dislocating the salaryman doxa." Both within and beyond Japan, salarymen have been deployed as powerful and popular symbols of the postwar recovery, economic power, masculinity, or Japaneseness in general.[6]

For most of the postwar era being a salaryman indexed a particular system of employment akin to labor monogamy. First, unlike the majority of workers in Japan, salarymen were offered so-called "lifetime employment" (shūshin koyō), an implicit guarantee from employers that any man hired as a salaryman would have a position at the company until his retirement. This singular, normative, and life-long commitment between a worker and an employer might seem to breed inefficiency, but for many workers it was an unmarked norm that justified the loyalty due to employers (Abegglen 1958, 11; Cole 1971, 52; Kelly 1986, 603; Rohlen 1974).[7] Japanese courts have repeatedly refused to allow employers to lay off or fire employees with impunity, further supporting extended employment for workers in this protected class (Foote 1996; Song 2014, 69). An employee leaving a position was equally unlikely, so much so that it would be imagined as a stigmatizing "divorce" (Dore 1983, cited in Moriguchi and Ono 2006, 163). Second, the majority of a salaryman's salary was calculated based on years of service to the company (nenkō joretsu), rather than on merit. Aware of such a formula, salarymen could accurately predict how much money they would be making in every future year (Allison 1994; Rohlen 1974). Third, salarymen's work lives were shaped by frequent transfers within a company and between branch offices. While salarymen could expect that they would regularly be transferred, they couldn't easily predict their division within the company or where, geographically, they would be working. The logic behind this strategy suggested that employees who had first-hand knowledge about more than just one particular specialty would be more well rounded and better prepared to fulfill the company's needs (Rebick 2001, 124), while the arrangement also allowed for a flexible labor force within the structure guaranteeing lifetime employment to some. So as not to interrupt children's schooling, salarymen often moved alone and left their families behind (Fujita 2016). For all these reasons, during Japan's economic recovery and boom, salarymen's lives were represented as predictable, possibly a little boring, but intensely secure if measured through salary and employment stability.

The salaryman's symbolic importance has never been matched by actual employment statistics. Salarymen were, and to some extent still are, ubiquitous as symbols, but relatively few Japanese people ever experienced work lives in this form. Throughout the postwar, various studies have suggested that 20 to 35 percent of employees were in "lifetime" positions with the attendant guarantees, seniority pay, and regular transfers (Ono 2009; Song 2014, 61; Tachibanaki 1987, 669). The actual number of salarymen is difficult to calculate because although "salaryman" has long been an incredibly recognizable and powerful social category, it is not one that is used explicitly in employment contracts. The promise of lifetime employment for certain male workers was always implicit, a sense that came with particular jobs available at larger companies, rather than a contracted guarantee. Salarymen fell within the categories of "regular" employees (as opposed to part-time, contract, or dispatch employees), but that category also includes workers who did not stay with the company for the course of their careers, such as female workers categorized as "office ladies" (Ogasawara 1998). Brinton confirms that "No explicit contractual agreement exists, either for the employer not to dismiss the employee or for the employee not to quit and seek employment elsewhere" (1993, 131).[8]

As the gendered terminology might suggest, the secure trajectories associated with salarymen were foreclosed for female workers, although female labor was fundamental to the Japanese economic miracle. Despite the popular image of Japanese women as "only" housewives, female labor and in particular female part-time labor facilitated the lifetime employment system. In 1980, for instance, 64 percent of women between ages forty-five and forty-nine were in the paid labor force, a number that rose to 71 percent in 1990 and approximately 75 percent by 2010.[9] However, although a majority of women worked for pay at some point in their lives, especially between 1970 and 2000, many quit or were forced out either when they married or when they had their first child (Brinton 1993; White 2002; Ogasawara 1998). Mandatory "retirement" at these moments had been written into women's employment contracts until the 1960s.[10] After court cases forced a change in contracts, causality in these decisions is unclear. Some women surely left employment because they wanted to, but others did so unwillingly or in response to the demonstrable lack of promotional opportunities for female employees, or because strong norms suggested it was appropriate for women to "retire" upon marriage or childbirth (Atsumi 1988, 57). After having left a job because of family needs (or perceived family needs), parallel needs pushed women back into the labor market. Partially to cover the high costs of children's education and other family expenses, many women returned to the workforce as part-time employees after their children were in school, intentionally choosing part-time positions that allowed them to prioritize family work (ibid., 55). This pattern of labor force participation until childbirth and a later return to paid work was labeled the "M-curve" for the shape it made over a woman's lifetime and was particularly pronounced from about 1970 until 2000 (Japan Institute for Labour Policy and Training 2014, 26).

During that period, female workers tended to be treated as a flexible labor force, the "cushions around the core" that enabled lifetime employment for a minority of men, or as "a safety valve" and "shock absorbers" to mitigate fluctuations in the market (Johnson 1982, 13; Kelly 1991, 406; Miller 2003, 181). Brinton (1993) convincingly argues that female labor was fundamentally necessary to the Japanese economic miracle in two ways: first, the unpaid domestic labor done by women enabled and supported the male labor force; second, the paid positions held by women were designed for easy hiring and firing, allowing labor markets flexibility without threatening the lifetime jobs given to male workers. In the 1980s, marriage was "jokingly referred to as women's 'lifetime employment,'" phrasing that reveals links between employment opportunities for women and marital norms (Brinton 1988, 325). In short, the stable jobs possible for *some* male workers were made possible through unstable jobs held by *many* women, in addition to the unpaid domestic labor they provided.

Reinforcing Gender through Tax and Salary Structures

Japan's intimate political economy is further constructed and enforced through tax law and common salary structures that reward a gendered division of labor conforming to normative marital forms. In addition to the gendered hiring policies mentioned above, only male workers were eligible for salary augmentations explicitly labeled as "family allowance," that is, extra money for workers with families to support. Many if not most companies offered additional salary to married male workers so that they might better support wives and children: in 1991, Shiota found that 89.3 percent of companies surveyed offered family allowance and that it averaged 16,113 yen per month (about $120 at that time) (Shiota 1992, 37; Nakamatsu 1994, 92). In this practice, companies were creating and reinforcing gendered norms they assumed to be natural; female workers, even female breadwinners, were ineligible for this additional salary.[11] Salary structures directly reflected workers' gender: married male workers were automatically assumed to be breadwinners and rewarded for that status, while female labor was restricted as ancillary and merely augmentative no matter the worker's family situation.

The national tax structure further reinforces these gendered labor assumptions by offering substantial financial incentives for married women who limit their paid labor. Begun in 1961, "Allowance for Spouses" (*haigūsha kōjo*) permits dependent spouses, most commonly wives, to deduct their earnings under a threshold from the primary earner's taxable income. If a spouse earns less than ¥1.03 million ($10,300) per year, ¥380,000 ($3,800) is automatically deducted from the breadwinner's taxable income.[12] Since 1987, through the "Special Allowance for Spouses" (*haigūsha tokubetsu kōjo*), a breadwinner gains additional deductions if their dependent spouse earns less than ¥1.41 million ($14,100). In practical terms, this tax system rewards people who are heterosexually married and chose to labor in patterns conforming to the gendered ideals espoused in the Japan, Inc. model. It incentivizes dependent spouses to actively seek lower-paying jobs, positions with salaries that will not push them over the threshold and out of the "dependent" category, thereby creating a demand for low-paying jobs that might otherwise be unattractive (Adachi 2018, 111). Moreover, many companies that offer "family allowance" calculate eligibility for those benefits through these tiers, meaning that a wife who makes more could jeopardize both her husband's tax reduction and his additional "family allowance" income. Because of such strong incentives for women not to earn over this amount, it has been called the "painful wall" of one million yen (*butsukaru itai kabe*) (Fuji 1993).[13]

Although this tax code does not stipulate the gender of the dependent spouse, survey data suggest that 40 percent of employed married women qualify for this tax deduction; male recipients are not counted (Yamada 2011, 544). We can tell that men and women are shaping their labor around these incentives because of the spike in the number of female workers who make just at or under the dependent spouse tax threshold (Takahashi et al. 2009). Ishii-Kuntz et al. (2004, 786) found that in their sample of heterosexually married couples with small children, a husband's salary accounted for 88.5 percent of household income. This tax policy, even without gendered hiring requirements written into the law, pulls women into the labor market but rewards them for choosing ancillary, lower-paying positions. Therefore what seem like tax "benefits" for female workers instead "reinforce the sex role division in society" (Nakamatsu 1994, 92) and, as I explain in chapter 5, have particularly deleterious effects for divorced women needing jobs to support themselves and any children. Other economic policies, including the pension system, further reward families that conform to normative gendered divisions of labor.[14] These highly gendered patterns of remuneration and taxation shaped marriage norms through labor patterns despite Article 14 in Japan's Constitution, which explicitly articulates gender equality, and an equal employment opportunity law (Danjo koyōkikai kintōhō) that went into effect in 1986. Although the EEOL has been revised, it remains a list of recommendations that requests employers to voluntarily comply and has therefore has prompted few systemic changes (Abe 2011; Assmann 2014; Boling 2008; Gelb 2000). Throughout Japan's postwar recovery, economic transformation was facilitated through a labor market built on, and actively reinforcing, a restrictive model for marital relationships that manifested this gendered division of labor.

MR. YAMAGUCHI: TRYING TO BE A GOOD HUSBAND

Mr. Yamaguchi has lived for decades in a "normal" marriage and is now trying to manage the risks that style of intimacy has brought into his life. He is so open and forthright about his worries that his wife might divorce him that sometimes I can't tell if he's kidding or not. He's not. He's really worried and doing what he can to make sure his wife never wants a divorce. As he explained to me with awareness of the irony, most of what he was doing in 2005 to be a good husband consisted of doing exactly the opposite of what he did in his younger years. So far, his method is working and he has a good relationship with his wife, but it takes effort and feels like a substantial revision of their relationship. He's paying attention to the media that suggests all sorts of risks in marriages like his and trying to strategize with friends about what they can do.

In a lot of ways, Mr. Yamaguchi was a typical salaryman with a fairly typical family. Born in 1943, he grew up in the immediate aftermath of World War II. This places him within the generation who, as children, bore the misery of a war for which they had no personal responsibility. Mr. Yamaguchi grew up in Aichi Prefecture but attended the elite Kyoto University, which put him on track for a successful career. Reflecting common hiring practices, Mr. Yamaguchi was recruited directly from university and began his "lifetime" salaryman position immediately after he graduated with a degree in engineering.

He and his wife met through a matchmaker (*omiai*) and married when he was twenty-seven, and they had two children in quick succession. Working in a company that rapidly became a telecom giant, he was regularly transferred between different divisions and was asked to live outside of Japan for years. The transfers were part of the job, and not surprising, but living outside of Japan was especially challenging for his wife and their children. Living in upstate New York in the 1980s gave the Yamaguchi children opportunities to learn and use English but was isolating and challenging for Mrs. Yamaguchi. In parallel with Kurotani's (2005) analysis, Mrs. Yamaguchi found it harder to raise her children and support her husband when they were outside of Japan. There were some other Japanese families around, but she had to tutor their children to keep them on track with the Japanese national curriculum, and she worked hard to find food and other products that would have been easy to get in Japan.

Throughout this time, Mr. Yamaguchi worked. As in Japan, he put in long days at the office, sometimes longer now because they were staying late to be able to coordinate with colleagues still in Japan. Looking back, when he tells me about his family's time in the United States, Mr. Yamaguchi emphasizes how much was being asked of his wife, in particular, but stresses that he didn't fully understand that in the moment. They were all doing what they had to do, what they were supposed to do, and his focus on work felt appropriate and responsible. Working hard was how he knew how to be a good husband and father, although he worried out loud to me about the negative repercussions those previous actions are now having on his marriage. After he was transferred back to Japan, he worked for another decade or so before he hit his company's mandatory retirement age.

Sixty-eight when I first met him at a public talk, he seemed far younger and full of tremendous energy. He was practically the poster child for an ideal retirement: happily attending all sorts of events that he never had time for before, manifesting his natural curiosity. His worry was that work had taken him too far away from his wife, in particular, or that they were tied together only through their children or basic needs for each other. Aware now of things he didn't see in his younger days, he is deeply appreciative of all his wife had done and continues to do but wasn't fully sure how to express that to her in ways that would make her happy. From the very first moment I met him— when he spontaneously started talking to me in an elevator as we left the same event, as I explained in this book's introduction—Mr. Yamaguchi seemed more willing to communicate verbally than most people, but this wasn't something his wife shared or especially enjoyed. She seemed, instead, to put up with his talkativeness and desire to join events, preferring to stay at home and socialize with friends she already had. For this reason, I could never tell if Mr. Yamaguchi's fears of divorce were well founded. On the one hand, being aware of the risk of divorce seems to mitigate it. But on the other, as Mr. Yamaguchi suggested, he and his wife weren't really used to sharing time with each other and she seemed happier when they continued on with their own activities and interests.[15] Mr. Yamaguchi understands and tried to respect his wife's preferences for separation and independent hobbies but worries about what would be best for her, himself, and their marriage.

Marriages Built through Disconnected Dependence

Hiring, salary, and tax policies have inscribed Japan's intimate political economy into normative family life, making certain family forms and styles of intimacy seem superior. Particularly for generations of Japanese people building families in the 1960s, 1970s, and 1980s, strong social norms dictated a disconnection between gendered spheres of influence. Both spouses were supported, in social terms, by the other's complementary set of responsibilities. Researching in the 1980s, Edwards (1989) created an evocative phrase to capture the particularities of this relationship: complementary incompetence. Because labor norms discriminated against married women and mothers to push them out of full-time labor, the average woman was unable to find a career that enabled her to support herself. Men, on the other hand, were not taught basic domestic necessities like how to do laundry or cook nutritious meals. Even if a particular man had domestic skills or knowledge, the demands of his work schedule would likely make it impossible for him to feed and clothe himself. Thus, Edwards convincingly argues, Japanese spouses in the 1970s and 1980s were linked together partially through their complementary needs and abilities—her need for a financially viable salary and his for the domestic assistance required to earn such a salary. Many spouses found such dynamics normal, ideal, and satisfying (Ishii-Kuntz 1992; Lebra 1984).

Compared with more contemporary intimate relationships, these older styles of intimacy embody disconnected dependence, framed by both centripetal and centrifugal forces on spouses. Gendered labor policies, demands placed on male employees, and family norms pushed men and women to be structurally dependent on each other. Judged solely by the archetypal ways married couples shared money—a husband earned money but dutifully turned his paycheck over to his wife, who took care of family expenses and quite likely gave her husband a small weekly allowance—Japanese spouses were fundamentally linked.

And yet these strong social centripetal forces were met, in practice, with equally common disconnections between the spouses. While they might need each other, many spouses didn't want to spend too much time together. When I talk with older female friends in their sixties and seventies about their husbands, what I hear are often hilariously crafted narratives of annoyance and incompetence: husbands are punch lines and are regularly made fun of, especially if they are around "too much." Indeed the ethnographic record contains many examples of Japanese wives suggesting that a good husband is "healthy and absent," an idea that was voted "phrase of the year" in 1986 (Ueno 1987, 80; White 1987, 151).[16] In ideology, labor realms, hobbies, friendships, and spheres of responsibility spouses were largely disconnected (Borovoy 2005; 2010, 67; Imamura 1987, 13; Ishii-Kuntz and Maryanski 2003). In these ways, discursively and in practice, typical marital relationships for most of the postwar period were framed through disconnected dependence: spouses absolutely needed each other and fully recognized that dependence but often led social and emotional lives that were fundamentally disconnected from each other. In the 1990s and earlier, these patterns were normal, unremarkable, and evidence of a healthy marriage.

Marital sexuality, as described in my interviews and represented more generally in the media, furthered a sense of spouses largely disconnected from each other at that time. Although married couples were expected to have children, many interlocutors described a sense that after children were born, it wasn't unusual for couples to stop having sex. When describing this dynamic to me, people often drew a similar diagram—an inverted triangle with each of the upper corners representing one spouse, linked together by marriage, and the child as the third point below them. As they described, once a child is born, spouses become parents and lose or diminish the connection they had with each other. While such tension between marital and parental roles is not unique to Japan, marriages built on disconnected dependence situated sexuality as one realm in which spouses might be disconnected. Although they didn't think it was ideal, interlocutors explained that it was not wholly unusual for seemingly "good" marriages to include little sex between spouses and/or extramarital affairs, especially by the husband, a point supported by the ethnographic record (Allison 1994; Laurent 2017, 114; Moore 2010; Moriki 2017, 45).

By the early 2000s, I heard about marriages framed through disconnected dependence mostly as people complained—about the bad marriage they had, what they didn't like, and whom they had decided to leave. Older women especially verbalized their ongoing burdens caused by the domestic responsibilities and care work that continued to fall on them after their husbands retired. More than a few wives in their sixties and older very clearly identified the ultimate lie embedded in the social contract they had agreed to upon marriage: if man was to lifetime employment as woman was to household responsibilities, only one of those people would ever really get to retire. Unless other family members stepped in to help, a woman with a retired husband had just as much housework and responsibility, if not more, and now also had her husband underfoot and in the way. For spouses who spent many of their married years in separate spheres, this physical and temporal proximity could lead women in particular to consider divorce more seriously.

NOMURA-SAN: AT THE END

Nomura-san is one such woman struggling to balance the new realities of her marriage with her sense of responsibilities. She is in her early eighties, with three adult children and two grandchildren on whom she dotes. Her husband was a doctor, with an income that pushed them into far wealthier circles than they had been born into, but Nomura-san's life was shaped by his constant requests, incredibly high standards, and unwillingness to do much of anything for himself. In addition to the normal cooking and cleaning responsibilities for any housewife, Nomura-san was responsible for all the details of her husband's life: if he went to play golf, she had to remember to pack his favorite pair of gloves and maybe a spare; if he traveled overnight, she was responsible for his entire suitcase and anticipating whatever needs or wants might come up during the trip. His demands were constant, whether stated or unstated. Nomura-san understood all this as her job, but as she got older, she had less patience for the precision of his demands and grew frustrated that he wouldn't cut her any slack given her advancing age. On some level, she thought there was nothing to do about his personality: he was the first and only son (*chōnan*) born into his family for two generations, and also the youngest of all his siblings, so he was spoiled from birth.[17] By the time I met them, when they were in their seventies, she seemed resigned to making do and spun epic poems of complaint about her husband as soon as he was out of earshot.

This changed one day when she said, quietly but with a serious expression, that she had something to tell me about her husband. Mr. Nomura had always been a drinker. His drinking had moved years ago from fun, to necessary for his professional masculinity, to troublesome, to a marital burden for Nomura-san to bear. A week before they'd gone to some function where'd he gotten drunk. As usual, she managed to get him into their car and drive him home, something that she hates because she knows her eyesight is slipping and she's terrified she'll get into an accident one of these nights. But he passed out in the car, and when she got home, she physically couldn't lift him. Alone, late at night, with a passed-out husband who is probably twice her weight, Nomura-san finally managed to get him into their foyer. This area, called the *genkan*, is where the family leaves their shoes to keep dirt out of the house and is metaphorically most similar to an American trash area—it is the domestic space that stays dirty in order to keep the rest of the house clean. Nomura-san's husband fell asleep in this dirty space and she woke the next morning to find that he'd soiled himself and slept all night in the filth.

Nomura-san has long told me stories about her husband, but this version felt very different. She wasn't laughingly angry and it didn't feel like a narrative of his absurdity. Her story ended when she leaned toward me and said, emphatically, "This is a reason, right? This is a reason" (*Kore wa riyū ni narimasu yone? Kore ga riyū desu*). We had been friends well before I began this project on divorce and didn't really talk about my research much, so it took me an embarrassingly long moment to realize that Nomura-san was asking me to confirm that she had finally found a good reason to leave her marriage. This reason was not just her husband's alcoholism or selfishness, or the fact that she had been dealing with both of these for decades, but rather her new physical inability to lift him. She had been dealing with all those other difficulties by relying on her own physical strength and, for the first time, it had failed her.

Nomura-san was furious with her husband—mad about his unending selfishness and how that translated into his behavior toward her—but when she obliquely brought up the possibility of divorce it wasn't only a reflection of her anger. That anger wasn't new, and therefore wasn't motivating her sudden decision to mention divorce for the first time. Instead, divorce entered her mind because she simply couldn't sustain their relationship as it had been: she was no longer able to give him the physical care he apparently required, and their marriage had been at least partially based on such an exchange. Even if she resented it, she felt responsible for his daily needs, and this particularly horrible episode made clear how her own aging made that work less possible. Reflecting her awareness of popular media describing the increased risk of divorce among older couples (*jukunen rikon*), but also her sense of what is necessary to sustain a marriage, Nomura-san wondered aloud if she had perhaps encountered the final straw, piled as it was on a lifetime of frustration.

A Burst Bubble and Economic Restructuring

Despite the terminology now used, the economic bubble bursting did not happen in a single moment, nor was the shift immediately identified as the beginning of an economic crisis. Between 1989 and 1992, yen became less cheaply available, contributing to inflation of housing prices and land prices, and corporations were left underwater with mortgages for high prices that properties would never be able to reach again. As Grimes describes it, "borrowers became unable to pay back loans collateralized with land and securities whose value was plummeting" (2001, xvii). After the bubble burst, as a result of ineffective policies, the Japanese economy hovered around recessionary levels for more than a decade, a period labeled the "lost decade" or "the Heisei recessions" after the era's name in Japanese. From 1992 to 1999, average real GDP growth was one percent (Mori, Shiratsuka, and Taguchi 2001, 54). As the government and the private sector attempted to spring the nation out of recession, they instantiated substantially new ways of organizing, legislating, and encouraging labor. While millions of people lost wages or work altogether, the Japanese labor market was radically re-formed.

These most recent antecedents to contemporary labor patterns largely revolve around changing employment opportunities, especially for younger people. When Japanese companies were faced with dramatic profit loss in the mid-1990s, they were more likely to protect their lifetime employees by retaining benefits for older workers and offering many fewer options for younger workers (Brinton 2010; Song 2014). Rather than laying off or reducing the benefits of lifetimes employees, companies instead kept supporting those older generations of male workers and significantly slowed the hiring of new lifetime employees. These decisions to support older male workers reflect the continuing expectation that such men were breadwinners or, in Japanese terms, the central pillar that holds up a house (*daikokubashira*) (Hidaka 2011, 112).

Instead of hiring a new generation of regular, full-time employees, as was typical in previous decades, employers instead increased positions for temporary contract workers (*haken*) or part-time workers (*pāto*). In 1991, only 20 percent of workers were in nonregular positions, but that figure grew to 30 percent in 2003 and continues to grow through the present (Japan Institute for Labour Policy and Training 2016, 14). By 2007, 55 percent of women in the workforce, and almost 20 percent of men, were in nonregular positions (Song 2014, 30). Younger workers, men and women alike, faced job prospects akin to those common for women in previous generations—perpetual part-time work with few benefits and little predictability—and new categories of "contract" labor. In this latter type, workers are hired to complete work that had previously been done by full-time and lifetime employees; these newer workers might be working full-time hours but are paid a fraction of the salary (Driscoll 2009, 300; Keizer 2008, 413).[18] These changes in practice were both codified and expanded in 2003 with passage of a renewed Dispatch Workers Law, allowing companies leeway to convert more full-time positions to contract jobs, while also being allowed to hire contract workers for a longer continuous period before being legally required to offer them full-time employment (Araki 2007, 277).[19]

Rhetorics of Responsibility

In the midst of such changes in the labor market's structures and opportunities, the 2000s brought a new popular consciousness surrounding "self-responsibility" (*jiko sekinin*). The term was popularized by Prime Minister Koizumi Jun'ichirō when he suggested that the Japanese economy would never recover from recessions unless individual citizens began to take responsibility for themselves. This rhetoric aligned with global neoliberal policies designed to free the flow of capital across national borders, often to the benefit of nonlocal investors. Elected in 2001, Prime Minister Koizumi undertook a massive program of privatization, emphasizing particularly the Japanese Post Bank. The publicly owned bank of the Japanese post office system was, at the time, the world's largest financial institution, with 240 trillion yen in holdings as of July 2002 (Scher and Yoshino 2004, 121). This accounted for approximately 30 percent of all Japanese household savings and, combined with the life insurance also offered, the post office held "a quarter of Japan's personal financial assets" and "virtually every" Japanese citizen has a postal savings account (Porges and Leong 2006, 386; Imai 2009, 139). In a nation with comparatively high savings rates, these patterns created a large supply of capital sitting, as it were, in the Post Bank's coffers (Garon 2002). Although Koizumi justified his call to privatize this bank as a necessary step to recover from a lingering recession, people with whom I spoke also described the move as resulting from international pressure, particularly from the United States. Because it was a public company, foreign capital was unable to access the Post Bank's funds; if the bank were privatized, its potential profits could be available to Japanese or foreign investors.

After Koizumi dissolved parliament and called a new national election, the summer of 2005 was full of campaigning targeted at creating popular support for the privatization of the Post Bank (Nemoto, Krauss, and Pekkanen 2008; Maclachlan 2006). In the midst of this campaign, in attempts to explain and popularize a movement toward private-sector ownership, Koizumi emphasized ideals related to independence and individuality. Specifically, he argued that truly mature people had "self-responsibility" and relied on themselves rather than their families, communities, or government to achieve what they needed (Takeda 2008; Thorsten 2009). Thus newly articulated ethics of "self-responsibility" were linked with the promise of economic recovery, particularly through a privatized Post Bank. Koizumi's plebiscite election on the possible privatization was a fantastic success for him, and even members of his own party who had voted against an earlier version of the law changed their votes. In everyday terms, one result of this election is a continuing discursive focus on self-responsibility as a measure of maturity and success.

Intimate Ideals in a New Economy

A hugely popular entertainment franchise begun in 2004 demonstrated links between self-responsibility and the intimate political economy. In it, the romantic hero is a new kind of worker and a new kind of man imagined to be capable of a new kind of relationship. The story, told in various media forms including a movie, a television show, a manga series, and online bulletin board systems, is collectively titled "Train Man." The narrative began on March 14, 2004, on the popular online bulletin board system called "Channel Two," which is akin perhaps to Reddit in sheer numbers of users and rapidly updated content. On that day, in a post, a person using the handle "train_man" (*densha otoko*) told a story and asked for advice.[20] An extreme and antisocial nerd (*otaku*), train_man was riding home from buying geeky figurines when a drunken salaryman began to harass and threaten women in his train car. Gathering his courage, train_man finally got brave enough to step up to the man when he harassed a young woman whom train_man found to be quite beautiful. Train_man didn't accomplish much, but after the police arrived and stopped the harasser, the women were so grateful to train_man that they asked for his mailing address to send him thank you cards. On the bulletin board post, train_man asks his unknown readers for advice about how to respond to this and how to possibly make himself attractive enough to win the heart of the beautiful young woman. The rest of the narrative plays out his attempts to enact the advice he gets from his online audience and, depending on the media iteration, he either succeeds in winning the girl, improves his life, or imagines the whole thing. This story, told and retold in various media forms, occupied a central segment of mainstream popular culture in 2005, as I began my fieldwork. It is a remarkably warm-hearted story suggesting, among other things, that even internet connections with strangers can produce lasting and meaningful relationships. Although there is no evidence to suggest that the original events ever took place—that they were "real" instead of fictional or staged—the story broadly suggests that real human connection (*ningen kankei*) is possible even through the internet.[21]

For our purposes, the story also represents a sea change in idealized forms of Japanese masculinity. The entire narrative is prompted by a drunken, threatening salaryman harassing random women. In this moment, the former hero of the Japanese economic miracle has become a belligerent, entitled drunk who apparently does nothing productive. Throughout the film, all representations of salarymen are equally negative: they are either drunk, rude, or in crisis because their work computer is overrun with pornography. In contrast with the generalist salarymen, train_man appears to be a specialist with a tremendous amount of computer knowledge, and he certainly doesn't join any of the obligatory drinking sessions that are typical for salarymen. And yet, importantly, he is the romantic hero of the film. After a makeover prompted by suggestions from his online friends, and after he learns the obligatory lesson that he should still be himself to win the girl he likes, train_man does exactly that. He wins her heart without conforming to stereotypical markers of masculinity. Such a representation was one of many that suggested a different kind of man was newly attractive, and capable of a new kind of relationship, in early twenty-first century Japan.[22]

Since then, it has become common to characterize such supposedly "weak" men as "herbivores" (sōshoku)—as opposed to carnivores—because they enact masculinity in ways that disrupt or refuse earlier models for masculine silence, emotional distance, and patriarchal control (Charlebois 2013; Miles 2019; Slater and Galbraith 2011). In derogatory terms, they are wimpy. This label could be an insult or a new badge of pride, and it's equally possible to find people who relish the distinction from older performances of masculinity or who identify such a "loss" of masculinity as evidence of Japan's decline (Frühstück and Walthall 2011, 8). Men and women are cautiously trying out these new gender ideals, debating the benefits and drawbacks of, say, marrying a financially secure salaryman versus a potentially sensitive part-time worker. Studying how masculinity matters to Japanese men in irregular employment, Cook (2016) found that men and women both struggled with contradictions between their romantic ideals, personal goals, and employment requirements for any potential spouse. People who challenge normative gender models—men by refusing to find full-time employment, women by seeking careers—often still hold normative standards for their potential spouses. Thus Takeshi, a thirty-five-year-old surfer who works part-time jobs, disparages both younger female surfers and his female coworkers as unacceptable marriage partners. Instead, he desires a woman who will simultaneously let him maintain his uncommon lifestyle while also conforming to "older gender norms" herself (ibid., 118). Such double standards are not unique to men. A thirty-year-old married woman on a career track asserts her simultaneous beliefs in "equal rights" for men and women, but also that she would be embarrassed if her husband held a part-time job (ibid., 120). In these examples we see not only human contradictions, and the gaps between people's standards for themselves and their intimate partners, but also the piecemeal and stuttering process of changing romantic norms.

AOYAMA-SAN: DIVORCING JAPAN, INC.

Aoyama-san, a woman in her late thirties living in a small city in Shikoku, is unusual for a number of reasons, including her forthright conviction about what makes a good marriage and therefore why she decided to divorce. Residents there describe the city as having a small-town feel, and although the population is about half a million people, it's very common to run into people you know around town. This small-town atmosphere still impacts the ways in which Aoyama-san experiences her divorce; getting divorced in such a small community assures that everyone knows your story. Indeed, I was introduced to her precisely because some people in the community knew her story and thought it might be helpful for my research because she is a divorced, noncustodial mother. As I discuss further in chapter 4, joint child custody does not exist in Japan, and in the current moment child custody is awarded to mothers about 80 percent of the time. A noncustodial mother is therefore relatively unusual, and I came to understand Aoyama-san's choices as evidence of her strident refusal of formerly mainstream norms.

Aoyama-san does not have custody of her two daughters because she did not ask for it. Instead she bargained away custody in negotiations with her ex-husband to get him to agree to a divorce. Although it is rare for mothers not to have custody, the act of bargaining or bribing in the course of divorce negotiations is utterly typical. In this way, Aoyama-san's story conforms to some key patterns while challenging others. Her divorce, specifically her motivations to seek a divorce, enact newly common and recognizable reasons for wanting to leave a marriage.

Aoyama-san grew up in Matsuyama city and married a man who became a government worker. It was a good job and they had two daughters. Aoyama-san was a full-time housewife, focused on raising her daughters and providing support to her husband. As she tells it, at one point, she simply got sick of the restrictions on her life. She didn't want to be a housewife and didn't want to be in this kind of marriage, a relationship that conformed very much to what I have labeled disconnected dependence. She wanted to have a marital relationship that was emotionally connected and felt like it would change her for the good, an emotionally and personally transformative relationship that would allow her to become a better self. Her marriage wasn't the kind of relationship she wanted.

When she first mentioned divorce to her husband, he was incredulous. Why on earth did she want a divorce? There was a significant gap between her definition of a successful marriage and her husband's. To him, in ways that reflect the ideal of disconnected dependence I explained above, any marriage that functioned marginally well and didn't include domestic violence or extramarital affairs was an inherently successful marriage.[23] Why would she consider leaving a marriage that was, by this definition, working just fine? By her husband's standards, in a casual sense, she simply had no grounds for divorce. There was no reason to judge their marriage as anything less than successful, and although Aoyama-san explained her reasoning and her standards of a good marriage, he was not convinced. As far as he was concerned, this divorce should not happen.

Because her husband wasn't supportive of their divorce, she had to persuade him to agree. This dynamic is extremely common, and many people told me about the methods they used to effectively bribe their spouses to agree to a divorce. In Aoyama-san's case, the bribe she offered was that she wouldn't ask for custody of either of their daughters. Because Aoyama-san agreed not to seek custody, and did not ask for financial support, her husband agreed to the divorce. In practice, after their divorce, Aoyama-san still sees her daughters quite regularly—multiple times each week—and her ex-husband's mother moved in with her ex-husband to take daily care of the girls.

In the course of telling me about the reasons she found her marriage unsatisfying, Aoyama-san reflected on the etymology of the word "husband" (*danna*; literally, master) to explain why she came to see heterosexual marriage as fundamentally problematic. As she explained, this common term embodies expectations that husbands are fundamentally responsible for, and superior to, the women they marry.

> Do you know the meaning of "husband" (*danna-san*)? It probably originated in Japanese brothels. In the Edo period, there were brothels in the Yoshiwara district of Tokyo. Prostitutes called their male patrons "my sponsor." Therefore, when we use *danna* for "husband," it means he is the wife's sponsor. [...] To me, it carries a really strong connotation of ownership.

Aoyama-san elaborated on the distaste and discomfort she felt with both the typical terminology surrounding heterosexual marriages and the common styles of intimacy found within those relationships. In her interpretation, risk comes not just from the ways specific people embody their roles as a husband or wife, but in the terminology used to describe those relationships. The terms themselves, and the way that language sets up expectations about gendered responsibilities and roles, imply dangerous ideologies that can ruin marriages even between two very well-intentioned individuals. In ways that were confusing to her ex-husband, she saw their marriage as fundamentally flawed despite the absence of extramarital affairs or domestic violence. Refusing that style of intimacy, and the very common terms used to describe their relationships within it, Aoyama-san embodies a newer rejection of previous intimate norms.

A New Search for Intimacy

Amidst debates about newly contested gender norms and the shifting labor market, in the early 2000s a neologism describing new ways to find and sustain intimacy burst into Japanese popular consciousness. The word *"konkatsu"* was suddenly everywhere. It competed as a finalist for the most important phrase of 2009, was discussed regularly on talk shows and in private conversations, and became a trendy term highlighted in a television drama title and the popular media (Fuji TV 2009; Yamada and Shirakawa 2008). Coined by a journalist and a prominent public intellectual, *konkatsu* describes a new attitude and energy around marriage. The term both reflected behavior the authors already witnessed and modeled potential actions that, they suggested, could improve Japanese marriages, families, and the nation-state.

Konkatsu defines a self-conscious search for a marriage partner that mimics the market ideology surrounding employment: the term asks people to search for spouses like they search for jobs. To Japanese speakers, the link between marriage and employment is obvious in the phrasing. *Konkatsu* is an abbreviation for "marriage hunting," *kekkon katsudō* (the shortened term takes the middle two characters), which refers to the long-standing term describing "job hunting," *shūshoku katsudō*, often abbreviated to *shūkatsu*. In both phrases, "hunting" or "searching" is described with the same word, and only the object of that hunt varies.[24] "Job hunting" (*shūkatsu*) connotes more than just a search for employment, and instead describes the highly regularized pattern of events required to land elite and stable jobs like salaryman positions. In both employment and intimate realms, the term "activities" (*katsudō*) immediately signals a regularized schedule of required activities targeted toward a goal and a vast wealth of self-help goods marketed to those hoping to be successful. It is a difficult rite of passage, a key step on the way to becoming a social adult (*shakaijin*). To look for a marriage as if it's a job means, in this context, to take it seriously and do what needs to be done: make oneself physically attractive, buy the right clothes, attend the required meetings or parties, and all while performing a particular kind of seriousness and constant presence of mind focused on the end goal. Although Japan has a long history of arranged marriages and dating parties, *konkatsu* was framed as a new technique for finding and sustaining marital partnerships, implicitly suggesting that the previous methods were no longer working (Applbaum 1995; Lebra 1984).

Searching for a spouse as if you're searching for a job became popular at a moment when both marriages and the labor market faced extended, intersecting crises: compared to a few decades before, in 2008 there were fewer good jobs and a higher likelihood that marriages would end in divorce. These two trends represent disintegrating but overlapping social contracts, embedded within Japan's intimate political economy. By the mid-2000s, the terminology and associations previously used to describe employment security smoothly transferred into the intimate realm. By replacing "job" with "marriage," the new terminology suggests marriage as a goal that will produce the lifelong security no longer commonly available through lifetime employment. In actual practice, given the divorce rate, marriages are statistically less likely to provide the lifelong stability that previously signaled security.[25] Although this might at first seem like a contradiction, it also prompts an expanding definition of "security." Rather than measuring security in terms of the length of a marriage, some people understand it as a depth of emotional support and commitment. A secure marriage, or an intimate relationship that provides security for one or both partners, can be judged by the affective ties and emotional connection it includes, rather than merely its duration. Judging by this standard, the typical long-term salaryman marriage wasn't necessarily secure, a fact rendered more obvious when retired men like Mr. Yamaguchi must struggle to keep their wives from leaving them. Despite, or because of, Japan's substantially restructured labor market, popular attention to the intimate political economy highlights links between employment and intimate relationships.

Do Women Buy Out of Marriage?

In many cultures, people are socialized to ignore the constitutive presence of money in intimate relationships. Scholars have noted how quickly people in different cultural contexts minimize financial and market influences in loving relationships, as if noting that most dates require money will automatically turn everyone into prostitutes. Describing these dynamics in northeast Brazil, Rebhun (2007, 111) says, "People claimed a total separation of sentiment and economics, while in practice, when asked how you know someone loves you, people described showing love by sharing food, money, clothing, access to credit, employment opportunities, labor, and child care—which I saw as economic transactions—while they were reluctant to so label them." In popular understandings such as these, intimacy and economic exchange are represented as two "hostile worlds" that would destroy each other if they came into contact, despite the fact that in practice "[m]oney cohabitates regularly with intimacy, and even sustains it" (Zelizer 2005, 28). In the examples presented in this chapter, rather than refusing to acknowledge money's role in intimate relationships, a vocal segment of the population presents divorce as entirely about money, what Zelizer labels a "nothing but" perspective, as in intimacy is about nothing but money (Zelizer 2005, 30). As I explained in this chapter's introduction, more than a few men confidently informed me that a woman's wealth was the strongest predictor of divorce.

When men and women contemplate divorce, or attempt to avoid it, their models for ideal, problematic, or risky relationships necessarily reflect Japan's intimate political economy. In the earlier postwar period, being a husband or wife—let alone a "good" husband or wife—was made possible only through particular forms of employment. In that paradigm, a good husband necessarily labored such that his wife could focus on domestic responsibilities or work for pay in a part-time position. Disconnected dependence was not only normative but also lauded as evidence of a strong marriage. In the early 2000s, men and women are pointing to this same model now as a negative example. What was previously a sign of strength has become a risk for divorce.

Wouldn't it be nice if divorce were caused by something as simple as a woman reaching a certain salary threshold, an automatic trigger point after which there was no way to save the marriage? Such a mechanism would certainly obviate the guilt or responsibility either spouse might feel for ending the relationship. As we've seen in this chapter, money is necessary but not sufficient for anyone to leave a marriage. When people are commenting on money's imagined role in divorce, rather than describing an accurate picture of how marriages collapse, they are instead noticing the intertwining of marital possibilities, styles of intimacy, standards of employment, and state policies that long made certain relationships look stronger, better, and more natural. Moreover, they are noticing that key parts of those intertwined social contracts have disintegrated, making it less likely that men will desire, or be able to attain, the secure lifetime employment more available a generation before.

For these reasons, "money" is far too simple an explanation for divorce in contemporary Japan. But if we understand "money" instead to be a shorthand for Japan's intimate political economy, and as a gesture acknowledging how previous norms are fracturing, it begins to make more sense. Rather than some magic force prying women from otherwise secure marriages, the intimate political economy feels like ground shifting beneath everyone's feet.

Two Tips to Avoid Divorce

One Hundred Reasons for Later-Life Divorce, a marital advice book published in 2006, offers more than just a list of the most common reasons for divorce among people over sixty years of age. After enumerating the "top ten" reasons for divorce given in a television program on the topic, the authors ask the reader to identify the spouses' mistakes, a game that mostly consists of figuring out what the husband is doing wrong. In a section including a reenactment of a middle-aged husband's return from work one evening—complete with script and still photos—the text recommends keeping an eye out for the "reasons for divorce" (*rikon riyū*) and then provides a quiz about what isn't working in this marriage. In this opening to a longer scenario, the husband manages to do three things that are presented as both entirely typical for a man of his age and dangerous risks for his marriage. First, this husband doesn't return his wife's greeting (*aisatsu*) when she welcomes him home. Second, he pulls off his clothes to lounge around in his underwear. And finally, when asking for a drink, he calls his wife "mother," as in "Mother, do we have any beer?" (TBS Program Staff 2006, 72). While this denotational pattern has long been a very common practice in Japanese families, many contemporary sources suggest spouses are creating tectonic risks in marriages when they call each other "mother" and "father."

On surveys asking men and women why they decide to get divorced, the most common reasons given are diverging personalities (*seikaku no fuicchi*), abuse, addictions, or serious debt.[1] Yet in counseling sessions I attended, on television programs about divorce, and in conversations focused on marital problems, those causes were acknowledged but downplayed. Instead I repeatedly heard two tips presented as dependable ways to avoid divorce. Despite their seeming simplicity, both push against extremely common relational prac-

第62位 私を「お母さん」と呼ぶ　第66位 服を脱ぎちらかす　第68位 挨拶をしない

FIGURE 2. In a guidebook showing negative examples, reading right to left, a middle-aged man returns from work, doesn't greet his wife, lounges in his underwear, and calls her "mother" (TBS Program Staff 2006, 72)

tices between spouses. First, as recommended in the above exchange, spouses should not call each other "mother" and "father." Second, rather than conveying affection through actions, spouses should explicitly say "I love you" to each other. That was it: don't say one thing but do say something else. Although these tips might seem small or easy to enact, they recommend tremendous shifts in styles of intimacy that get to the heart of how people understand themselves in relationships.

Why are these tips so popular? What problems do they identify and attempt to solve? In suggesting ways to avoid divorce, these tips reframe dependence in intimate relationships as risky and problematic. When a husband calls his wife "mother," or doesn't say "I love you," he is conforming to previous models for intimacy in which spouses were dependent on each other but largely disconnected. Like the fictional husband mentioned above, contemporary representations describe men in those relationships as old-fashioned, selfish, and satisfied with being dependent on the very wives they take for granted. In contrast, with these two tips, marital guidebooks and counselors suggest spouses should restructure their relationships so as to be independent people who actively choose to be together. Through seemingly small changes in behavior, these tips recommend enormous shifts in the ways spouses think of themselves and of their relationship together.

Despite their popularity, these tips are far easier to articulate than to manifest. In practice, I found many people struggling to even imagine intimate relationships that conformed to the ideals suggested in these two recommendations—let alone to create those relationships in real life. Instead, as I argue in this chapter, these popular tips epitomize tensions Japanese men and women perceive between intimacy and independence. Older models for intimacy in Japan suggest that spouses should be fused into "one body" (*ittai*), so deeply connected that even verbal communication is unnecessary. Although that model remains popularly recognizable, newer styles of intimacy suggest that

spouses should instead be connected as two loving, but fundamentally separate, selves. As people try to reduce the risk of divorce, and try to calculate
what makes a "good" relationship, they often draw on three contradictory
models for relationality: rhetorics of companionate marriage that suggest
spouses should be best friends; neoliberal ethics that define a good person
as entirely responsible for himself; and Japanese cultural norms that label dependence (*amae*) as a positive marker of maturity. I theorize this fraught intimacy through separation as *connected independence*, a new, elusive ideal for
relationships that reflects broader social concerns about the risks and benefits
of interdependence. This chapter traces how people in contemporary Japan
negotiate, moderate, and refuse contradictions between competing models
for intimate relationality. As they work to mitigate the risks of divorce and
understand themselves in relation to others, spouses are trying to figure out
how to be intimate without being dangerously dependent.

Disconnected Dependence and Love Like Air

"Love like air" (*kūki no youni*) is one older Japanese idiom that idealizes intimate relationships as best when they are un- or understated. In this belief—
common enough to be recognizable to even those who don't hold it—the best
relationships are those in which partners understand the love they share for
each other through actions rather than words. Within this logic, articulating
love is a catch-22: if a person verbalizes emotion too frequently (or maybe *at
all*), that means they are overcompensating for lacking emotion. Verbalizing
an emotion automatically calls the emotion itself into question. If you really
love someone, you have to demonstrate it through actions rather than merely,
and quickly, stating it as a given. In its most positive understanding, "love like
air" is reassuring because it is always present but not ostentatious or cloy-
ing, and it suggests a mature, secure love that does not need to be constantly
reiterated. Such understandings link deeply intimate feelings with nonverbal
"telepathic" communication (*ishin denshin*), which describes the ways that
truly intimate people can communicate without speaking. Although these expectations are still articulated in the current moment, they are more typically
associated with what is now described as "traditional" or "old-fashioned" ways
of thinking about marital relationships, described in the previous chapter as disconnected dependence.

Japanese cultural norms in the early postwar era described representations of such relationships as ideally romantic, and this romance was facilitated
through air-like communication. In such historical representations, spouses

who worked hard at their separate responsibilities and rarely needed or wanted to verbally communicate with each other were held up as beautiful examples of mature love. Ella (Embree) Wiswell, researching with her husband John in Suye village in the 1930s, heard a group of younger married men comparing romantic love with married love to suggest that the latter was more subtle, stable, and constant (Smith and Wiswell 1982, 179; see also De Vos and Wagatsuma 1961, 1210). In contrast to an immature or childish "puppy love," for instance, Lebra's interlocutors in the 1970s described mature love as occurring between spouses who lived largely separate lives but did so for each other's benefit (see also Smith 1999). Indeed it is precisely because spouses understood themselves as fundamentally dependent on each other, as two halves of a single social unit, that their intimate communications were so subtle:

> Because husband and wife are viewed as being *ittai* (fused into one body), it would be unnecessary to display love and intimacy between them. To praise rather than denigrate one's spouse would amount to praising oneself, which would be intolerably embarrassing. In this interpretation, aloofness is not a matter of deception but *a sign of* ittai *feeling*, or an extreme form of intimacy. Many Japanese seem to convey this view when they wonder how American spouses can express their love for each other without embarrassment. (Lebra 1984, 125, emphasis in original; see also Vogel with Vogel 2013, 13)

In this logic, the deep (and socially necessary) links between husbands and wives bind them such that verbal communication of affection feels saccharine and embarrassing. Compared with marital advice given in the more contemporary moment, the patterns of belief and behavior described here imply causation as much as correlation; when spouses don't need to verbally communicate with each other, that could be both a sign of the maturity of their relationship and a way to make their marriage even stronger. Less verbal communication, in these older descriptions, is held up as a measure of and tool for marital strength.

In these representations of nonverbal marital intimacy, "love like air" is often linked with telepathic communication (*ishin denshin*). Glossed as "tacit communication" or "telepathy," it describes an ideal and constant communication that needs never to be clearly articulated (Befu 2001, 39). Telepathic understanding was understood as a beautiful manifestation of deep intimacy between people, a loving mind meld that renders mere speech evidence of unmet intimate understanding. Intimate relationality through nonverbal communication was not limited to spouses or sexual partners; ethnographic research has found telepathic communication idealized among family members in other situations (Tahhan 2014). For instance, Japanese nurses providing end-of-life care describe family members communicating with each other nonverbally. Because Japanese medical professionals were long unlikely to inform a patient of a terminal prognosis, nurses imagined that patients came to understand that they were dying through telepathic communication with family members (Konishi and Davis 1999, 184).[2] Therefore telepathic communication, which was once idealized as evidence of the best kind of marriage, needs to be understood in relation to a broad cultural context that privileged nonverbal communication.

Connected Independence and Love Out Loud

Although tacit or unstated affection remains a recognizable cultural form, in the contemporary moment marriage counselors are likely to emphasize "communication" (*komyunikēshyon*) as a key measure of marital quality. In Japan as other places, "communication" has become a key idiom in which counselors and spouses find inherent risk and possible salvation (Evans 2012, 123; Yan 2003). In contemporary marital guidebooks, on websites, on television shows, and in my conversations with people, creating and sustaining marital love are regularly premised on rhetorics of "communication."[3] While tacit "love like air" can be attractive or reassuring, marital problems and impending divorces can also be demonstrated through silence. Moreover, an unkind spouse could use "telepathic communication" as an excuse to be coldly silent, demanding, or uncaring. Contemporary ethnographic research confirms that many people associate hegemonic masculinity with silence (Nakamura 2003, 168).

In one example of the pervasiveness of "communication" rhetoric, on a website devoted to sharing marital tips directed at middle-aged couples, "communication advisor" Uchida uses broad definitions of "communication" to frame what he describes as key ways to protect and save marriages. For him, words, actions, and hearts should all be understood as vehicles for communication; in all of these examples, communication is the key frame through which marital relationships should be understood.

> Communication with words is absolutely about conversations. Is a couple able to play [conversational] catch-ball? I think some spouses don't even have the word, or ball, to throw to their partners. [. . .] But I think that, by far, the most necessary communication is with hearts and souls. People talk a lot about "telepathic" communication, but that only happens at really high levels, with a lot of skill. It tends to create fights between partners, because they can't tell how poorly they communicate and one says, "I thought you had understood my feelings!"[4]

In this model, communication is clearly key, but its definition is also broad enough to include almost every action imaginable to save or protect a marriage. Moreover, Uchida specifically advises against the telepathic communication that was recommended in previous generations. The point is not that improving communication improves marriages but that, in many counselors' tips, "communication" becomes the general rubric through which marital advice is framed.

The National Chauvinistic Husbands Association (Zenkoku teishu kanpaku kayokai), which became a media darling in 2006, also outlined the ways through which communication could save marriages. Founded in 2005, the group rose to prominence during the national reconsideration of conjugal relationships that occurred on the eve of the 2007 pension law change. As outlined on the group's website, the association members are husbands who recognize and want to change problems in their marital relationships. In a play on twelve-step recovery programs, this group enumerates a hierarchy of traits that demonstrate a husband's recovery from chauvinism. The list provides an example of common expectations that contemporary marital problems stem from male (mis)behavior, as well as a summation of standard indicators of marital risk. For our purposes, the fundamental point is the qualitative difference in the three highest levels below the "platinum master level"; these highest degrees of transformation come when men become able to *speak*.

Starting level—A man who still loves his wife after more than three years of marriage.
Level 2—A man who shares the housework.
Level 3—A man who hasn't cheated or whose cheating hasn't been found out.
Level 4—A man who puts "ladies first" principles into practice.
Level 5—A man who holds hands with his darling wife while taking a walk.
Level 6—A man who can take seriously everything his darling wife says.
Level 7—A man who can settle any problems between his wife [*yome*; literally, bride] and his mother in one night.
Level 8—A man who can say "Thank you" without hesitation.
Level 9—A man who can say "I'm sorry" without fear.
Level 10—A man who can say "I love you" without feeling shy.
Platinum master level—A man who proposes again.[5]

In this self-consciously performative example, antichauvinistic enlightenment comes not when men can say "thank you," "I'm sorry," or "I love you" with *true feeling* but when they are able to say them *at all*. Conforming to a model of "love like air," in which spouses love each other but never articulate those feelings, this model for advancement never questions a man's love for his wife—seemingly, the men who don't love their wives wouldn't be interested in the group or wouldn't get past the introductory level. Instead of asking men to rediscover their love to save marriages, this chart asks men to *explicitly articulate* the feelings they are assumed to already have, suggesting that such articulations are the hardest things for men to do and the surest way to save a marriage.

The need to communicate love and affection in such explicit—and verbal—ways reflects new models for relationality between spouses. While the earlier norms suggested the best style of intimacy was for spouses to be fused into one body, thereby obviating the need for any verbal communication, the current models suggest that even if spouses feel like they shouldn't have to verbally communicate with each other, such communication is vitally necessary for a healthy relationship. Spouses who say "I love you" to each other are not just verbalizing their love but are also simultaneously demonstrating their need to talk, thus attesting to the lack of any fusion between selves. Needing to speak suggests that spouses are fundamentally separate beings who, nevertheless, work to care for each other. In contrast to the older patterns of relationality and intimacy, this pattern of *connected independence* emphasizes the complicated web of connections and disconnections through which spouses build a relationship with each other. In this model for intimacy, spouses are ideally linked through emotional and affective ties rather than highly gendered structures of labor. Saying "I love you"—both having loving feelings and being able to share them out loud—marks relationships as aspiring to this newer kind of ideal.[6]

These norms embody companionate romance, in which spouses are supposedly best friends who share a great deal with each other. Here we see husbands and wives who understand intimacy to be constructed through ongoing connections, such as shared hobbies, emotional honesty, and deep confidences. Such transitions between models for intimacy echo the popularity of companionate romance in other cultural contexts, where people shift from preferring "respect" to "trust" as the backbone of a marriage, or replace a sense of "duty" with "desire" (Ahearn 2001; Collier 1997; Hirsch 2003). For instance, Bloch (2017, 26) found that many Japanese people, particularly those who are younger, seek a "gratifying emotional relationship." Gratifying here has a very different definition than for generations earlier and refers to explicit verbal communication wrapped with other companionate ideals.

SADAKO: LITTLE PHRASES HELP A MARRIAGE

Sadako, a semi-professional marriage counselor, described the work she and her husband needed to do around this specific point. In her midthirties and living a few hours from Tokyo, Sadako turned herself into an unpaid online marriage counselor. With a website advertising her willingness to answer questions, she estimates that she's exchanged emails with many thousands of clients over the few years she has been dispensing advice. Her training for this position was, she explained to me, the practice that came with listening to her friends, watching TV shows, and reading popular magazines. Her ideas about what makes a good marriage, and therefore the advice she dispenses, frame verbal communication as an important signifier of a healthy relationship. While her husband puttered around their kitchen assembling lunch for us and their infant daughter, Sadako contrasted their current happiness with how they used to treat each other.

> In those days, I thought we were "normal." But I can say, when I look back, that we had fallen out of love with each other. We barely talked. That was before we had kids. My husband worked late and came home late. As I served his dinner, he didn't even say "Thank you for the meal" or anything. He just ate, took a bath, and went to bed. I got so irritated and took my frustration out on him! Then, I found out that there were many married couples living that way, but I didn't think our marriage would work out. So, I calmed myself and decided to clean up my act. I started making a point to smile every day and greet him, saying things like "Welcome home" and "I'm home."[7] Little by little, my husband got better at responding. I talk with him as much as I can. Because I think that conversation is the most important thing for a married couple.

Sadako brought up her own marriage to demonstrate how common patterns of noncommunication are and how problematic they can become. According to her, not communicating, especially if spouses assume their feelings are clear and obvious, causes trouble and increases the likelihood of divorce.

FUJITA-SAN: TALKATIVE AIR

Fujita-san, a happily married man in his midthirties with whom I talked in 2006, shared opinions and experiences that demonstrate the potential gaps between theories and practices surrounding the stakes of intimate communication. When I asked him directly, Fujita-san articulated the idea that better, stronger relationships were those that were built on air-like relationality. He suggested that a person who was so crass as to say "I love you" was doing something that was at once unconvincing, cinematic, and potentially American.

ALLISON: Did you propose [to your wife]?
FUJITA-SAN: I did in a roundabout way. I did, but it was none of this "Will you marry me?" kind of stuff. See, I knew that she wanted to get married.

So we let it take a natural course. Just naturally, we discussed marriage. "What are we going to do?" "When could you move?" "When should we?" Those kinds of things were what we were talking about. Things like, "OK, so, next year in March would be good, huh?" Kinda like that. It wasn't like how it's on TV or in the movies! There was none of this "I love you" stuff. Sometimes we call each other "people like air" (*kūki mitai na hito*).

ALLISON: What does that mean?

FUJITA-SAN: Basically, if it wasn't there, we'd be in big trouble. It's air, so if it wasn't there, we couldn't live. But its existence is not intrusive.

The typed transcript fails to represent the mincing sarcasm with which Fujita-san delivered the key phrase in this quote: *I love you*. Although many Japanese people regularly use so-called English "loan words," Fujita-san rarely did (Stanlaw 2004). He does not speak English and generally described himself as an undereducated everyman who had been working in a suburban barbershop since he graduated from high school. This context, and my previous interactions with him, made his abrupt switch even more striking when he said "I love you" (*ai rābu yū*) with an English-derived pronunciation rather than the myriad ways to say a similar idea without referencing English. Although Japanese television dramas (to which he explicitly refers) could also include such outright articulations of affection, Fujita-san's switch into an English register made me think he was picturing the line being delivered by an American celebrity, a screen-sized Brad Pitt making a treacly declaration.

While Fujita-san presented himself as part of a quiet partnership demonstrated more through action than words, in practice his experience told a very different story. In introducing his marriage to me, he described sharing deeply affective ties with his wife, saying, "My friend became my wife" (*Tomodachi kara okusan ni nattatte kanji*). Ten years into their marriage, with a son who is four years old, Fujita-san remained glowingly happy about his relationship. Atypically, he and his wife both live and work together; she also cuts hair in the same barber shop, so they regularly see each other for many hours of every day. Although in the quotes above Fujita-san represented their relationship as one that rested on tacit communication so strong that they did not really need to discuss their decision to marry, in practice that exact time of his life was characterized by tremendous amounts of speaking. Fujita-san described his decision to marry his future wife as stemming from a series of absurdly expensive phone bills:

> I decided to marry her because of financial reasons. Every day, for work, I used to go to Chiba to pick her up and drop her off. Gas fees and tolls cost me a lot.

But the worst was a phone bill. There were no cell phones at that time. I once got an ¥80,000 ($800) monthly charge! We talked on the phone every day. But I didn't want to impose a financial burden on her because she is younger than me. So when she called me, I hung up right away and called her back. But over ¥80,000 was too much. That was more than my rent.[8]

Although Fujita-san first characterized his relationship as one in which understanding occured without speech, in practice he had an obvious measure of precisely how verbal their relationship was. In this example, we see two divergent understandings of how a marriage proposal was prompted, discussed, and settled; his first characterization of their relationship as ideally air-like is rapidly revised to include so much talking that it became financially burdensome. I interpret this seeming contradiction to reflect Fujita-san's deep happiness with his marriage. In trying to represent it to me, he employed the rhetoric typical of "old-fashioned romance" while describing a relationality built through constant connection and verbal communication.

Terms of Endearment

While communication has become a key idiom in which counselors and spouses find inherent risk and possible salvation, the second common tip to improve marriages recommends connections built through particular terms of endearment. Current Japanese literature on marital problems and risk emphasizes the dangerous identifications created by using parental kinship terms for spouses, but previous ethnographic literature about families presented these behaviors as standard actions that demonstrated the relative importance paid to parent-child relationships. Describing village life in Suye in the mid-1930s, John Embree found it common for family members to be addressed using kinship terms from the youngest generation's perspective (Embree 1967 [1939]). Thus a man living in a house with his son, daughter-in-law, and grandchildren would be called "grandfather" (ojīsan) by everyone, not just his grandchildren (Embree 1967 [1939], 86). Ella Wiswell described similar patterns of a daughter-in-law calling her mother-in-law "mother" (kaka-san) (Smith and Wiswell 1982, 199). Unmarried couples used "you" (anata) to speak to each other, which Embree glossed as "thou" or "dear" and Wiswell characterized as an "affectionate" term (Embree 1939, 86; Smith and Wiswell 1982, 176). In both cases, the implication was that most married couples begin to call each other "mother" and "father" soon after marriage, possibly even before they have children, and using "you" (anata) was an intimate gesture that embarrassed some people.

In her research almost forty years later, Takie Sugiyama Lebra found that merely asking people how they addressed their spouses and family members embarrassed them (Lebra 1984). Based on ethnography conducted between 1976 and 1980, her results mirror what many of my interlocutors, in 2005–6, described as "normal" (*futsū*) practices in more traditional or conservative homes. We get no sense from Lebra that the practices were worrisome to any of her interlocutors; their embarrassment seemingly stemmed from being asked to explain intimate terms (Lebra 1984, 127). Compared to the neutral (if shy) tone that Lebra's interlocutors used to describe being called "hey!" (*oi!*) or "mother," my interlocutors, twenty-five years later, used these same practices as evidence of the inherent problems of dependence and disrespect in Japanese marriages and the necessity that men change their attitudes toward women.

Chiharu-san was one of many men and women who went out of her way to make sure I knew Japanese men are likely to call their wives only with "hey." Chiharu-san was in her early fifties and occasionally participated in gatherings at the Kanto Family Center. Firmly working class, with three children, and divorced from her husband, she simply did not have the money to participate more regularly in therapy groups. During a day of hanging out—eating lunch, window shopping, and sharing fruity desserts—our conversation ranged over a number of topics. In the midst of talking about the general state of marriages in Japan, she looked up and said, "You know about 'food, bath, sleep,' (*meshi, furo, neru*) right? How Japanese men talk to their wives?" She went on to tell a hypothetical story that many other people had also described: When a husband comes home, he'll first request food from him wife by saying only "food!" (*meshi*) before demanding a "bath!" (*furo*) and "sleep!" (*neru*) in similarly abrupt language. (Earlier in this chapter, Sadako referenced this same trifecta as evidence of a marital problem.) In the same train of thought, Chiharu-san, like many other people, continued by mentioning that these same men are likely not to refer to their wives as anything at all—"They just say 'hey!' (*oi*)." As she told me these scenarios, Chiharu-san did what other people had done when they mentioned them to me: she gestured toward my notebook and suggested that I "write this down" because it was a key to understanding Japanese marriages and marital problems.

These examples mirror more general understandings about why and how divorce happens by placing the onus on men. But, further, Chiharu-san's insistent scenarios simultaneously suggest that she believes key evidence of marital difficulties can be found in the words a husband speaks, or doesn't speak, to his wife. The hypothetical husband's words *for* his wife—hey!—and his words *at* her—food, bath, sleep!—have become key symbols of the quality of marriage and a common shorthand for structural problems faced in contemporary relationships. For Chiharu-san and women like her, neoliberal ethics of individuality were attractive because they seemed to undercut such demanding dependences.

OSADA-SAN: I AM NOT YOUR MOMMY!

Osada-san, a woman in her forties I first met at a training course for people who want to become counselors, used her ex-husband's attempts to call her "mother" to characterize how their marriage had been problematic, if not doomed, from the beginning. After they both graduated from prestigious universities in Japan, she and her husband met while working in Hong Kong. At the time, she was thirty-two, hadn't dated anyone, and wanted to get married. Her husband was five years younger and they dated briefly before he proposed. She said that he proposed as a reaction to a letter she wrote saying that she didn't want to continue the relationship if he wasn't thinking about marriage. In conversation with me, at a cheap chain restaurant crowded with high school students, Osada-san described his proposal in a fancy Ginza restaurant and the changes that occurred once she became a wife. After quitting her job, she went with her husband to live in the United States for a year while he completed a business degree. It was a very stressful time for her, and although they were trying to have children, she found that she was unable to get pregnant "because of the stress."

This talk of having children prompted Osada-san's first representation of what was wrong with her husband and their marriage. Although she and I both knew that the story she was telling would end in her divorce, her narrative up to that point had been neutral, if not slightly romantic. It was a not unhappy story of a couple meeting, getting married, and starting a life together. But as she told me about her husband's willingness to step into the role of her "baby," Osada-san characterized his desire to be dependent as repulsive, while also describing their marriage as ultimately untenable, though she felt it was typical for many husbands in Japan.

ALLISON: Did you want kids?

OSADA-SAN: I wanted kids.

ALLISON: Did your husband?

OSADA-SAN: Yes, he did . . . But, he said, until we have children, "I can be your baby." I don't want such a big baby, I thought. A dependent child (*amae ko*) . . . There are lots of Japanese men who think like this, you know? Men who want to substitute their wife for their mother. Men who want their wives for their mothers. So, after we got married, he started calling me "Mommy" (*kāchan*). He said, "Mommy, Mommy!" *I am not your mommy!*

Osada-san's tone became poisonous as she yelled the final phrase of reported speech at me. Over the steady chatter of high schoolers talking, her normally breathy voice became guttural as she almost growled her response—or what she had wanted to say—when her husband offered to become her baby: *I am not your mommy!* Describing it to me almost ten years after her divorce, she understood her husband's misidentification of her as his mother to be the first sign of trouble in their marriage. Although this naming practice was once very normal, Osada-san articulated an opinion increasingly typical in the contemporary moment: the expectations inherent in a husband calling his wife "mother" suggest untenable degrees of dependence.

Osada-san is now enrolled in a weekend course to become a therapeutic counselor, but she did not talk with a professional counselor when she was thinking about divorce. Instead of reflecting on the ideas of any number of contemporary counselors who use this pattern of identification to index divorce risk, Osada-san described her reaction against her husband calling her "mommy" as visceral and uncontrollable, as a reaction to something that felt gross and strange. Even if it would have been completely typical for her parents' generation, she immediately felt that being called "mommy" by her husband spelled trouble for their marriage.

Loving Dependence

When Osada-san wanted to explain the problems she saw with her husband, and other Japanese men, she used the term *amae*. This word implies a loving dependence, like a child's belief that a caring parent will take care of their needs, and was first popularized by psychologist Doi Takeo (Doi 1971, 1973). Writing in the 1970s, Doi theorized *amae* as fundamental to loving bonds and a method for caring and empathetic understanding. Paralleling Freud's identification of childhood attachments as key dynamics through which to understand adult interactions, Doi suggested that *amae* begins for everyone in infanthood. Initially, *amae* describes an infant's attachment to their mother, their desire to be loved and taken care of, and their unwillingness to separate (Doi 1973, 20). (Doi's theory presumes a female caregiver.) In his theory, as Japanese children grow up, *amae* remains a largely positive form of attachment cultivated and welcomed in relationships beyond that with an original caregiver. Intimacy and connection between people "is based on reciprocal recognition of, and response to, the other's wish for dependence and indulgence" (Mass 1986, 3). Dependence in this sense—both seeking indulgence from other people and being willing to enable it upon yourself—builds relationships and social ties. Although it could be abused or performed badly, dependence was understood as a positive social building block (Borovoy 2012).

Rather than being automatically immature or problematic, as they might be described from Western perspectives, relationships built on dependence "permeate" Japanese society and enable people to rely on each other (Doi 1973, 65). Learning how to facilitate dependence—on others, and by others on oneself—is a key component of socialization. Reflecting on the continued importance of rhetorics of productive dependence in the late 1990s, Borovoy (2005, 23) suggests: "The notion that one need not 'look out for oneself' but rather can achieve one's ends by presuming on the good graces of others suggests the possibility of harmonious human relationships that do not entail a curtailment of self-interest." For Borovoy's interlocutors, mostly wives struggling with their husbands' alcoholism, social expectations of dependence between husbands and wives made it particularly difficult for the wives to enact the "tough love" demanded by Alcoholics Anonymous methodology. In other contexts, happily married couples described dependence (*amae*) as a reason husbands avoid domestic responsibilities; even if a wife would like a more helpful husband, she might excuse his lack of help because of his dependent personality (North 2009).

Created at a moment of national reflection about the nature of Japaneseness, Doi's theory of *amae* was rapidly picked up as justification for culturalist discourse of Japanese uniqueness. In the wake of losing World War II, the terms of armistice constitutionally prohibited Japan from having any offensive military forces and forced the emperor to deny his divinity. These tremendous changes prompted reconsiderations of what linked Japanese people together, what precisely made them Japanese. As a result, Japanese scholars, politicians, and public intellectuals contributed to discourse eventually labeled *Nihonjinron*, or theories of Japaneseness. Broadly, *Nihonjinron* discourse fundamentally assumed Japanese people to be homogenous, sharing innate orientations to the world (Borovoy 2012; Kelly 1991, 396; Manabe and Befu 1993). Starting in the early postwar period, Japanese and foreigners alike were deeply committed to representing "the Japanese" as so fundamentally different from everyone else that mere "culture" was an insufficient explanation. In a diverse set of projects, authors attempted to prove that *all* Japanese people shared some unique characteristics.[9] As might be expected with any totalizing model of cultural difference, the tautological results would have been laughable if they weren't taken so seriously.

Doi had not initially framed *amae* as something uniquely Japanese, but it quickly got pulled into *Nihonjinron* discourse. In his work, Doi (1973, 28) first described dependence as fundamental to all humans but uniquely cultivated by Japanese society. For instance, he suggested that American children are trained to suppress their dependence and are rewarded for independence, whereas the inverse is true in Japan. But when it was translated and published in English as *The Anatomy of Dependence*, Doi's theory of *amae* quickly became used to justify representations of Japanese collectivism and groupthink, two of the most pernicious stereotypes leveled during Japan's unpredicted postwar economic recovery. By that dubious logic, Japanese appreciation for and cultivation of dependence reflect their innate inability to exist as individuals. As part and parcel of *Nihonjinron*, the term *amae* came to stand for unquestioned stereotyping masked through pseudoscientific language and shallow analysis intended to reiterate limited understandings of "the Japanese."[10]

Because of this history, during my research when men and women used *amae* to describe tensions they felt in their marriages, I sighed. As in Osada-san's example above, I most commonly heard the term being used to describe problematic marriages in which husbands took advantage of, relied too strongly on, or were too demanding of their wives. Although I always took seriously what people told me, at first this felt like the equivalent of an American anthropologist going to China and discovering yin/yang. To me, *amae* so clearly stood for culturalist nonsense that it could never be helpful in my analysis. But I eventually came to understand contemporary Japanese discourse about *amae* and the risks dependence brings as entirely honest and also a possible rejoinder to neoliberal rhetoric privileging individualism. Although I could not hear it immediately, when people used this term to talk about marital problems, they were using it to very different ends than had been popular during the heyday of *Nihonjinron*. Rather than describing Japanese people as homogeneous with innate similarities, in these exchanges men and women were using the term to emphasize conflict and diverging opinions about styles of intimacy.

When Osada-san used "dependence" to disparage her ex-husband and Japanese men generally, she was using an insult with particular resonance in neoliberal rhetoric. Because neoliberal ethics presume all people should be independent and responsible for themselves, it declares anyone dependent to be troubled, troubling, and undeserving. Rather than an intimate dependence, the dependence most commonly targeted in neoliberal contexts is defined through use of welfare or other state services. In the American context, Fineman (2004) claims that although dependence is fundamental to human existence, emphasis on autonomous individualism has prompted associations

of dependency only with weakness. This logic is particularly clear in social welfare policies that stigmatize recipients, imagining that mature adults
should not need such support (Cockburn 2018). In the disapproving logic of
the American Judge Judy, for instance, *any* use of state services immediately
connotes dependency: on her television show, welfare recipients are represented as "morally unsound citizens who cheat taxpayers" (Ouellette 2009,
234).[11] Working in the US, scholars have made clear that political discourse
disparaging dependence necessarily targets women and people of color (Fraser and Gordon 1994).

   In everyday conversations with me, Japanese women used *amae* as an an-
alytic category to pry apart, critique, and reconsider previously unremarkable
styles of intimacy. For them, *amae* became a frame through which to judge
problematic husbands, at the same time as it enabled a broader critique of
normative styles of intimacy. Describing the causes of her divorce, Osada-san
leapt from her husband's willingness to become dependent on her to what she
saw as general male tendencies that make marriages untenable for women.
Rather than a positive characteristic shared by all Japanese people, such us-
ages reshape *amae* into a tool with which to reconsider relationships, gender
disparities, and patriarchal norms.

ETSUKO AND YANO-SAN: ROMANCE IN DEPENDENCE

Although much of the professional marital advice suggests that people, especially women, should be unhappy when their spouse has a dependent relationship, having a romantic partner become dependent is not always considered unattractive by people in relationships. The relationship between
Etsuko, a thirty-seven-year-old woman, and Yano-san, her forty-five-year-old
boyfriend, demonstrates the mercurial attractiveness of romance with someone who likes to be indulged to the point of dependence.

   Etsuko and Yano-san met through social media on *mixi* and began emailing, then talking on the phone, and finally meeting for dinner. Despite own-
ing his own successful design firm, in his interactions with Etsuko, Yano-san
seemed unwilling to do much for himself. He never cooked, or cleaned up af-
terward. I once saw him open the refrigerator while holding a bottle of wine,
look confused, and then yell "Etsuko, fix the wine!" and put the bottle down
on the counter. As their relationship progressed, Yano-san liked to know
where Etsuko was at most times and began calling her if he wasn't sure what
she was doing. One time, she told me with frustration, he had called twenty
times over a few hours while she was in a meeting. That annoyed her but their
relationship continued.

Once, while Etsuko and I sat chatting, she came up with a new game: determining the "real" ages of all the people we knew, regardless of their biological age. First, she pronounced the dumber of her two cats as still two years old, the other cat as six, and then that she and I were both probably about seventeen. (She's not wrong.) Yano-san, she thought, was about four years old, and then the game continued with us deciding the ages for all our mutual friends and their spouses. Since that time, whenever Yano-san did something remotely mature, Etsuko made a crack about how he was possibly nearing a birthday. But when he did what he was prone to, and called her ten times an hour because she wasn't answering, he got pushed down a year. What interests me about this joke is that it didn't make her want to stop dating him. She was completely aware that he could act like a selfish child—and actually noticed that fact so much that she made jokes about it—but that didn't diminish her commitment at all.

For Etsuko, one story epitomized exactly what she wants in a man, and how dependence can be attractive. One evening, Taiji, one of Etsuko's friends, brought four pieces of different types of cake to share. After presenting the gift, Taiji asked Etsuko, "Which type would you like?" Etsuko countered that any of the pieces were fine with her and that she would choose after Taiji did. He demurred, again, saying that she should pick the one she wanted first. When she told me this story later, she said that this exchange was already enough to annoy her. "But then it continued!" she told me incredulously. Even after Etsuko had picked the piece she most wanted, and then offered the box again to Taiji, he refused again, this time saying, "Well, which piece do you want to eat *tomorrow*?" As Etsuko told me this story, the morning after the interaction, she literally screamed in frustration and yelled "that's *enough!*" (*mo ii*) while making chopping motions in the air. She was *mad*. She was mad that Taiji was so intent on being nice and unselfish that he had become annoying.

Lucky for her and this storytelling, Etsuko had a relationship with what might be considered Taiji's diametric opposite, at least in terms of dependence: Yano-san. After Taiji went home, Yano-san came over to the house. There were two pieces of cake left in the box that Taiji had brought and Etsuko gestured toward them and suggested they could eat cake. She went into the kitchen to put on water for tea and, by the time she came back, Yano-san had already eaten half of the piece of cake that he picked. There was no asking what piece she wanted, no asking what piece she might want tomorrow. Yano-san knew what he wanted, took it, and started eating. And Etsuko *loved* this. *This*, she told me, was how men should be. Sure, it might be annoying when Yano-san called her incessantly, but she would take his expectations for indulgence and borderline dependence any day, especially over Taiji's infernal willingness to be flexible, or to anticipate her needs. That was just irritating. Selfishness, and the dependence that comes with it, was much more attractive to her.

The Attractiveness of Dependence

Etsuko was far from the only woman who described the romantic potential possible within dependence. Midori-san, a woman divorced from her abusive husband a decade before I met her, surprised me by asking to be introduced to any available men I knew. She had been alone for long enough, she said, and was looking for someone with whom to share a partnership. Using a metaphor of a bicycle built for two riders, and invoking classic images from ideals of companionate love, she described wanting a man with whom she could share daily struggles and "peddle together."

> I'm a woman and my partner should be a man. I would like to have a relationship we could work together. Like riding one bike together. I want to have that once again. No, wait, not *again*—for the first time! I never had that while I was married. As far as sexuality is concerned, having kids would be impossible for me now. Particularly the sex part. I just think it's too late. But that's my dream now. Applications for boyfriends are now being accepted! I'm available. Can you introduce anyone to me? (laughs)

She didn't mind if this hypothetical man leaned on her because she planned to lean on him, and that is what love is about. For her and other women, dependence is a key ingredient of romantic love even when, and precisely because, they contemplate the emphasis on individualized selfhood suggested by neoliberalism. To be an independent person requires a particularly reliable intimate partner.

Although Etsuko's patience with and attraction to dependence mirrored patterns more typically associated with older generations, her ambiguity toward Yano-san's behavior represents a common tension in intimate relationships. On one hand, some women voice frustration with norms of *amae* that make their husbands feel comfortable calling them "mother" and expecting maternal attention. On the other hand, though, as many women told me, "it's nice to be needed," and having dependent intimates can feel like companionate romance. Although such tensions between unhealthy dependence and a satisfying interdependence might happen in any cultural context, the normative expectations of *amae*, and the links between dependence and intimacy, make it particularly salient in Japan.

Within this context, the "simple" tips to strengthen marriages represent a complex negotiation of neoliberal ethics, cultural norms, and personal desires. These recommendations find traction against people's attempts to discover and enact the intimate relationships that will make them most happy. Happiness came for some women as they shared with me their husbands' outrageous dependence, listing in great detail the shocking everyday chores that men could not accomplish without them. Even if a woman did not enjoy the activities of making her husband's every meal or packing his suitcases whenever he traveled, there seemed to be some limited pleasure in the retelling, in the conversational competitions between women talking about their incompetent, dependent husbands.

In an even more straightforward way, other women, like Etsuko, continue to have complicated relationships to intimate dependence. Rather than subscribing to an impossible neoliberal ideal that only people who don't need other people should form relationships, many women find dependence to be a space of real romantic possibility. Loving someone is about allowing them to relax into dependence, and companionate ideals in and beyond Japan suggest that spouses who need each other are those who are most likely to be happy. In contrast, neoliberal ethics of disconnection and independence give Japanese women the vocabulary to articulate their dissatisfaction with particular relationships, but few people find pleasure or happiness embodying such ideals. In the current moment, for many Japanese women contemplating intimate relationships, neoliberal ideals are more pleasurable to articulate than to embody.

Divorce for "My Self"

In the course of my research, by far the most common explanation I heard for divorce was that it represented an attempt to regain a lost sense of self. Although no uniform judgment exists regarding valid or invalid reasons for ending a marriage, many people who had been divorced or contemplated it explained things by saying they had lost their sense of self (*jibun ga nakatta*). As introduced above, Midori-san was one such divorced woman who described her need to recover and protect her self as a motivation for her divorce. Now in her late fifties, Midori-san divorced almost fifteen years before, leaving her husband when their son was in high school and their daughter in junior high. As she described it to me many years later, her desire to regain her quintessential self-ness (*jibunrashisa*) motivated her decision to divorce. She felt she couldn't be herself or feel self-confidence within the marriage.

Although her life since her divorce has become something of a quest for self-awareness through therapy groups, Midori-san's divorce also enabled her to leave a husband who had been physically abusive for years. When she described why she got divorced, Midori-san was much more likely to discuss her attempts to find her true self and self-confidence, though explanations for divorce due to domestic violence have been more acceptable for a longer period of time. When Midori-san got divorced in the early 1990s, common attitudes still criticized divorced men and women (though primarily women) for failing to fix the marriage, or for giving up too soon. Numerous interlocutors described domestic violence as one of the only acceptable explanations for divorce during this time period. One son of a divorced woman said his mother was stigmatized because her bruises were literally not visible enough, and therefore neighbors couldn't understand why she was "abandoning" her marriage. Although Midori-san had lived through a violent marriage, her current descriptions and explanation for divorce diminish the violence and emphasize her quest for selfhood. Contrary to patterns when she divorced in the 1990s, such a quest for self has become a more common, and more widely intelligible, explanation for why people leave their marriages. Midori-san's multifaceted explanation is both completely true and utterly reflective of changing understandings of problematic intimacies in contemporary Japan.

When people describe protecting their "self" as a reason for divorce, they echo neoliberal emphasis on the self but also complicate longstanding theories of Japanese selves as fundamentally relational. In psychology, sociology, and anthropology, Japanese understandings of how selves relate to others have been analyzed as deeply contextual. Quoting Geertz's characterization of the "Western self" as a bounded distinctive whole, Lebra (2004, 4) defines Japanese selves as always in opposition to their interlocutors. Rather than imagining a fully mature adult as someone who is entirely consistent in different contexts, Lebra and others instead describe Japanese subjectivity as ideally dependent on the situation, meaning that people are socialized to imagine and perform different selves in different contexts. Describing how pronouns are constantly shifted in relation to interlocutors, Smith (1983, 77) suggests "there are no fixed points, either 'self' or 'other,'" and terms of address simultaneously reflect and create relationships as they are employed.[12] In these theories, it is not just normal but ideal and a sign of maturity for a Japanese person to understand themselves (literally, their self) differently in different contexts. Such flexibility might be true in practice in other cultures, but in Japan it is explicitly taught and managed (Cave 2007; Kondo 1990; Lebra 2004).[13]

When men and women used discourse about their selves to explain a divorce, however, they referenced a new model of selfhood. Rather than a relational self, expected to shift based on the context, some described a more static self being hurt, smothered, or reduced through a problematic marriage. Of course, there was variety in people's descriptions, both in the selves they described and the relationships that stifled those selves. But styles of intimacy balancing dependence with individualism pushed people to understand their selves and subjectivities as consistent across contexts. We can see this in Midori-san's narration: when she described lacking a sense of her self during her violent marriage, she was imagining a self that could and should have existed but was somehow stymied by the relationship. Within this rigid notion of selfhood, she felt the need to leave her relationship, rather than renegotiate it with her husband, or stay in the marriage but work to recover part of her identity outside the relationship. Amidst neoliberal calls for greater flexibility and self-responsibility, some Japanese men and women paradoxically have come to understand their selves as less relational, increasingly rigid, more likely to be harmed, and therefore more in need of the protection divorce can bring.

What Connections Are Best?

Since the early 1990s in Japan, public policies and private rhetorics have increasingly privileged neoliberal ethics of individual responsibility, self-reliance, and reduced dependence. In political discourse, employment opportunities, and advice books, people are ever more recommended to cultivate independence. At the level of policy, neoliberalism creates a preference for private control and ownership, but it recommends a similar independence for individuals. According to such a perspective, selves are most successful when they are self-reliant and responsible for their own needs (Gershon 2011; Muehlebach 2012). These kinds of policies can translate into fewer state-funded support systems but also, at the level of the family, into constructions of familial relationships that are not premised on dependence. The neoliberal ethical system persistently prioritizes individualism and individual responsibility as the marks of a successful adult person. Following this logic, the strongest marriages link people who could otherwise function independently. Such a push for independence conflicts with ideals of romantic intimacy, particularly "companionate marriage" in which spouses are ideally best friends linked through affection. Rather than being founded on family obligations, reproduction, or a sense of duty, companionate marriages are based on a sense of partnership or emotional intimacy.

For people struggling to save marriages or initiate divorces, popular models for relationality create tempting, but potentially contradictory, recommendations. Behaviors that were common and recommended a generation before are now imagined to weaken the relationship, hurt people within it, and increase the risk of divorce. Connected independence, as a rejoinder to previous styles of intimacy, might be popularly discussed, but it is far from universally accepted. Although the vast majority of people with whom I talked in the course of this research still wanted to be married or fall in love again, they also tentatively espoused the value of being alone, or, more specifically, the value of being able to be alone. Almost no one wants to be alone, but many more want to be *able to be* alone, or be connected on their own terms.

The ability to be alone, to stand independently of the structural ties that created fundamental marital dependencies just twenty years before, has increasingly become a marker of successful adult maturity and happiness. But such a balance is hard to find. It is similarly hard for men to walk the line between feeling masculine (which might require particular types of employment less available now after neoliberal restructuring), acting like the kind of man they want to be, and not being divorced by their wives. As divorce becomes more visible, and individual people contemplate the possibility that their marriage will end, they work to balance connection and dependence, selfish individuality and childish reliance, in efforts to create sustainable marital and family relationships.

PART II

Legal Dissolutions

3

Constructing Mutuality

When Natsuko decided to divorce her husband, she did not hire a lawyer. She did not pay for legal advice or hire a professional advocate because she could accomplish the divorce herself, with a straightforward form including basic biographical data about herself and her husband. She could pick up the form from her local government office and fill it out in five minutes, by signing it, affixing her name stamp (*inkan*), and asking the same of her husband.[1] Returning the form to the local government office would finalize the divorce; neither Natsuko nor her spouse needed to be present when it was turned in. Unless she wanted to, Natsuko would never have to interact explicitly with lawyers, judges, or mediators during the process.

What may seem unusual in this scenario is actually what makes this divorce entirely typical in contemporary Japan. Statistically speaking, this is how most divorces are accomplished, with a two-page form filled out and submitted by spouses. These divorces are labeled "mutual," "uncontested," or "no-fault" (*kyōgi*) in legal terms, meaning that both spouses agree to the divorce and it requires no attribution of guilt. In 2005, when I began this research, 89 percent of all divorces were accomplished using this method (NIPSSR 2017b). By 2015, that figure had dropped to 87.6 percent, but throughout the postwar period over 90 percent of divorces were accomplished this way (ibid.). Divorcing in this manner is therefore both a legal norm and a cultural standard.

When a divorcing couple signs and stamps a divorce form they are acknowledging both that they want to be divorced and that they have already agreed to the terms of the divorce. In comparison with American experiences in which involving the legal system can mark the *beginning* of conflict over how to arrange alimony, child custody, and the division of property, in Japan the legal system becomes directly involved only at the *end* of the process.

Two signatures and name stamps mean that the couple has established terms to which they both can agree, and the family law system is largely organized based on the assumption that spouses will work out all the potentially thorny details on their own.

Such relative bureaucratic ease stands in sharp contrast to the prolonged debates, negotiations, and conflicts that occur as people work to accomplish a divorce. This chapter examines the legal processes of divorce in Japan to characterize the negotiations and conflicts that occur, most typically outside the legal system, as people try to agree to divorce. Because legal precedents require that both spouses indeed *agree* to divorce, many protracted negotiations occur as a spouse who wants to divorce attempts to convince the other to agree to it, often by promising material property, making no financial demands, or offering other bribes. Although many of these negotiations occur in divorces that are, eventually, registered legally as "mutual," that eventual mutuality masks substantial private conflict and negotiation that are themselves intimately, and constantly, shaped by legal categories and ideologies.

Legal categories and ideologies operating on Japanese families are not immediately obvious because Japanese families are fundamentally structured by laws but, in practice, are often disconnected from those same laws. Since its creation in the late nineteenth century, the Japanese Civil Code has legislated the particular forms families can take, and also administered social policies through households. In these ways, families are directly involved in law both as units delineated by codes and as the delivery mechanism for other laws. And yet despite such imbrication, much of the family law system is designed to create distance between legal processes and members of any given family. In the legal process of accomplishing a divorce, courts are unlikely to attempt to resolve, or aid in the resolution of, extant problems within a family. Instead, the family court system is designed to wait until family members have reached their own solutions, at which point family court mechanisms confirm their agreement. The basic assumption behind this legal system—that it is better for families to work out their problems without any systematic legal involvement—reflects the saying "Law does not belong in families" (*hō wa uchi no nakani hairanai*) (Burns 2005, 53; Fukushima 1997, 50).[2] Ignoring the myriad ways families are always already shaped by law, this restriction refers to laws and legal mechanisms explicitly designed to help families settle conflicts. As my ethnographic research illustrates, when spouses fundamentally disagree about vital topics—for instance, about whether they should divorce or not—the family law court has few extant resources to aid them, and instead pushes them to come to an agreement on their own.

To many divorced or divorcing people with whom I conducted research, this all makes a good deal of sense. The typical person with whom I spoke expressed little to no frustration with the family law system. Even when they told me long, painful stories about the extended negotiations they had to go through to get their spouses to agree to divorce terms, few people faulted the legal system. Instead they believe this process to be normal and described feeling relieved that they didn't have to interact with the legal system any more than they did. In this way, legal structures and social norms construct a dynamic that gives people good reason to stay as far from the family court system as possible.

In this chapter, I argue that the contemporary legal process to accomplish divorce demonstrates the contradictory pulls embedded within Japanese family law: pressure to keep law disconnected from families that manifests in the divorce process itself, but also a long history of intertwined connections between metaphorical "family," state policy, and actual families. It is precisely the myriad legal structures surrounding contemporary families and their members that construct the divorce process in ways that, ostensibly, remove the state and legal system from those same processes. Although legal structures do not necessarily work to make themselves invisible, they are designed to provide little of the assistance that divorcing spouses arguably might need and, in this absence, reinforce the belief that divorce is best settled within families. Therefore, although divorce remains a fundamentally legal category, in contemporary Japan the legal system is shaping the process both through its absence and presence simultaneously.

Creating a Family Nation

The legal process of becoming divorced in contemporary Japan is shaped by laws and legal structures first concretized when the modern Japanese nation was created. Japan's modern period began in 1868 with the Meiji Restoration, a time of political turbulence and reinvention, when families, both literal and symbolic, were moved to the center of the new nation. In their attempts to build a new nation that could repel powerful threats to its sovereignty, statesmen built national cohesion and patriotic loyalty to the emperor by describing the national population as one large family, while also restructuring individual families to conform to invented but supposedly traditional forms. These laws, which defined certain family arrangements as required, created a newly universal "stem family" system (*ie seido*) and the concurrent "household registration" (*koseki*) system that tracked all citizens through their family membership. Although family law has since been radically revised, Meiji-era laws first concretized in this moment of national reinvention continue to influence the ways that family is imagined, experienced, and legislated in the contemporary moment. Before moving on to describe how divorce is accomplished in the present, in this section I explain how modern Japan was built using family metaphors, at the same time that national laws reshaped and restricted actual families to render them uniform. My intention is to demonstrate how legal structures have long been involved in families, a historical truth that runs contrary to contemporary expectations that families and law should be somehow separate.

The early decades of the Meiji period (1868–1912) are marked by self-conscious attempts by the Japanese ruling elite to build a demonstrably modern nation. The "unequal treaties," first signed in 1854, gave European powers and the United States privileged access to trade in Japan, low trade tariffs, and rights of extraterritoriality for foreign citizens (Gordon 2003, 50). The new Japanese government attempted to recover its sovereignty by convincing the American and European powers that Japan, too, was a modern, civilized nation. To those ends, leaders embarked on an intense period of exploration and importation, traveling around the Western world to identify characteristics that defined a civilized nation—as defined by those nations controlling the unequal treaties—before building equivalent structures in Japan (Jansen 2000, 355; Mukai and Toshitani 1967, 33; Nish 2008). As might be expected, formal political organization was a substantial part of the accepted definition of a modern nation, and the Japanese government focused on creating political structures and legal codes, including a Constitution, promulgated in 1889 and influenced by French and German law (Oda 2009, 6).

Throughout this process of national reinvention, family became the dominant organizing metaphor for the new nation. This metaphor linked filial loyalty (*kō*), a recognizable and familiar characteristic to the Meiji population, with loyalty to the emperor (*chū*), thereby constructing what came to be called a "family nation" (*kazoku kokka*) (Gluck 1985; Matsushima 2000; Smith 1974, 32). Citizens were instructed to show allegiance to the emperor as if he were the nation's father and to understand the diverse national population as members of an extended family. These new ties appealed to a common belief in "the importance of an extended family with common ancestors" that linked disparate populations, even though "in practice there were differences [in actual families] according to local and class customs" (Isono 1988, 184). By employing this central symbol for national unity, the elites of the new Meiji state walked a fine line: they acknowledged but minimized the differences that had crosscut the Japanese population for centuries, particularly differences across regions and between prescribed social classes, which had been legally formalized during Tokugawa rule.[3]

Within this context of national reinvention, impinged sovereignty, and a powerful metaphor of family connecting a newly interlinked population, the details of actual family law embedded within the Civil Code took considerable time to work out. Working under the gun—almost literally—of American and European powers to demonstrate that Japan was now a modern nation, Japanese politicians and bureaucrats first tried to create a recognizable form of government. Compared to the Constitution, the Civil Code was much more contested and took longer to create (Hatoyama 1902; Mukai and Toshitani 1967). This extended process reflects the fundamental conflict within the creation of the Meiji state: while wanting to demonstrate modernity and civilization in order to combat the threats embedded in the unequal treaties, Meiji statesmen also wanted to maintain traditions they thought to be axiomatically Japanese, although such traditions were neither as universal nor as old as some thought (Epp 1967, 34). From different perspectives but with parallel concerns about the new Civil Code, traditionalists were joined by statesmen worried about excessive government influence on families, liberals who wanted to create more rights for people in enervated positions within the family, and nationalists who worked to limit the influence of foreigners and foreign legal systems (ibid.). These perspectives combined to delay the promulgation of the two sections of the Civil Code relating to family life until 1898: three years after the rest of the Civil Code, ten years after the promulgation of the new Meiji Constitution, thirty years after the political movement that prompted the national reformation.[4] When it was promulgated, the Meiji Civil Code required that all Japanese citizens be located within a family and that all families organize themselves in the "stem family" (*ie*) system and register in the "household registration" (*koseki*) system. Japan's family nation was born.

Legislating Families through the *Ie* and *Koseki* Systems

Despite contemporary expectations that the law should not be involved in families, Japanese laws have long structured how families can be organized through the interlocking "stem family" (*ie*) and "household registration" (*koseki*) systems that built normative family forms and the mechanisms to police them. In the current moment, only the *koseki* system remains legally operative, although the *ie* system continues to influence how families are imagined and legislated. In contemporary families, and at moments of divorce, many people frequently refer to this historical, but now legally defunct, *ie* system when describing what makes a family "normal" or describing what is best.

Ie means both "home," the literal structure in which a family lives, and the multigenerational "family" that might be expected to live in such a home. But the "*ie* system" was a set of national legal regulations that required all Japanese families to follow certain patterns of organization and hierarchy (Kitaoji 1971, 1036; Ronald and Alexy 2011). When enacted in the 1898 Meiji Civil Code, the law required families to be multigenerational groups headed by a male family member, who was also the family's official representative. Women were legally "incompetent" and unable to make decisions that contradicted the household head (Akiba and Ishikawa 1995, 589; Smith 1987, 6). All family members required the household head's permission to make decisions such as whom to marry and where to live, as well as what work to take, and the household head legally owned all household property (Masujima 1903, 538; Wagatsuma 1977).[5] When a household head was no longer able to hold the position, which could occur at the moment of death or sometime before, his responsibilities would pass to his designated heir, most ideally his eldest son. Younger sons, if not designated as the heir, were legally required to move out of the family's main home (*honke*) and set up "branch" households (*bunke*). Sometimes these younger sons were given gifts with which to start a new branch household, but legally the household head owned all household property. If there was a viable male heir, daughters were legally required to leave the family by marrying into other families and taking up a role within that lineage. In these ways, the idealized version of the *ie* system was not only patrilineal but also patriarchal, patrilocal, and based on primogeniture. To members of the *ie*, these rules and attitudes played out as privileging the "vertical" relationships between ancestors and descendants, rather than the "horizontal" relationships between spouses or siblings (Isono 1988, 184). In theory and design, "men may come and men may go, but the *ie* was supposed to go on forever" and potentially "personal" decisions were also made based on what would be best for the *ie* lineage (ibid.). Similarly, for people living within the *ie* system, gender and birth order mattered a great deal, and firstborn sons, especially, were given structural privileges that translated into all sorts of daily benefits, from eating or bathing before other relatives to being allowed to receive more education.[6]

When the *ie* system was codified into national law in 1898, its singular method to organize families was only one option among many in practice in Japan. Although the Meiji statesmen who instantiated the legal requirement presented it as reflecting universal practices, this ideal of patrilineal stem families organized through primogeniture and female outmarriage had occurred within elite samurai families, a small segment of the population. Families in other social positions, from merchants to farmers, peasants, and outcasts, had a great variety of family ideals and practices, which often included more formal power and responsibility for women (Mackie 2014, 203; Matsushima 2000, 21; Smith and Wiswell 1982, xvi). The Meiji Civil Code therefore required *all* Japanese citizens to organize their families as only *some* samurai families once had, a process that obliterated diverse practices at the same moment one pattern was universalized as Japanese tradition (Hayami 1983; Ikegami 1995; Uno 1991).

To operationalize the newly universal household system, the Meiji government simultaneously expanded the *koseki* household registry system that had already been in place in some parts of Japan.[7] At root, the *koseki* system was and remains a method for the government to monitor its citizens through households, recording three types of information about every Japanese citizen. First, the system records all major life events such as births, deaths, adoptions, marriages, and divorces as they occur over the course of people's lives. Second, it locates all citizens within a particular household, thereby connecting them with earlier and later generations of the same family. Third, it locates these families in geographic space, tying any individual person not just to their relatives but also to where those relatives lived. The *koseki* system counts citizens but locates them within household "*ko*" units to do so, thereby making households a fundamental unit of society (Chapman and Krogness 2014, 2).

Although the *ie* and *koseki* systems were perpetually updated, they both underwent major changes in the immediate postwar period.[8] The stem-family system was perceived to be so integral to the Japanese state that, during the Allied occupation following World War II, it became a key legal and social structure targeted for removal. Specifically, the *ie* system seemed dangerous to newly democratic Japan because the links between family forms and the nation-state were explicit and ideologically powerful. Families, symbolically and literally, had been so instrumental to the creation of imperial Japan that they became equally central to the reformation of the nation after defeat (Oppler 1949, 318; Wagatsuma 1950). In June 1946, politician Katayama Tetsu made the relationship explicit by saying, "By establishing an improved family system a new Japan will be born" (Steiner 1950, 174). In the postwar Constitution, the *ie* system formally disappeared but the *koseki* system remained in place with some modifications. For instance, within the *koseki* record, households were no longer allowed to include more than two generations, thereby further disconnecting the updated *koseki* from the previous *ie* system (Krogness 2011, 67).

Although the *koseki* system might seem like a neutral record of information, in practice, it created a strong sense of what a "normal" family was, as well as multiple avenues for discrimination. Krogness (2011) argues that contemporary Japanese people continue to prefer family forms that conform to the most normative patterns within the *koseki* system. Asking people to describe their sense of *koseki* and "normal" families, he found that they were very likely to believe that a family that looks normal on the *koseki* is the best kind of family. Even though it is no longer a legal requirement, people still expect that a man will be the official household head and would be suspicious of, or embarrassed about, a *koseki* that does not obey that pattern. In an interview, Krogness asks a woman to clarify what she meant when she said that a "proper" (*chantoshita*) *koseki* was one with no stains (*oten*). He continues:

> A good *koseki* will not put an uncomfortable spotlight on its registrants. Remarkable *koseki* are those that are somehow "marked" by unusual data (e.g., a female [household head], divorce items, a sister deleted from the parental registry due to childbirth [while unmarried]) or even by lacking data (e.g., no name in the father column, or a birth date marked "unknown"). Unclear and unusual, they can potentially weigh down its current and future [household] members. (Krogness 2011, 82)

In this case, the format of recording family membership continues to impact people's understandings of how families should and should not be organized. Because divorce is recorded in the *koseki*, it is one of the many possible "stains" that might induce people to choose other paths to keep their family clean on paper.[9] The *koseki* system has also created and sustained discrimination, particularly toward people whose ancestors were among the "untouchable" class (*burakumin*, *eta*, or *dōwa*) or Korean immigrants (Hankins 2014; Neary 1997, 65; Tsutsui 2018, 179).[10] In these ways, people continue to imagine "normal" families as those that adhere to the unmarked *koseki* categories. More broadly, and visible in examples throughout this book, many people still reference the norms constructed through the *ie* system, even though it has not been a legal requirement for decades (Akiba and Ishikawa 1995, 590).

The Legal Steps to Divorce

In the current moment, the legal process of becoming divorced is primarily characterized by efforts to push spouses to make decisions on their own, with little intervention or help from professionals within the system. Almost

90 percent of spouses accomplish the legal requirements surrounding divorce through private negotiations, and only approach the legal system after they have made their agreements. In this section, I describe the required legal steps to accomplish a divorce in the contemporary moment, the paths shaped explicitly and implicitly by the structure of the current family law system.

There are four legal types of divorce in Japan, and 99 percent of divorces fall into only two of these categories. "Mutual" or "uncontested" divorce (*kyōgi rikon*) is by far the most common, accounting for 87.6 percent of all divorces in 2015 (NIPSSR 2017b). The process for this kind of divorce was described in this chapter's opening passage: it requires both spouses to fill out a simple form, sign it, stamp their name stamps, and turn it in to a local government office. In this, divorcing couples are not asking for permission nor requesting a divorce from the government's authority, but informing the state of a fact that has already been decided (Krogness 2014, 149).

Such a process of notification, however, does not mean that the government representative is required to accept all notifications that are submitted. All types of notifications, ranging from birth to marriage to divorce, can be refused if the government worker identifies a problem.[11] In the case of divorce, a notification can be refused by the government office if one spouse has previously registered a "divorce nonacceptance request" (*rikon fujuri todoke*). Because the "mutual" divorce form is so simple and can be submitted by anyone, the process is ripe for forgeries. Name stamps are extremely official but readily available for sale at inexpensive prices, meaning a nefarious spouse could easily forge a stamp and signature and accomplish a divorce without actually negotiating the details, or over the refusal of the partner (Jones 2007b, 204). To reduce this likelihood, any married person can submit an official form to the local government office saying that he or she does *not* want to be divorced. This request on record at the office should prevent any divorce notification from being accepted. In the course of my research, I heard of cases where spouses turned in this "divorce nonacceptance" form but found out, months or years later, that they had nevertheless been divorced without their knowledge and against their will. In one case involving a non-Japanese husband whose Japanese wife was trying to divorce while they lived in her hometown, his "divorce nonacceptance" form was lost in the local government office. After the wife forged his signature and stamp to complete a divorce form, and the husband unknowingly lost custody of their children, he believed the local government staffers had conspired with their "native" daughter to exact a divorce upon him. Once the divorce notification was accepted and registered—months before he was even aware of what was going on—it couldn't be rescinded and the divorce was legal. The particular structure of the "mutual" divorce process, relying on a simple form with no requirement for in-person confirmation, makes this possibility for forgery very real.[12]

As will be illustrated in examples included in the next section, a spouse might want to forge a divorce or prevent a divorce for a myriad of reasons. Precisely because the legal divorce process includes little space for negotiation, and agreements are supposed to be reached in "private," spouses are expected to settle a number of questions between themselves, ranging from whether to get divorced at all to child custody and property division. Forging a divorce form obviates the need for such difficult negotiations, about which people might feel ill prepared or embarrassed. Alternatively a spouse might submit an official "divorce nonacceptance" form to forestall any possible forgery as a way to ensure s/he doesn't lose official custody of children, property ownership, or legal rights through an unwanted divorce.

To accomplish a "mutual" divorce without forgery, both spouses must agree to the divorce terms, and if unable to do so their divorce negotiation moves into the second legal category of divorce: "mediated" (chōtei). In 2015, 9.6 percent of divorces fell into this category, a figure that reflects a rise in the last decade. When spouses do not agree—either about terms of a divorce, child custody, or whether they should divorce in the first place—they enter into chōtei mediation sessions with representatives of the local government. The ultimate goal of these sessions is to get the spouses to agree: to bring them to a point where they will agree with each other enough to either complete the divorce or return to the marriage. Importantly, the structure of this mediation mimics the ideals embedded within the "mutual" divorce described previously: although divorce includes spouses being guided to agreement by mediators, the structure provides little authority or assistance to manifest a complicated agreement. Instead, previous research and my ethnographic work demonstrate that the chōtei process produces stressful pressure to reach a decision.

The key figures within the chōtei divorce process are the mediators themselves who, rather than being professionals trained in psychology, family therapy, social work, or law, are instead upstanding members of the community required to be over the age of forty, though they are typically older (Bryant 1995, 9). Through these requirements, the family law system is attempting to mimic a type of "private" mediation that might ideally occur in a small town. The system suggests that the people most helpful to a divorcing couple are those who have successful lives and accumulated wisdom that comes with age. In practice, many people in mediation feel judged and pressured by the mediators, with whom they are unlikely to share experiences or worldviews. Because of their older age and respected community status, mediators are quite likely to be more socially conservative than the couples they are mediating and also very unlikely to have been divorced themselves or have divorces within their extended family (Bryant 1995). Despite the rising divorce rate, even now a personal experience with divorce might disqualify a potential mediator from the position (ibid.). Bryant conducted participant observation within such mediation sessions in the 1980s, and her detailed description of the mediators echoes what my interlocutors described occurring in the early twenty-first century. Every single person who had experienced *chōtei* mediations expressed frustration with the process, mostly focusing on the mediators themselves. Among my interlocutors, people found the mediators possibly well intentioned but unable to provide real help at a moment when assistance or advice was very obviously needed. One man switched into English to emphasize his frustration: the mediators he said weren't particularly knowledgeable or helpful; they were, pointedly, "*just* old, *just* [having] white hair." In the first moment the family court system offers assistance to divorcing family members, it does so by involving generally unhelpful, undertrained community citizens who often try to compel resolution.

The mediators, however underqualified, are further elevated because they control a good deal of the *chōtei* process. Although every divorce case brought into *chōtei* mediation falls under the jurisdiction of a particular family court judge, in practice judges rarely participate in the mediation sessions themselves (Minamikata 2005). Typically divorce mediation sessions are scheduled once every four or six weeks, giving spouses time to reflect between sessions, but also drawing the process out and requiring each session to include substantial review about what was discussed or decided previously. Spouses in mediation to accomplish a divorce, and those trying to avoid one, told me that they were frustrated by this drawn-out scheduling. Of the many people who described such sessions to me, only a few had had the experience stretch beyond three or four sessions. As they described them, the sessions were so painful, humiliating, and exhausting that no one wanted them to go on for very long. I know many spouses who began mediation resolutely refusing divorce and yet succumbed after a few sessions, simply to end the unpleasant process. When I was conducting this research, most spouses in mediation were there because they couldn't agree on child custody, a topic I will explore in greater detail in chapter 4.

The remaining two legal types of divorce are extremely rare and include less than 2 percent of divorces in recent decades. If spouses cannot agree—if one spouse wants to divorce and the other refuses—it is possible for a judge to grant a "judicial" (*saiban*) divorce. Although some high-profile Supreme   . Court decisions have involved judicial action to grant a divorce refused by one spouse, these remain rare, accounting for just 1.1 percent of divorces in 2015 (Bryant 1992; NIPSSR 2017b). Finally, the least common type of divorce is a *shinpan* divorce, a divorce by family court decree. These divorces are granted, for instance, to a person whose spouse can't be found and occurred in less than 0.2 percent of divorces in 2015 (NIPSSR 2017b).

Throughout this process and the legal categories of divorce, the legal system's primary focus is getting spouses to agree, preferably on their own but with assistance if necessary. As shown in figure 3 and table 1, even as the absolute number of divorces has increased, "mutual" divorce remains the most common experience by far. But it has been underexamined in extant literature on Japanese family law precisely because it seems to occur outside the purview of the court system (Bryant 1992; Takezawa 2003; West 2011). For this reason, in this chapter, I focus on these "mutual" divorce experiences.

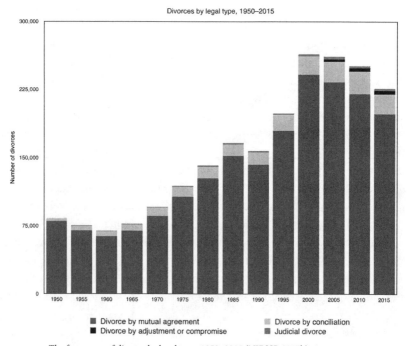

FIGURE 3. The frequency of divorce by legal type, 1950–2015 (NIPSSR 2017b)

TABLE 1. Number of divorces, by year and legal category, with percentage of total (NIPSSR 2017)

Year	Total divorces	Divorce by mutual agreement (kyōgi)	Divorce by conciliation (chōtei)	Divorce by adjustment (shinpan)	Judicial divorce (saiban)
1950	83,689	79,995 (95.5%)	3,276 (3.9%)	25 (<0.1%)	433 (0.5%)
1955	75,267	69,839 (92.8%)	4,833 (6.4%)	27 (<0.1%)	568 (0.8%)
1960	69,410	63,302 (91.2%)	5,413 (7.8%)	43 (0.1%)	652 (0.9%)
1965	77,195	69,599 (90.2%)	6,692 (8.7%)	41 (0.1%)	863 (1.1%)
1970	95,937	85,920 (89.6%)	8,960 (9.3%)	64 (0.1%)	993 (1.0%)
1975	119,135	107,138 (89.9%)	10,771 (9.0%)	54 (<0.1%)	1,172 (1.0%)
1980	141,689	127,379 (89.9%)	12,732 (9.0%)	46 (<0.1%)	1,532 (1.1%)
1985	166,640	151,918 (91.2%)	12,928 (7.8%)	59 (<0.1%)	1,735 (1.0%)
1990	157,608	142,623 (90.5%)	13,317 (8.4%)	44 (<0.1%)	1,624 (1.0%)
1995	199,016	179,844 (90.4%)	17,302 (8.7%)	66 (<0.1%)	1,804 (0.9%)
2000	264,246	241,703 (91.5%)	20,230 (7.7%)	85 (<0.1%)	2,228 (0.8%)
2005	261,917	233,086 (89%)	22,906 (9.6%)	185 (0.1%)	3,245 (1.2%)
2010	251,378	220,166 (87.6%)	24,977 (11.4%)	84 (<0.1%)	2,473 (1.0%)
2015	226,215	198,214 (87.6%)	21,730 (9.6%)	379 (0.2%)	2,383 (1.1%)

Easy Divorces Take Time

For a small minority of couples, the divorce process goes smoothly, without conflict. In this section I trace two divorces that include an unusually small amount of explicit conflict. Although both processes were fairly smooth, they share an important characteristic: both initiators waited many months between formally requesting a divorce and completing divorce forms. Their divorces took a good deal of time to complete, even if that time was not beset by fractious conflict, as will be narrated in later examples. These examples, although unusual, demonstrate how legal structures shape divorces that appear to occur outside their influence, pushing the instigating spouse to wait as long as it takes for his or her spouse to agree.

MARIKO: LET TIME CONVINCE HIM

First introduced at the beginning of chapter 1, Ando Mariko married her college boyfriend when he agreed she should keep her career after their marriage.

Their marital tension occurred because her husband expected her to be responsible for all household labor on top of her demanding work as a financial consultant. After Mariko made the decision to move out, it took about nine months before her divorce was finalized. Most of that time was spent as her husband came to terms with the impending divorce. Because Mariko had moved out, her husband was no longer able to afford the rent for their apartment, and he had to move as well. She feels like he was waiting for a couple of months, expecting her to come back. Once he truly understood her intentions, and believed that she really wanted a divorce, they signed the paperwork on their own. Mariko explains:

> I think our case went smoothly, without any specific obstacles. After I moved out, we met up for dinner together three or four times. But I clearly told him that I had no intent to reconcile, and he finally believed me. Ultimately, we didn't use a lawyer or mediator. We just did the divorce ourselves. We had no joint property such as savings or a bank account, and we both had contributed to paying the living costs during our marriage. I'm forgetting the details now, but I know we split most things. So we had nothing financial to contest. If we had, things might have been different, though.

Although she explicitly describes the divorce as relatively easy, she is quick to link that ease with a lack of complicating factors. Important to her were that not only did they not have children, but they hadn't really had a wedding ceremony. Had they had children as her ex-husband wanted, Mariko thinks she would have stayed married no matter what for the good of their children. If they had had a big marriage ceremony, it might have been harder to get divorced because of the social pressure to stay married. Either way, Mariko seems quite happy with a divorce that she describes as relatively painless, and she maintains a friendly association with her former husband. Now she feels that they are "good as friends."

For her, the process of getting divorced required the time it took for her husband to realize that she wasn't coming home. Although she had told him clearly when she moved out that she would like a divorce, he didn't really believe her and wasn't ready to accept it until months had passed. She got the divorce forms but waited to fill them out until her husband had agreed. She didn't want to push him and instead invested time to convince him that she wasn't coming back. Once that convincing was accomplished, and after he had verbally agreed, she brought the paperwork and they both filled it out together. She didn't want or need to engage professionals and instead feels lucky that other possible incentives to stay in a dissatisfying marriage—children and a public commitment ceremony—hadn't happened. For Mariko, divorce was relatively easy to accomplish because she needed only to be patient. It certainly helped that she had the financial resources to rent a new apartment and that she could afford, literally and figuratively, to wait.

WADA-SAN: FOR THE BABY

Like Mariko, Wada-san is a woman who describes her divorce as a good thing that was accomplished with relative ease. Married to her husband in 1990, Wada-san quickly had a daughter and was a happy mother. She wanted children and would have gladly had more if the circumstances of her life were different. In contrast to the prediction that Mariko made above, Wada-san was compelled to leave her husband precisely because she had a child. By her account, her relationship with her husband had become full of vicious fighting, partially as a result of his work schedule and his disconnections from their family:

> At the time, I was very angry at him. We had these big, terrible fights that made our daughter cry. It was just awful, the worst. But, you know, Japanese men are at their offices all day from Monday until Friday. They stay at the office until late each night, and socialize after, drinking and hanging out with their colleagues. My husband never helped me at all when I needed him. I didn't ask him to come home early every day. Only once in a while, I wanted him to come home early to go grocery shopping or run errands for me. Even on weekends or holidays, he went out without us. He acted like a jerk right before our divorce. So mean and nasty. He bought himself clothes and shoes without consulting me, saying, "I need this stuff for work." It wasn't fun. [. . .] I thought that women had to put up with tyrannical husbands. But now I know it's not right. Right? I wasn't his maid.

Feeling isolated and underappreciated, Wada-san began to think seriously about divorce. With the terrible fights she was having with her husband, she started to feel that leaving the marriage would be the best thing for her daughter. When she narrated her decisions to me, a decade after the divorce, she framed her thinking in relation to her daughter's need to live in a safe and peaceful home, and her own to be with a partner who thought of her as more than a maid. After making her decision and telling her family, she moved out of the house she shared with her husband, taking their daughter as well.

Despite her husband's surprise when she first asked for a divorce, she represents their divorce process as simple and easy. She went to the local government office and picked up the divorce forms, filled them out, and sent them to her husband. She explained the process as follows:

While we were separated, I signed and stamped the divorce form and mailed it to him! And then about one year passed. I got a phone call from him and he said, "I submitted the form." He sounded better. I think that he finally realized that we both could start new lives. He knew I would never come home and he would have to live on his own. But he sounded better and upbeat. We've become friends.

Although she doesn't mark it as particularly meaningful, the year it took to get her divorce forms completed merits attention. Her husband was processing a request that took him by surprise, and he needed time to agree. Luckily for Wada-san, she had the time and was willing to give it to him. She felt no particular need to hurry their divorce, and moving out of the house with their daughter reduced Wada-san's worries. Looking back, she finds this divorce process to be friendly, almost cheerful. It took a good deal of time to wait until her husband was ready to sign the forms, and their divorce was officially registered as one of mutual agreement.

Compared with the many other narratives of divorce I heard, these two descriptions include remarkably little conflict around the fact of divorce itself. These represent atypically easy divorces. The process did take time because neither woman was interested in hurrying her husband to sign the forms. These narratives contrast with the next example, in which a woman grows increasingly frustrated with the time it takes to get her husband to agree to divorce.

NORIKO: STILL NOT DIVORCED

Noriko is a woman in her midthirties who participated in an inexpensive, informal counseling group. When we'd first met, she mentioned that she was about to get divorced and was very happy that the process would soon be finished. She was planning it, she said then, and had already moved out of her husband's house and picked up the necessary forms. The only delay was coming from her husband, and he said he didn't want to get divorced because he was worried that his parents would be upset. Noriko understood, but still felt there was no way to save their marriage and hoped that the divorce would be settled soon. When we first met she announced to a counseling group, "I will be divorced in three days!" because she had planned, with her ex-husband, to submit the divorce form together on a specific day.

Yet when we met four months later to talk about her experiences being married and divorced, Noriko began to talk animatedly even before I was able to get my recorder turned on. She was really upset that her husband refused to sign their divorce papers, though he had (verbally) agreed to the divorce.

In contrast with the previous examples, Noriko felt that time was no longer necessary to the process and that her husband was simply avoiding a promise he'd made to turn in the forms. She was livid.

> At the end of last year, I went to my parents' home to tell them about my decision. I said, "I'd like to break up [with my husband]." They said, "Well, if this is what you've decided, we understand." So that was settled. But, *he* . . . He hasn't yet talked to his parents. It's OK if he doesn't talk to *my* parents, but he didn't talk to *his* parents. [. . .] I told him that I would tell my parents because I thought it would be better. Then I asked him to tell them [his parents]. And he said "Yes, I'll tell them." So, I set the date to submit the form, January 25th of this year. I took a day off from work to get it all done, turning in the form at the local government office, switching my surname on my driver's license at the DMV, and going to the bank to switch back my name. Things like that. I assumed it took the whole morning to go around switching back my surname on the register [*koseki*] and on my driver's license. I scheduled all those errands for one day. But first, I called my father in advance to tell him about the form submission. I said, "Tomorrow we're turning in the form."

Despite her hopes and what she'd told her father, Noriko was unable to divorce because her husband still hadn't signed the forms.

In addition to her mounting frustration as her divorce continued to linger unfinished, Noriko-san was upset because even after her husband finally submits the divorce forms, she still has to wait six months before she can remarry, although her husband could legally remarry the same day, if he wanted.[13] Her awareness of gender differences in family laws made her more anxious to get her divorce completed, despite the fact that she wasn't dating anyone. On principle, Noriko wanted her divorce as soon as possible, so that if she met someone new, she could remarry. She was aware that the legal system stipulates different laws for men and women, and because of this she was more motivated to complete the divorce. In all of my conversations with her, Noriko never wavered from her conviction that her marriage was over, but her husband refused to agree or, worse yet, would agree to the divorce but never follow through by turning in the divorce forms. Noriko-san said she would think about appealing for court-ordered mediation, but thinks that such a process ultimately might be even more difficult and drag on longer than simply waiting for her husband to come around.

Fighting for Signatures

For the vast majority of people, accomplishing a legal divorce is a difficult process because it takes time, energy, and money to get both spouses to agree.

Agreement does not come easily, and most do not conform to the patterns experienced by Wada-san and Mariko. Many people have to work hard to convince their spouses to agree to a divorce and typically move through various types of informal mediation or negotiation, possibly including threats or bribes. In my research sample such protracted, private negotiations were absolutely the norm. Most people went through a great deal to get a divorce form signed and turned in, and in this section I describe two cases representing a spectrum of experiences.

SAKURAI-SAN: PROLONGED AFFECTION

Sakurai-san is a woman in her midfifties who lives in Tokyo and works as a Japanese language (*kokugo*) instructor at a small women's college. Sakurai-san described her divorce as an unusual one because she never really got angry at her husband, and she still isn't. Although at times she thought the divorce was a good idea, she was more likely to describe it as something unfortunate, that couldn't be helped, rather than being necessary or inevitable. The divorce couldn't be helped because her husband had a lover that he wouldn't leave, and Sakurai-san found this unacceptable. She would have forgiven her husband after she found out about his affair, but she was unable and unwilling to accept the other woman's continued presence in their life together.

Sakurai-san met her future husband when she was twenty-two and staying in a youth hostel. After Sakurai-san and her husband married, they moved to live about thirty minutes away from his family in Osaka. As her husband worked from home designing sports equipment, she took various part-time jobs. They both wanted to have children, but soon after their marriage, Sakurai-san found out that she was unable. Although she does not explain her divorce with this infertility, she does think that it would have been easier for them to stay together if they had become parents together. As evidence she points to her ex-husband's second wife—the woman with whom he had the affair—and the two children they have together.

Sakurai-san had discovered her husband was having an affair when she accidentally ran into him with a woman on the street one day and started to wonder. She eventually confronted her husband, who promised to end the relationship, but Sakurai-san later discovered that he hadn't. She talked to her own parents and moved out of their marital home and back to Tokyo. At this point in her storytelling, she narrated their intricate negotiations about the divorce papers. Neither she nor her husband really wanted to get divorced, but because he wouldn't end his relationship with the other woman, they finally decided there were no other options.

We'd been separated but not divorced for years. But I started thinking about my own future without him. So I hired a divorce lawyer who was the son of my mother's friend. My husband came to negotiation meetings [at the lawyer's office] and we talked about how much alimony should be when we got divorced.[14] But during the negotiation, I had mixed feelings because we really didn't hate each other. If he wanted a divorce, I would agree to it. But I . . . how should I put it? I didn't want to get divorced. I still really cared for him, and if the marriage could continue, I wanted it to continue. But if he still had a relationship with the other woman, it would be impossible. To me, it was all up to him.

At this point, Sakurai-san's divorce seemed heartbreaking but a foregone conclusion. Her husband refused to leave his girlfriend, Sakurai-san's one demand to maintain their marriage.

The lingering affection that Sakurai-san and her husband felt for each other made the process harder to complete. After she completed the legal form, her husband needed only to add his own name stamp and drop it off at the local government office in order to enact the divorce. But that turned out to be a difficult step that required more time:

About the divorce papers: I stamped my name on them and left them to him, and then I went back to Tokyo. But he never stamped his name on the papers. He just kept them by himself. Finally, after about a year, he submitted them. But even after he submitted the papers, he gave me Coach brand goods for my birthday. Do you know Coach? Even after we turned the forms in, he sent me some really expensive melon fruit that he'd bought on a business trip. His indecisiveness kept me from moving on in my life. When I look back now, it just annoys me. But at that time, it was hard for me to move on because he had a really good heart. So, it was dragging out and dragging out.

Sakurai-san's experiences complicate our understandings of negotiations behind uncontested divorces in at least two ways. First, her narration describes the lawyer they hired to help determine a divorce agreement to which they could both agree. Because they eventually filed a "mutual" divorce request, the state has no record of this lawyer's involvement and no suggestion that their mutuality included expensive private mediation that went on for more than a year. Second, even after they agreed on a divorce settlement and alimony arrangement, and Sakurai-san had signed the form, her husband waited over a year to submit it. At that point, there was very little Sakurai-san could do to impel her husband to submit the form. If she had wanted to ensure his cooperation and their immediate divorce, she could and should have insisted he sign the forms in front of her and turned them in herself.

At the time, she says, she found his delay almost romantic—or, at least, an extension of the continuing romantic potential for their relationship—but, looking back, it makes her angry. She now equates his refusal to turn in the papers with the inappropriately intimate (and expensive) gifts he continued to buy her after they were divorced. Both of these actions made the divorce more difficult by extending their emotional relationship with each other. For her, like many other people, divorces are easier to understand and accept when they are characterized by animosity and conflict (Hopper 2001). Because divorces are supposed to mark the end of irreparably bad marriages, divorces marked by continued affection between former spouses can be less easy to understand or accept. In terms of the argument of this chapter, Sakurai-san felt that her ex-husband used their continued affection to muddy the waters of their divorce, making it more complicated by his refusing to make a clean break. The structure of the legal system made this ambiguity possible.

TANAKA-SAN: ESCAPING FROM VIOLENCE

In terms of the lingering affection Sakurai-san describes for her ex-husband, she couldn't be more different from Tanaka-san, another divorced woman in her late fifties. Despite their categorically different experiences being married and getting divorced, Tanaka-san also described the extended conflicts that occurred before she was able to convince her husband to sign and submit their divorce form. Tanaka-san's marriage was one of the most violent I heard described: she and her children experienced regular physical, emotional, and sexual abuse by her husband.

Tanaka-san was married in and continues to live in a very small town two hours by express train from Tokyo. Located in an economically depressed area, the town's primary employer is a concrete factory that releases dark soot into the air, covering laundry hanging outside to dry with a heavy gray dust. Tanaka-san's husband usually worked shifts from midnight until around the early afternoon. When he got home, he would expect his wife to be waiting for him, and if she wasn't he would blame the children. Tanaka-san regularly slept in her clothes and carried medical records in her purse, to be prepared to run away if she ever needed to. When we talked, more than five years after her divorce, she was still dealing with the lingering effects of the violence she endured.

After more than twenty years of marriage, Tanaka-san decided to finally get divorced for a few reasons. Primarily it was because Daisuke, her younger son, had to be admitted to the hospital that made her realize the domestic

violence and stress were "destroying" her son's health. She didn't mind suf-
fering through the bad relationship herself, and in the following narration,
she describes how much she endured (*gaman*). But when the marriage began
to take a physical toll on her children, such that they were hospitalized with
major problems, she decided that it was enough.

But deciding that she finally wanted a divorce wasn't actually enough to
end the marriage; she also had to convince her husband to agree to sign the
"mutual" divorce forms. Her husband had been baiting and taunting her with
divorce forms for years. He knew that because she didn't work outside the
home it would be difficult for her to support herself and her children. Knowing this, he would not threaten to divorce her but *dare her to divorce him*,
taunting her that she couldn't live without him. After saying "no" for years,
and refusing to call his bluff when he practically begged her to sign a blank
divorce form, she finally changed her mind and agreed. In her narration,
Tanaka-san stated that her husband did not actually want to get divorced.
Instead he used divorce, as symbolized by the form, to remind Tanaka-san of
her *inability* to get divorced and of her financial dependence on him.

When Tanaka-san finally took him up on his disingenuous offer to divorce, he was reluctant to sign the same form that he had been waving at her.
Having threatened her for years with the possibility of divorce, he was both
crying and enraged when she completed the form.

> Although he had always said, "Give me the form right now! I'll sign!" His
> eyes were glowing red as he actually signed it. We had been financially com-
> fortable with his income. I hadn't worked [for a salary]. So he believed that
> it was not possible for me to live without him. He belittled my ability. He
> believed that I would have financial problems if we separated. He had goaded
> me many, many times to bring him the forms. So I finally handed it to him.
> "Here's the divorce form." At that point, he was sobbing.

In this case, her husband did sign the form, stamp his name stamp, and submit
it to the local city office. Tanaka-san moved back in with her parents, who
live in the same small town as her ex-husband, and has been taking care of
them as they age. Since the divorce, her older daughter has been divorced
twice and is now much closer to her father than to Tanaka-san. Daisuke lives
away from home but visits his mother and maternal grandparents when he
returns and has absolutely no contact with his father and very little with his
sister. Perhaps surprisingly, Tanaka-san's ex-husband has continued to pay
her ¥200,000 ($2,000) per month by automatic bank transfer. In the nine
years since their divorce, her ex-husband has proposed remarriage a number

of times, saying that it need only be a paper marriage and would be a way for him to make her the beneficiary of his will and pension payments. As Daisuke told me, his mother is not at all interested in this and certainly doesn't trust her ex-husband enough to marry him again, even if it's only on paper.

What Makes Mutuality?

This chapter has traced the mechanisms through which "family law" has been constructed in Japan and the impacts those mechanisms have on people seeking divorce in the contemporary moment. In these cases, we have seen how family disputes are regularly represented as fundamentally disconnected from legal processes, even as law continually shapes families. This paradoxical disconnection and fundamental imbrication between family law and the rest of law situates Japan firmly within a common pattern of "family law exceptionalism." This term describes how, in many different cultural contexts, judges, lawyers, and potential litigants exclude family conflicts from the legal realm.[15] Halley and Rittich (2010, 754) summarize these patterns by saying, "family and family law are often treated as occupying a unique and autonomous domain—as exceptional." Despite law's seeming disinterest in "interpersonal relations" in various cultural contexts, family law exceptionalism is no less constructed for being so common, and such exclusions manifest a wide range of social results (Strathern 2005, 86).

In Japan, family law exceptionalism manifests very clearly in the divorce process, pushing people to negotiate on their own. The five disparate examples above demonstrate the diverse range of experiences masked in the process of settling a "mutual" divorce. For Japanese people getting divorced in the early 2000s, the legal process of becoming divorced could include myriad forms of negotiation, ranging from easy silence while spouses contemplate what to do to threats, bribes, or confusing liminality. While none of these actions take place within the formal legal system, they occur precisely because of the way the family law system structures divorce. Because couples are expected to come to an agreement on their own, their ostensibly extralegal negotiations attest to the constraints of the legal system.

The vast majority of people with whom I spoke felt the legal system worked well, or at least well enough not to merit much mention.[16] Only Noriko, extremely frustrated because her husband had broken his promises to turn in the divorce paperwork, expressed any dissatisfaction with the family law system, and it's possible that she will feel differently after her divorce is final. Quite correctly, Noriko pointed out the ways in which the legal system regulates men and women differently, but her anger was directed as much at her failing soon-to-be-ex-husband as at the system that made their ongoing negotiations necessary. For most Japanese people seeking divorce, by their own definitions, the family law system works. That it works by pushing negotiations and conflicts out of the formal legal sphere, by reinscribing disconnections between families and law, remains an expected part of the process.

Families Together and Apart

As far as anyone knows, Koizumi Jun'ichirō has never met his youngest son, Yoshinaga. Although it would be sad or surprising to hear of any father never meeting his son, the details of this particular case might be especially striking. Koizumi was, from 1999 to 2006, prime minister of Japan and remains a popular politician from the conservative Liberal Democratic Party. He has never met Yoshinaga because this son was not yet born when Koizumi divorced his former wife, Miyamoto Kayoko. They had married in 1978 and quickly had two sons. Kayoko was six months pregnant with their third son when Jun'ichirō divorced her in 1982.[1] He received legal custody of their two elder sons, and Kayoko retained custody of their unborn child. After the divorce, the two elder sons did not see their mother for thirty years, despite her public requests for contact, and Koizumi has never met his third son, who is now in his thirties (Asagei Plus 2016; Reitman 2001). Because Yoshinaga was raised by his mother, who has legal custody, he shares her family name and is Miyamoto Yoshinaga. Occasionally the tabloid press will publish stories about Yoshinaga or his mother, but for the most part, this custody arrangement and the separation caused by it aren't scandalous. This family history certainly hasn't threatened Koizumi's political success, even as a conservative.

Koizumi's divorce and postdivorce parenting haven't negatively impacted his political career because, although far more extreme than typical, his experiences do not radically deviate from custody patterns in contemporary Japan. Talking about divorce in Japan, I grew accustomed to people outing themselves as children of divorce who are totally disconnected from one parent. Some framed it as an inevitable loss that they only began to question as they had children themselves; others represented it as a daily hurt they couldn't talk about without insulting their custodial parent. More than a few described a total loss of contact with one parent as a statement of fact, something that happened in their childhood but was too far in the past to really engage. Younger people, especially, described losing a parent through divorce as a pain they weren't expecting, couldn't fully understand, and often couldn't mention.

For a substantial number of children in Japan, their parents' divorce means that they will lose all contact with their noncustodial parent. This way of being a divorced family—what I label the "clean break"—is a recognizable but contested model for dealing with the complications those families face. Although the logic is far from universally accepted, this model is described by those who support it as an attempt to reduce conflict. If divorced parents never have to see each other because one parent effectively disappears, so this thinking goes, the child will not have to manage the difficult emotions and disagreements that occur when two former spouses try to share family responsibilities and lives that continue to overlap.

Managing messiness, pain, embarrassment, and possible conflict is, in every cultural context, a significant part of the transition from marriage to divorce (Simpson 1998). Precisely because marriage is far more than an economic transaction or legal status, the transition out of it prompts powerful emotional reactions ranging from glee to deep regret and wounded betrayal. The processes of *becoming* divorced and *being* divorced require complex negotiations on two levels: first, spouses must literally negotiate a divorce agreement, which, as described in the previous chapter, almost always includes challenges and conflicts. Second, former spouses must figure out how to relate to each other—if they want to relate at all—with a new identity status, often when one or both partners hold anger about the current situation or what happened to get them there.

For divorcing parents, these negotiations necessarily include explicit or implicit decisions about how they want to relate to their children, and custody decisions can become flash points of tension, conflict, and stress. They must decide, independently and together, how to be parents when they are no longer spouses (Simpson 1997, 733). Rather than being a process of natural or entropic disintegration, divorce with children especially requires labor to unbuild and rebuild relationships. Unlike childless divorces, these cases are complicated by the added layer of potentially oppositional needs: what divorcing spouses need or want, and what their children need or want, can overlap or be entirely contradictory. In the 60 percent of divorces that occur between parents with minor children in contemporary Japan, the potential contradictions between what divorced parents and children need are central to debates about custody.

Following the previous chapter's examination of the legal and extralegal processes of becoming divorced, this chapter analyzes how divorced Japanese parents and their children imagine, negotiate, and enact their family relationships after a marital split. These diverse arrangements are all impacted by a legal restriction for sole custody after divorce. Although we will see parents who create de facto shared custody arrangements, the law's insistence on sole custody substantially influences all families. I argue that the range of tactics parents use in response to the legal assumption of sole custody reflects debates about how connection—specifically ongoing connections between kin in divorced or separated families—can be helpful or harmful to children after divorce. On one end of the spectrum, some people believe that children's interests are best served by severing all contact with the noncustodial parent, as if that parent had died in an accident. This logic tries to minimize the tremendous social, psychological, and emotional work that a child would have to do while shuttling between two parental homes, meeting new stepparents and siblings, explaining their unusual family situation, or mediating between two fighting parents. On the other end of the spectrum, some believe that real harm comes to children who suddenly lose a parent, and therefore work to maintain functional relationships even after divorce. In this thinking, maintaining connections after divorce might be messy and difficult, but it ultimately is necessary for children's social and psychological development. These debates reflect changing ideals for parenthood and families, while situating either ongoing connection or sudden disconnection as a solution to the messy realities of families after divorce.

Legal Structures of Child Custody

The complex realities of divorced families in contemporary Japan stem from the fact that joint custody is never a legal option. When parents of minor children decide to get divorced, the custody of those children must be held by a single individual. In the present moment, as a result of parental agreements and court orders, more than 80 percent of custody is held by mothers (NIPSSR 2017b). Although the legal requirement for sole custody is increasingly being called into question by parental activists, the logic and rationale for this truth reflects both structures of the family law system and the ideologies of the *ie* system that underlies it. In this section, I describe how those systems operate, although, as will become clear in this chapter's later examples, many people work outside and beyond these legal frameworks as they organize their families.

When two married people have a child in Japan, that child's custody is jointly held by both parents. The shared nature of this parental relationship simultaneously reflects the legal privilege given to married couples and obscures the granular nature of child custody in Japan.[2] Divorce quickly exposes both of these characteristics. Legal custody of any child actually consists of two different types of custodial responsibilities, *shinken* (literally: parental rights) and *kangoken* (literally: custody and care rights). *Shinken* refers to the right to make legal decisions for a child, for instance where they live or go to school. *Kangoken* describes the right to live with and make everyday decisions for a child, for instance when a coresident parent decides what a child will eat or when their bedtime is. When parents are married, both parents simultaneously hold both types of custody over their child. When parents divorce, however, only one person can hold either of these types of custody.[3]

Although joint legal custody is never possible, these two forms of custody do not have to be held together, so one divorced parent might hold "parental rights" (*shinken*) and the other hold "custody and care rights" (*kangoken*) of a single child. Such a shared arrangement is the closest parents can come to building a legal joint custody. In practice, this might mean that both parents consult each other about all decisions, but they don't have to because their legal parental responsibilities are discrete. Although it is legally possible for divorced parents to each be responsible for one type of custody, in practice the vast majority of postdivorce child custody places both *shinken* and *kangoken* with a single individual. In 2015, for instance, among the divorce settled through court mediation, just 0.5 percent had "parental rights" and "custody and care rights" separated and awarded to two different people (Supreme Court 2015).[4]

When parents make the uncommon choice to give "parental rights" (*shinken*) to one parent and "custody and care rights" (*kangoken*) to the other, likely they are structuring that arrangement to increase the chance that both parents will remain connected with the child. One mother told me that exactly this type of unusual arrangement had been suggested to her and her ex-husband by their lawyer. In their case, with two daughters, the father holds *shinken* for their older daughter and *kangoken* for their younger daughter, while the mother holds the inverse custodial responsibilities. As the mother happily told me, their lawyer had brilliantly created a structure that made it more likely the parents would cooperate with each other and functionally share custody. Laughing, this woman compared their lawyer's creativity to the seventeenth-century "hostage system" (*sankin kotai*) in which the Tokugawa shogun held underlings' family members in the capital to guarantee loyalty.[5] Referencing a recognizable historical example, she compared it to her own custody arrangement as a system intentionally structured to keep potential warring parties in functional harmony with each other. Her family's unusual arrangement has worked so far, and she is grateful to their lawyer for suggesting it.

The restriction against any child's custody being held simultaneously by multiple people stems from a legal fiction at the heart of the *koseki* household registration system: a person must be in one, but only one, household. As introduced in the previous chapter, the household registration system requires that all Japanese citizens be registered into a legal household through tracking of births, adoptions, marriages, divorces, and deaths. This system combines what theoretically could be two separate records: each citizen's personal biographical data are embedded within figurative households consisting of family units (Chapman 2011, 10). Importantly, the households so integral to the *koseki* system are fundamentally a legal fiction that does not necessarily translate into people's real residential choices. It is quite common, for instance, for family members to remain "in" a shared household registry even if they are actually living on their own in a separate residence (Hinokidani 2007, 119; Krogness 2011, 70). Therefore, in ways that are fundamentally imbricated in patterns of postdivorce child custody, legal households are vital to, and constantly policed by, the Japanese state at the very same time that the actual households where people live vary.[6]

In the moment of a divorce, and the ensuing postdivorce relationships, legal households are exceptionally influential as a structuring abstraction even as they're being reorganized in practice. Divorced parents have to officially create their new families as if they are utterly separate entities—two distinct legal households where there was previously only one. Even if, in practice, both parents continue to have relationships with their children, thereby blurring the lines demanded by the legal system, those standards continue to exert significant force. For instance, if divorced parents who are informally sharing custody have a disagreement, the legal system will adjudicate it assuming and assigning sole custody to one parent. The legal household, with its requirements and programmatic boundaries, sets the norms with which divorced families must grapple.

De Facto Joint Custody

In my ethnographic research, approximately one-third of parents and former spouses with children eventually settled into de facto joint custody arrangements, creating and sustaining a workable arrangement that allowed the child(ren) to maintain regular contact with both parents. These arrangements involve idiosyncratic dynamics worked out within the family, and a system that works for one family might very well be infeasible for another. Although there remain points of tension between the former spouses, in general these de facto joint custody arrangements are only possible if both parents imagine the best scenario for their children to involve steady parental connection and work to make that possible. For these former spouses, as opposed to other parents we'll meet later in this chapter, being the best parent they can be requires enabling or allowing their ex to remain a connected parent as well, no matter the complications that scenario might bring. Because there is no legal structure that explicitly supports such arrangements, parents and their extended families must figure out ways to balance parental needs and preferences with those of their children, as well as how to handle family gatherings, financial responsibilities, new romantic relationships, stepparents or stepsiblings, and the children's residence. Although they can be hard to count in Japan, stepfamilies are increasing in number even if they remain largely invisible (Nozawa 2011, 2015a; Nozawa, Ibaraki, and Hayano 2006).

Since the early 2000s, a disparate movement to legalize joint custody has found increasing support, but there remains considerable debate about the risks and benefits of shared custody after divorce. For instance, in 2009, when the evening panel discussion program *Tuesday Surprise* (*Kayō sapuraizu*) aired an episode about child custody after divorce, the panelists and audience members who called in overwhelmingly voted that "Japan should have shared child custody" (*Nihon mo "kyōdō shinken" ni subeki*). Despite one panelist's extended invective about the risks brought by joint custody, 77 percent of those audience members who voted supported joint custody (Nihon TV 2009).[7] In contrast, a 2011 national survey reported that between 16 percent and 23 percent of divorced noncustodial parents have visitation with their children (MHLW 2011). The gap between casual television polls and the actual choices divorced parents make reflects more than unscientific surveys. Even parents who imagine (or hope) they will be able to maintain shared custody after divorce can see those feelings change when divorce becomes a reality. Cases of de facto shared custody demonstrate the extended effort, coordination, and flexibility required to sustain connections not immediately supported by law.

WADA-SAN AND OKADA-SAN: NAVIGATING BLENDED FAMILIES

Wada-san, the mother of a twenty-four-year-old daughter, is one parent who has worked hard to manage the complications of life as a divorced parent. As introduced in chapter 3, Wada-san left her husband when they were unable to figure out how to share domestic responsibilities or effectively communicate about possible solutions. In 1992, she moved out with Satomi, their baby daughter, and waited about a year for her husband to agree to the divorce. When he did, their divorce agreement gave her custody of their daughter and regular child support payments. Both parents were and remain committed to continued connection with their daughter, although she explains that it was rough going for a number of years. In the decades since the divorce, Wada-san's family has come to include many new family members. While her experiences might be immediately familiar to Americans, they are statistically unusual in contemporary Japan and demonstrate the possibilities of shared custody in practice if not in law. With her daughter, her ex-husband, his new wife and children, her new partner, and his ex-wife and children, Wada-san is navigating and negotiating connections to build relationships. She describes their choices as reflecting awareness of each other but also intentional distance.

A few years after her divorce, in the late 1980s, Wada-san began working at a technology company and met Okada-san. He was unhappily married with two children, and Wada-san says she was very cautious of becoming friends with him. She was worried that even just chatting at work would lead to something, and because she knew he was married, she didn't want to do anything wrong. She tried not to talk with him and found out later that he was feeling the same way about her. Eventually, after a few years, Okada-san left his wife and started a relationship with Wada-san. He moved in with her and her daughter and, at the time of our conversation, they had been living together for twelve years. They are not married and have no particular plans to marry. Throughout our conversations, Wada-san referred to him as her "partner" *pātonā*, a term that sidesteps some of the negative valences of more common words like husband (*danna* or *shujin*), boyfriend (*boifurendo*), or lover (*koibito*).[8]

Although they eventually grew into a genuine friendship, it took years and concerted effort for Wada-san and her ex-husband to build a relationship that enabled them to co-parent their daughter. During that time, they continued to share both money and time with their daughter. Wada-san explained that facilitating time between Satomi and her ex-husband wasn't particularly easy but felt completely necessary. In response to my question about if she and her ex-husband ever met up, she said:

> He and our daughter meet up, but I only communicate with him on the phone, not in person. He would say, "I'd like to see her on next Sunday." And I'd say, "Ok, sure. Please drop her off after you're done." They'd go somewhere to play, like an amusement park or somewhere. When it was time for her to come home, he would bring her back to the nearby train station. At the exit gate of the station, they would say goodbye. When I would ask her if she had a good time with her dad, sometimes she would tease me by saying, "Why does Dad have to leave?"

Although they didn't have a firm schedule for visits between Satomi and her father, they saw each other about once a month throughout her childhood.

These were mostly day visits, and Satomi didn't sleep at her father's house. At the same time, Wada-san was receiving monthly child support payments and made efforts to highlight these payments to Satomi, helping her understand that they were coming from her father.

> When we got divorced, we were renting our apartment. I didn't ask for alimony because I was the one who wanted the divorce. Also, neither of us had any money at that time. We really didn't have anything. After the divorce, he lived by himself, and I was on my own with our daughter. He has been paying child support to our daughter without missing a single payment. Every month, I go to the bank and withdraw the money with our daughter. I always say, "This money came from your dad. Thanks to him, we can afford your new clothes for the school trip and other stuff you want." I always say that to her.

Examining divorce in the United Kingdom, Simpson (1997) found that child support payments and visitation brought potential tension to divorced families because parents ascribed radically different meanings to them. Some fathers in Simpson's study understood child support payments to be in exchange for time, akin to renting their own children, and therefore resented having to pay. Mothers, on the other hand, who were already responsible for their children's everyday needs (financial and emotional), were more likely to understand child support payments as nonnegotiable contributions for the children's welfare. Extended arguments came about when fathers felt they were not "getting their money's worth" in terms of contact with their children and stopped contributing financial support to their ex-wives. In Wada-san's case, she doesn't report any extended tension perhaps because each side had very modest expectations: because there was no money, she didn't expect (or solicit) a big lump sum payment from her ex-husband. In turn, he spent about one day a month with their daughter, in a casual way. If she had demanded more money, or he had requested a more regular or frequent visitation schedule, things might have been very different.[9] For the time period—the late 1980s and 1990s—such a visitation schedule was entirely typical, if not more frequent than average. As will become clear with later examples in this chapter, conflicts increase when noncustodial parents want more time with their children through a frequent, fixed schedule.

Conforming to worries articulated within some Japanese media and scholarship, Satomi's biggest challenge around her parents' divorce was dealing with each of their new partners and the extended families they brought. One common argument in Japan against continuing connections after divorce suggests that children will not be able to handle (psychologically and socially) the complications that come with new partners, or the complex emotions occurring within blended families. Before she was ten years old, Satomi faced new relationships with both her mother's new partner (Okada-san) and her father's new wife and the children they had together. Wada-san explains that building these new bonds wasn't easy, quick, or necessarily fun.

> Before my ex had kids with his new wife, our daughter visited their house to hang out. Her stepmom really cares about her.[10] But my daughter is a bit obstinate. So she would tease her stepmother by saying, "He is my dad! Don't take him away from me!"

Okada-san moved into the house Wada-san and Satomi shared when Satomi was ten. In the beginning, they fought and disagreed with each other. Satomi felt and acted possessive of both her parents and was resentful of the effort it took to live with her mother's new partner. In this story, Wada-san was sharing a moment that demonstrates the contradictions present: Satomi worried that her new stepmother would somehow take her father away but was also comfortable enough to explicitly articulate those feelings. Wada-san used the moment as evidence of the strong relationship between Satomi and her stepmother, but her retelling also relates Satomi's worries. Wada-san says that their relationships improved over time, as Satomi came to feel that she wouldn't lose either of her parents, even if their relationships were changing.

Important in this blended family are strategic disconnections: some members of this broad, extended family rarely meet or have never met. Although Satomi regularly sees both her parents and their new partners, she has never met Okada-san's two daughters (her de facto stepsisters). Wada-san has never met Okada-san's ex-wife or his daughters (her de facto stepdaughters), nor her ex-husband's new wife and child. Okada-san hasn't met Wada-san's ex-husband. When I asked her about these avoidances, she had a hard time explaining the reasoning because it felt necessary and obvious to her. Everyone got along, and everyone seemed perfectly happy to know *about* each other, but Wada-san and her relatives felt that not everyone in the extended family actually needed to spend a lot of time together.

As a divorced father with two daughters, Okada-san more directly explained their connections and strategic disconnections by articulating the impossibility of becoming a "former parent" or "ex-father." Unlike the divorce process through which one can become a former spouse, he feels there is no way to ever undo the parent-child relationship:

> If I get divorced and separate from my wife . . . Well, I still care about her but she becomes kind of a stranger (*tanin*) to me. But my children won't become strangers to me. Definitely not. I will always care about my children. That's a universal feeling for parents around the world. At least, I think so.

The Japanese term he uses here, *tanin*, literally means "other person" and denotes a stranger or someone with whom the speaker does not have a relationship. Okada-san's point here is that even if he cares about his ex-wife, they aren't connected through blood, and therefore their relationship can be ended more completely than with his children. Goldfarb (2019) has convincingly argued that contemporary Japanese rhetoric about the supremacy of blood relations attempts to overcompensate for tenuous familial relationships that are always only socially constructed. Who counts as family—in the adopted families Goldfarb studies, or the divorced families I discuss here—is not merely determined by blood but by explicit and implicit choices made over the course of many years.[11] As the examples in the next section make clear, Okada-san's perspectives on the impossibility of fully disconnecting from one's children are routinely contradicted in practice.

The Logic of Clean Breaks

On the opposite end of the spectrum, approximately one-third of the parents with whom I did research decided that the best way to be a divorced family was for the noncustodial parent to remove themselves entirely from the child's life. Although this perspective is less popular than it used to be, it is still recognizable and is often the unmarked norm that must be argued against if parents want to attempt any alternative arrangement. These parents aspire toward, and work to create, a "clean break" between the child and noncustodial parent, as well as between the pre- and postdivorce family. Some parents made this unilateral decision in response to behavior they found problematic or worrisome: they felt their former spouse would be so unreliable, violent, or difficult that the best—or only—choice for themselves and their children would be to end all contact. Other parents, especially noncustodial parents who removed themselves from their children's lives, described the decision as extremely difficult but ultimately for the children's benefit.[12] In this logic, the leaving parent understands their own exit as a gesture of deep love for their children. To them, it seemed simply too hard for a child, especially a young child, to understand the complexity of divorce or to maintain relationships with two parents who didn't get along. In their narratives, leaving parents tended to represent their choice as a difficult but responsible decision that moved a potential burden from the child to the parent. Parents who chose a "clean break" represented this decision as a lifelong burden they took on so as to relieve their children of a perpetual trauma: a sudden break allows space and time for healing that continued contact would impair. To these parents, divorce forces the choice between an abrupt disconnection that will eventually heal into a scar and ongoing connection that will remain an open, festering wound.

Many people who voice support for the "clean break" ideology describe the risks that extended conflict can bring to parents and children. If a child's parents are required to stay in contact to facilitate shared custody, the argument goes, that opens the child up to regular, prolonged conflict. In a newspaper forum discussing the links between child custody and poverty, lawyer Hasegawa Kyoko delineates what she predicts as the negative impacts for children whose parents aren't able to get along but are forced to share custody:

> If the noncustodial parent and custodial parent disagree over parenting, it would create a deadlock that would hurt their child's well-being. If parents need to consult with the court every time they disagree, that will take a lot of time and energy especially from the custodial parent. That parent must earn a living, be responsible for parenting on their own, and deal with social stigma, financial difficulties, and an overwhelming daily schedule. Such negative impacts would override the possible benefits of improving the system of justice around child custody. (quoted in Yamauchi 2016)

Hasegawa here is articulating a position that reflects the gendered patterns in child custody and is, presumably, designed to protect mothers specifically. Linking the parent's and child's need, she's arguing that requiring a custodial parent—most likely to be a woman—to stay in contact with their former spouse increases the already substantial demands put on that parent. Those additional demands will take time and energy from the child's care and might require extra work to explain ongoing conflicts. In my experience, many Americans find even the idea of a "clean break" so harmful to children that it can be easy to gloss over the very real work Hasegawa identifies here, namely the ramifications of labor needed to heal, or at least maintain, tense relationships. Because emotional labor, particularly that occurring within families, tends to be gendered feminine and diminished as actual work, Hasegawa asks us to acknowledge the emotional and care work that custodial parents must do, and the impacts it might have on children. Of course, in an ideal situation, divorced parents can get along or hide their conflicts from their children. But for the not insignificant percentage of parents who cannot, shared custody pulls children into conflicts that a "clean break" would protect against.

Previous scholarship exploring Japanese families represents "clean breaks" as a normal, if difficult, pattern after divorce. In the Meiji era (1868–1912), family relationships were irrevocably severed with divorce (Fuess 2004). With very low rates of alimony, other financial exchanges (like inheritance), or contact between children and noncustodial parents, Fuess finds much evidence to support "the notion that the relationship between the spouses indeed ended at the time of divorce" (ibid., 98). When the Embrees worked in Suye village in the 1930s, they also knew divorced women who "had to leave their children behind in their [ex-]husband's house or in their natal house when they remarried" (Smith and Wiswell 1982, 275).[13] In the 1980s, a divorced mother echoed this sentiment when she explained that she didn't want alimony from her ex-husband, even though she needed the money, because "she felt it would maintain a relationship with [him]" (Rosenberger 2001, 79). Writing in the early 2000s, Kumagai makes clear that a "clean break" mentality was still operating, saying: "divorce of the spouses is pretty much equivalent to termination of the parental relationship with the noncustodial parent" (2008, 63; see also Ono 2010, 153). Comparing these disconnections to common Japanese construction methods in which buildings are regularly demolished and rebuilt, Nozawa (2011, 2016) evocatively describes these as "scrap and build families." In this way of thinking, both buildings and families are safer, stronger, and better when they are utterly demolished rather than transformed into a newer form. Although the "clean break" has never been a singular, unchanging ideal, these examples make clear that this model for parent-child disconnection after divorce is at least recognizable across historical periods and locales, if not common.[14]

National statistics back up these patterns, and throughout the postwar period, a significant number of children have had no contact with their noncustodial parent. In 2011, 50.8 percent of custodial mothers and 41.0 percent of custodial fathers included in a survey reported that their children never had visits with their noncustodial parent (MHLW 2011, 57–58).[15] The same survey shows that a significant minority of custodial parents are choosing to forgo any child support payments specifically because they don't want to have any contact with their former spouse: 23.1 percent of custodial mothers and 17.0 percent of custodial fathers said they did not ask for child support because they "did not want to engage with their child's other parent" (*aite to kakawaritakunai*) (ibid., 47).

Rhetoric advocating for "clean breaks" after divorce has shifted from the language of selfishness to that of annoyance and trouble surrounding visitation. When Bryant (1995) conducted research in the 1980s and early 1990s, court mediators and some parents described a noncustodial parent's wish to see their children as "selfish" (*wagamama*) because "postdivorce contact between noncustodial parents and children is harmful to the children" (Bryant 1995, 20). When I asked a similar question in 2005, many people used the term *mendōkusai*, which glosses as "troublesome" or "annoying." For instance, at a public protest advocating for legal joint custody in the Tokyo suburbs, one frustrated father articulated precisely this reasoning to explain why some custodial parents refuse contact with their former spouse. In his late forties, and expressing heartbreak at not seeing his young son for more than three years, this father answered with exasperation when I wondered aloud why custodial parents might be so unwilling to facilitate co-parenting. "[They think] organizing visits would be too annoying and messy (*mendōkusai*)." Such co-parenting would take time to organize and would require ongoing connections between former spouses, work that is obviated by a "clean break."

MIHO: IT MUST HAVE BEEN THE BEST CHOICE

Miho was six when her parents divorced. Telling me about it when she was in her midtwenties, Miho described the divorce with clarity about who was right and wrong and what should have been done. Although she was unaware when it happened, Miho found out later that one day her father had come home from work and requested a divorce. He wanted to marry a coworker, and therefore requested a divorce from Miho's mother. From Miho's young perspective, the divorce looked and felt very different than it did to any of the adults involved. To her, one day her father was there and one day he simply wasn't; she and her brother were not consulted about what kind of contact or connection they might want with their father.[16]

Her father's virtual evaporation was followed by other major changes in her young life: with her mother and older brother, Miho moved to live with her maternal grandfather, and eventually, her last name changed. This latter change was prompted by the requirement that all people listed within one legal family, with a single *koseki* household registry, have the same last name. When Miho's mother divorced, she decided to change her name back to her natal family's name, which meant that Miho and her brother also had to change their last names. This happened when Miho was in second grade and other students in her class started to bully her. Even though she didn't tell anyone about the divorce, they figured it out, and the bullying that began with her name change became a dominant pattern in Miho's life. Miho describes her life from that moment on as difficult and full of harassment. In fourth grade, Miho's mother decided to put her in a different school, hoping that would ease her trouble, but the bullying continued.

When she narrated all this to me from the perspective of her midtwenties, the years of bullying were what she highlighted as changing the course of her life. She was quick to link this bullying to her parents' divorce—the divorce, and her ensuing name change, were the ostensible catalysts for the bullying—but the divorce pales in comparison with the bullying. For Miho, the divorce was relatively quick and clean and she has never seen her father again. Although she described her father as a bad person because of how he treated her mother, she also says that he had been a very nice father to her up until that point. When I asked her if she would, or might still want, to see her father again, she described conflicted feelings. On the one hand, she had a good time with her father when she was much younger. On the other, she's incredibly angry about his apparent disinterest in her for the last twenty years and feels like she bore the brunt of the divorce in ways that her father never recognized. She reasons that she would, hypothetically, like to have some ongoing relationship with her father, but only if he's a good person. By virtue of the fact that he abandoned and ignored her for twenty years, he's probably not a good person, but she's not sure. The loss and longing she feels is more for a generalized idea of a father, not so much the particular father who seemed so willing to leave her.

Legal Support for Co-Parenting and Visitation

Legal interventions surrounding co-parenting and visitation look strikingly similar to those surrounding divorce overall: the legal system puts almost no restrictions on parents who can create and sustain their own arrangements but offers limited options and little support for those who need assistance.[17] Many parents, such as Wada-san and her ex-husband, devise functional and (relatively) happy shared-custody arrangements. But most "mutual" (*kyōgi*) divorce agreements, which account for almost 90 percent of divorces, lead to noncustodial parents having very infrequent contact with their children. When parents disagree about who should hold custody or how frequently a noncustodial parent should see their children, the family law system tends to prioritize the "clean break"—pushing parents who have unsettled conflict to entirely remove the noncustodial parent from children's lives. These determinations are attempts to protect children from the trauma imagined to be caused by witnessing parental conflict (T. Tanase 2010, 7). Such decisions, and the theories of conflict that underpin them, prioritize the types of conflict that come about through *connection* and fail to acknowledge the tremendous conflicts that can be caused through *disconnection*, specifically the sudden and total absence of a loved parent. Thus although the legal system putatively attempts to support children's best interests, by focusing primarily on the conflict caused through parental contact, policies that advocate or support a "clean break" leave children vulnerable to loss and longing that are largely ignored within the court system.

The vast majority of divorces are settled through private agreements negotiated by the spouses themselves, and although we might expect such personal arrangements to allow space for custodial flexibility, in practice this type of divorce strongly correlates with disconnections between children and non-custodial parents. According to a 2011 government report on single parents, compared with all other types of divorce, those who settle through mutual agreement (*kyōgi*) are less likely to have either child support payments or regular visitation for the noncustodial parent (MHLW 2011). Within the report's national sample, only 30.1 percent of custodial mothers with "mutual" divorces have a written child support agreement, compared with 74.8 percent of mothers with all other legal types of divorces (ibid., 45). As explained in the previous chapter, I understand this discrepancy to reflect the bargaining necessary to induce a reluctant spouse to agree to a divorce they might not want; many parents bargain away any possible child support in order to finalize a divorce they desire. Similarly, noncustodial parents in "mutual" divorces are much less likely to see their children: according to the Ministry's report, only 18.4 percent of children in these divorces have visits (*menkai*)[18] with noncustodial fathers and 14.1 percent with noncustodial mothers (ibid., 56), figures well below the frequency for all others types of divorce (48.2 percent for noncustodial fathers and 29.0 percent for noncustodial mothers in other types of divorce).[19]

If parents cannot agree on a custody arrangement on their own, they are required to begin mediation (*chōtei*) in which legal representatives negotiate an agreement for them. Precisely because of conflicts over custody and visitation, the frequency of these types of mediations has skyrocketed in recent decades, tripling between 1999 and 2009 (Kaba 2014; Tanase 2011, 563). These agreements give one parent custody, and the other should ideally have scheduled time with the child. Court-ordered visitation or shared-parenting time might be as infrequent as once or twice a year, but in 2011, among the approximately 30 percent of divorced parents who were currently participating in visitation, the most common frequency was "at least once a month" (MHLW 2011, 60; Tanase 2011).[20] At the same time, using standardized charts as a starting point, the noncustodial parent is assigned a specific child support payment, either as a regular monthly amount or as a one-time transfer.[21] If the parents are unable to agree—for instance, if both parents are requesting custody—the mediators and the judge involved will make a determination. Therefore, parents who cannot agree on their own open themselves up to a unilateral determination with the "clean break" model at its root.

All custody decisions, including those negotiated by mediators or parents on their own, are fundamentally shaped by the family law systems' limited enforcement mechanisms. If a parent violates their divorce agreement—for instance, by restricting visitation with a noncustodial parent, or failing to pay child support—the family court has few resources to induce agreement. Without legal "contempt" or a system to compel parents to uphold legal agreements, these negotiated pledges can easily become a list of broken promises (Kumagai 2015, 97; Shiori 2017).[22] In the pointed words of a US State Department flyer, "compliance with Family Court rulings is essentially voluntary, which renders any ruling unenforceable unless both parents agree" (US Department of State 2007, cited in Jones 2007a, 352). No matter what parents pledge in the agreements they make on their own, in family court mediation, or to judges, if they break that agreement, the family court can neither force them to comply nor substantially punish them. Two recent legislative changes have attempted to change these legal realities. In 2012, the Japanese Civil Code was updated to explicitly mention that "the child's best interest" (*ko no rieki*) should be given "highest priority" (*mottomo yūsen*) in custody determinations, although, as in other cultural contexts, what qualifies as a child's best interest remains subjective (Sadaoka 2011; Saito 2016; K. Tanase 2010; T. Tanase 2010, 17; Mnookin 1985). Some courts have fined parents who don't allow the visitation they promised—50,000 yen ($500) in Okayama Family Court in 2008 and 80,000 yen ($800) in Tokyo High Court in 2012—but such policies are inconsistent. At the time of this writing in June 2018, the Ministry of Justice has begun to consider the possibility of using force to remove children without the presence and permission of a custodial parent (NHK 2018).

In practice, these attempts at inducement have had little effect. Parents do not face systematic legal repercussions or punishment for breaking their promises surrounding custody, visitation, and child support (Kumagai 2015, 97).[23] The gap between negotiated custody agreements and actual practices is most obvious in judicial responses to parental abductions, when one parent—while married or divorced, holding legal custody or not—takes their child and restricts access to the other parent. Without enforcement capabilities to punish abducting parents, the family law system typically allows these unilateral moves to stand. Within the court system, an abduction is taken as evidence of extremely high parental conflict, which is to be solved through a "clean break," often facilitated through giving sole custody to the abducting parent and refusing visitation to the other.

Gender and Child Custody

In practice, legal negotiations and agreements follow deeply gendered patterns. Throughout the postwar era, mediators have been likely to assign maternal custody with increasing frequency, and now about 80 percent of custody is awarded to mothers. This increasing and systematic preference for

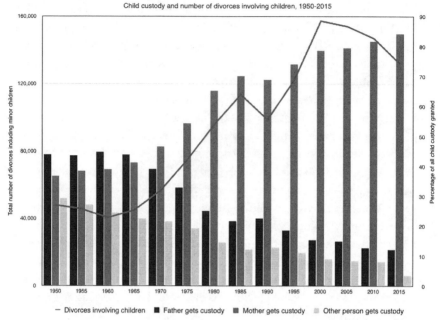

FIGURE 4. Trends in legal child custody, and the total number of divorces that include children, 1950–2015 (NIPSSR 2017b)

maternal custody represents one of the biggest changes in family law rulings in the postwar period and has become a significant flash point for many activists and reformers. It is a substantial deviation from historical patterns. For instance, from the Tokugawa era and through the early postwar era, because lineage was traced through paternity, legal agreements most frequently required children to "stay" with their fathers after divorce, rather than "leaving" the family with their mothers (Beardsley et al. 1959, 391).[24] If mothers were granted custody, it was most likely to be of daughters, who were expected to eventually leave their natal family upon marriage, or young children who were understood to be more in need of maternal care (Dore 1999 [1958], 153; Jones 2007b, 216). Therefore, in premodern and early modern legal decisions, custody was most likely to be directed to the paternal lineage and granted to fathers as representatives of that lineage. In practice, historical and ethnographic evidence suggests that children whose custody was held by their fathers might actually have been raised by other female relatives, such as paternal grandmothers and aunts, or maids (Fuess 2004, 94).[25]

In the contemporary moment, family law reformers regularly point to preferences for maternal custody as a fundamental inequity and evidence of structural bias against men.[26] Japanese and foreign fathers seeking custody or regular visitation describe legal support for contact with their children as vanishingly small (Sakuda 2017; Nishimuta 2017).[27] For example, in divorces that include high conflict, one common visitation policy is to grant a non-custodial father approximately two hours of contact with their child once a year. In many cases, if a mother suggests that the father might bring harm to the child, all visitations will be ended or moved to a "visitation center" in the presence of a third-party monitor (Sakuda 2017; T. Tanase 2010, 15). As might be obvious, it is extremely difficult for parents to rebuild or sustain relationships with their children under such circumstances. Moreover, the restricted and stilted nature of such interactions often serve as self-fulfilling prophecies, stressing relationships between parents and children to their breaking point.

Such minimal contact between children and fathers conforms to older models for parenting increasingly called into question. As explained in this book's earlier chapters, disconnected dependence was long a recognizable model for marital relationships, particularly in the 1960s through the early 1990s. This normative model for marital intimacy influenced relationships between parents and children, making it extremely common for mothers to be more directly involved in their children's daily lives. Common stereotypes throughout this period characterize fathers as being largely disconnected from children's everyday emotional, educational, and social development, casting them as figures who demonstrate their paternal affection through financial support and gruff discipline (Allison 2000, 24; Cook 2016, 108; Wagatsuma 1977).

Starting especially in the late 1990s, government campaigns attempted to shift these norms and push fathers to be more actively involved in their children's daily lives. Particularly famous was an advertising campaign running from 1999 through 2002, starting with a poster of a celebrity father holding his baby and the tag line "A man who doesn't raise his children can't be called a father" (*Ikuji wo shinai otoko wo, chichi to wa yobanai*) (Ishii-Kuntz 2015, 163; Nakatani 2006, 95). In the early 2000s, such reconfigured models for fatherhood coalesced around the neologism *ikumen*, which literally means "a man who raises [children]" and might be glossed as asking men to be "involved fathers" (Ishii-Kuntz 2013; 2015, 164). This new ideal is an explicit repudiation of previous models for fatherhood and parenting, suggesting that good fathers connect with their children as measured through time and emotional bonds. Although statistical measures make clear that *ikumen* ideals have not yet translated into radically revised gendered responsibilities in families, younger fathers especially articulated to me their involvement in their children's lives. For men who understand themselves as connected and involved fathers, legal interventions premised on the benefits of a "clean break" feel particularly like brutal and unfair assaults on their family relationships (Kawarada 2016; Koga 2016). Contemporary activism focused on family law reform demonstrates generational shifts in idealized fathering, as the assumptions and norms embedded in legal preference for "clean breaks" increasingly diverge from common understandings of what it means to be a good father.[28]

Contested Custody

On the surface, many cases of contested custody look like "clean breaks." In these situations, one parent takes their child(ren) and prevents contact with the other parent, unilaterally deciding on a "clean break." With very few exceptions, these unilateral moves are allowed, if not supported, by the Japanese judiciary and law enforcement. If a parent takes their own child, it is unlikely that child will be forcibly returned to the other parent. Although these situations ultimately look almost identical to "clean breaks"—with a noncustodial parent completely divorced from their child's life—they include agonizing, unwanted disconnections for so-called "left-behind" parents and quite likely the children, too. Some "taking" parents, by contrast, describe their decisions to take children as a necessity because of the family court system's structures, with few protections for parents or children and insufficient responses to domestic violence and other ongoing conflicts.

Although every case is different, the broad patterns of contested custody typically include certain key elements. If a married, divorced, or divorcing parent reports that their spouse has taken their child, police often refuse to investigate the situation. In one particularly striking example, the documentary film *From the Shadows* includes an exchange between an American mother and Japanese police officers (in a local police stand, or *kōban*). When the mother asks for police assistance finding the children taken by her estranged husband, the officer replies: "I'm sorry, we don't consider your case an abduction, or even a crime. We consider it a family matter, and we can't intervene in a family matter" (Antell and Hearn 2013).[29] Many Japanese left-behind parents have told me similar stories. Left-behind parents describe coming home to suddenly empty houses, their children and spouse simply gone. As the parent begins to figure out what happened, they might learn where their children physically are, but that information doesn't offer much help. Appeals to court agents, like judges or mediators, or to the police, are likely to push them into formal mediation sessions (*chōtei*). Because those mediations are themselves premised on the expectation of sole custody, that is the most common outcome. In simplified terms, a parent abducting their child triggers court mediation designed to award custody to only one parent, which can often be granted to the taking parent.

Why is taking a child not considered a crime, or at least evidence that the taking parent should not have custody? First, remember that the "clean break" has been a recognizable and idealized standard. Although parents are increasingly refusing that ideal, the legal system still maintains it as a viable method through which to organize families after divorce. In and of itself, a child losing all contact with their parent is not outside the realm of normal. Second, parental abduction can itself be used as evidence of the extreme conflict, or violent threat, present in a family. In this case, the taking parent's actions are understood to be a rescue or assisted escape. Japanese popular media regularly represents parental abduction as a necessary, if unfortunate, response to domestic violence (Nihon TV 2009; Tanase 2011). Third, many people believe the legal system is woefully unprepared to deal with the complex realities of violence within families. Because domestic violence has only recently begun to be taken seriously in law and law enforcement, many people have little faith that the legal system will act decisively enough to protect children from future violence. Therefore, media representations and popular perceptions suggest that any abducting parent must be fleeing violence. When I discussed contested "clean breaks" with men and women who had not experienced divorce themselves, their overwhelming response was to assume that the taking parent must have escaped violence that the court system wouldn't, or couldn't, fairly litigate. Fourth, Jones (2007b) convincingly argues that the court's ideological acceptance of parental abduction is merely cover for the court's inability to enforce its own judgments. If a parent consistently refuses to return the child, or allow promised visitation, or pay child support, the court has few formal mechanisms to compel them to do so. Jones (ibid., 253) describes a case in which a father refusing promised visitation simply hung up on a family court investigator, who turned to the children's mother and said, "There's nothing more I can do." By making the choice not to compel parents directly, the family court system suggests that such an intervention— for instance, police officers forcibly removing a child from a noncompliant parent—would be the absolute worst option for any child and therefore must be avoided.[30]

Parent activists, many of whom are fathers unable to see their children, have brought attention to these cases by writing and talking publicly about their pain. In organized groups, left-behind parents work to educate the public about custody laws, advocate for change, and support each other as they attempt to deal with total disconnection from their children. This commitment to educating other parents about the legal system stems from their own ignorance and the damage it caused: because they weren't aware that the legal system wouldn't prosecute parental abduction, many "left-behind" parents learned too late what could have helped them.[31] In public demonstrations at busy train stations, through websites, and with deeply personal narratives, these activists try to simultaneously inform the public of current laws and solicit support for a legal joint-custody option.

ENDO-SAN: PLANNING FOR THE FUTURE

Endo-san had been married and divorced, with no children, when he met the woman who would become his second wife. After they married, when he was in his late forties and his wife was almost a decade younger, they lived close to her family in Tokyo and soon had a baby daughter. Endo-san said they were both incredibly happy to have a child, and although he continued his regular (salaryman) white-collar job, he also wanted to be a different kind of father than his own had been. He wanted to be an involved father (*ikumen*), and everything seemed to be going smoothly until their daughter began school.

As Endo-san describes it, he comes from a family that puts a lot of value on education; his wife didn't, and when they decided to enroll their daughter in a private school, his wife began to become extremely anxious. She was, he says, insecure in her educational background and abilities needed to tutor their daughter in this high-level school. Even though their daughter was only in kindergarten, Mrs. Endo felt pressure and compared herself with other mothers, many of whom had elite educational backgrounds. She asked that they move to a different area in Tokyo, and put their daughter into a public school, but Endo-san was against the idea.[32]

He began to understand that Mrs. Endo had mental health problems, an opinion that he says his mother-in-law shared, but his wife refused treatment. At home, they would fight and she would occasionally call the police. When they arrived, Endo-san said, she would falsely accuse him of domestic violence, and although the police would often tell him privately that they believed his story, they had to record the accusation. Endo-san was never aware of any investigation into the claims, but the accusations remain officially recorded.

The tension in their relationship increased until Mrs. Endo decided to spend a few weeks at her mother's house, taking their daughter. Those weeks turned into months, and she refused to come home or let Endo-san interact with their daughter. Mrs. Endo eventually filed for divorce, which required court mediation sessions that Endo-san used to try to gain some contact with his daughter. Although his wife would promise contact in the mediation sessions, when time came for the visitation, she would refuse, with no penalty. After fighting for two years to see his daughter and to acknowledge her abduction, Endo-san has finally given up that particular battle. By the time we met, he hadn't seen his daughter in years and imagined it might be another decade or so before she is interested enough to come looking for him.

Endo-san worked within the family law system but grew disillusioned enough to want to stop all negotiations. When his wife first took their daughter away, Endo-san began the court-ordered mediation sessions. In these, Mrs. Endo was working to either convince Endo-san to agree to a divorce settlement or convince the court that there was some good reason for a judge to ignore Endo-san's refusal and allow the divorce. Endo-san made seeing his daughter a central claim in these negotiations and refused, for many months, to agree to anything that didn't allow him to see their daughter. He was willing, he says, to allow his wife to be the custodial parent, but he wanted to have some regular time with his daughter. Mrs. Endo could promise one thing in the negotiations and then simply refuse to hold up that deal, with no threat of formal punishment or being in contempt of court.

Endo-san, having done research, understood this possibility and was really quite angry throughout the process. He got even angrier when mediators questioned his basic character, saying things like, "You seem like you're an angry person. Is that good for your relationship with your daughter?" He said he wanted to answer, "You know why I'm angry? Because of this! Because of you!" but he tried to hold his tongue. Eventually, after many months, he came to understand that the system was stacked against him and there was nothing he could do directly.

He decided to let his wife do whatever she wants and instead do two things to prepare for the future moment when his daughter comes looking for him. First, he will work hard and make money to give her later, a choice conforming to a very normative model for paternal responsibility demonstrated through hard work outside the home. Second, although he is involved in the movement to legalize joint custody in Japan, he self-consciously refuses to let his activism become the kind of single-minded, righteous mission that it can for other parents in the movement. He doesn't want to let his grief make him feel or act crazy, by his own definition, and self-consciously stays away from the public displays of pain favored by some other parents. Instead, against his will, he has been pushed into being the type of father he had actively refused: disconnected from his daughter's daily life, working to earn money as a way to demonstrate his love, care, and responsibility. If she ever decides to find him, he is doing his best to be ready.

Does Continued Connection Help or Hurt?

For decades, scholars in different cultural contexts have debated the effects of divorce on children, families, and society more broadly. For instance, responding to a spike in the American divorce rate, itself prompted by the liberalization of laws to include "no-fault" divorce options, scholars from many disciplines focused specifically on what divorce does to or for children. Early research found strong correlation between divorce and various measures of difficulty for children: children of divorced parents were found to have trouble in school, higher dropout rates, and lower grades and were more likely to have troubles later in life. Later research nuanced these perspectives, walking back any assertion that divorce caused harm to children.[33] Sociologists and psychologists began to compare children of divorced parents with children of *unhappily* married parents (i.e., those in high-conflict marriages), finding little difference. At least in an American context, this research suggests that divorce per se doesn't hurt children but that being exposed to parental conflict, regardless of parents' marital status, and instability has lingering negative effects (Amato 2003, 2010; Clarke-Stewart et al. 2000; Pugh 2015, 187).

Common Japanese custody patterns further complicate our understandings of how conflict might hurt children after divorce. As I explained in this chapter, proponents of the "clean break" model understand it as a way to fundamentally reduce any conflict; if former spouses do not come into contact, their child cannot be harmed by ongoing conflict between them. However, such a model for conflict only acknowledges harm caused by contact and connection, ignoring harm potentially caused by disconnection.

This chapter has demonstrated both the logic of the "clean break" model and the methods parents use to create and sustain shared custody arrangements not formally supported by the legal system. Many Japanese mothers and fathers work hard on a daily, weekly, and monthly basis to maintain relationships with their children after divorce, or to facilitate connections between their former spouse and their children. My research shows that at least a significant minority of parents prioritize such continued connections and work to make them possible.

Since the early 2010s, discussions in Japanese popular media about child custody have increasingly highlighted voices advocating for continued connection between parents and children after divorce. In long-form news stories and interviews with parents, journalists represent the costs and benefits, risks and rewards, of complete disconnection through the clean break model. Once an unmarked standard, the "clean break" model now draws questions even as it remains a legal standard. These debates about what is best for children after divorce, how to protect both children and parents, fundamentally situate connection at the heart of the puzzle. Considering when and how connection helps children, or what harm it might cause, parallels broader questions about familial or intimate relationships in an age when self-responsibility is newly popular.

PART III

Living as an X

The Costs of Divorce

In 2006, Mae, a thirty-seven-year-old Japanese woman, was telling me about her unsuccessful job search as we walked to an art exhibition in Tokyo. Divorced for five years, Mae held a hair stylist license but struggled to find a permanent position. Given her training, she had recently applied to work for a company that made hair dye. But when she got to the final interview, despite her qualifications and a test that went well, she was told it wasn't going to work out. She was simply too old for the position, the interviewer said, and the company was reluctant to hire her because she would be older than her supervisor, a dynamic they expected would lead to inevitable tension. Such a hiring decision, particularly impacting older female candidates, is neither illegal nor uncommon in Japan, and Mae herself wasn't particularly surprised. As she narrated the negative result of the interview, Mae mixed language and gesture to convey the finality of what happened. She turned to face me, bent her elbows, and crossed her forearms into the shape of an X, while saying a single word: *batsu*. This word and the gesture that embodied it made clear the impossibility of her getting this job.

Throughout the postwar period, divorce has created a substantial and powerful social stigma in Japan. To be divorced, especially for women, was "a great failure, a lifelong shame" and made it harder to remarry, find a good job, or rent an apartment (Hardacre 1984, 119). Children of divorced parents have faced parallel stigmas that limit their options for work, education, and marriage. The lingering power of stigma is so strong that protecting children from it was long a common reason to avoid divorce (ibid.; Fuess 2004, 161; Kumagai 1983, 92; Ono 2006, 226). When Mae was rejected from a job for which she was perfectly qualified, it wouldn't have been unreasonable for her to imagine it might have had something to do with her divorce. But it could have been because of her age or gender, too. Being a divorced woman over thirty-five years of age made it extremely difficult for Mae to find a well-paying job.

In the last twenty years, the long-standing stigma around divorce in Japan has become tightly intertwined with poverty. At astronomical rates, divorce is likely to impoverish, and women are particularly likely to fall into poverty after divorce. In the early 2000s, an astonishing 74 percent of divorced women and 65 percent of divorced mothers had annual household incomes less than three million yen ($30,000), which put them in the bottom quintile of the general population (Ono 2010, 164).[1] Not only does divorce cause poverty, it is also caused by poverty: men and women of a lower social class, with less formal education and lower annual incomes, account for an increasing proportion of divorces. This effect continues into remarriage: when poorer people divorce in Japan, they are less likely to remarry, and therefore less likely to reap the financial and social benefits of being married (Ono 2010, 167). Amidst popular awareness of Japan's increasing economic inequalities, divorce has rapidly become a mechanism that exacerbates and extends poverty in highly gendered patterns.

For women in Japan, the costs of divorce can be quite high. Even as they are more likely to initiate divorce, and more willing to bargain with husbands who don't immediately agree to divorce, women disproportionally bear the negative repercussions of these intimate disconnections. As stigma surrounding divorce morphs into less explicit forms, the most substantial costs of divorce manifest in falling standards of living, decreased household income, and increased risks of poverty. Women generally, and custodial mothers specifically, face high risks of poverty amplified by two interrelated causes. First, Japan's gendered labor market is structured such that many divorced women must choose between temporary jobs that offer middle-class wages or permanent but low-paying positions. Second, the judicial system cannot guarantee or compel child support transfers, leaving many mothers with less financial support than their divorce agreements promise. For these reasons, risks and threats formerly caused by stigma now come from the poverty that divorce brings.

In this chapter, I focus on the lives of women to provide a portrait of lived realities after divorce. Many of these women actively sought divorce and remain happy with that decision, although their lives after divorce can tumble quickly into poverty, or inch dangerously toward it. Financial concerns have become more common, and in response these women employ a range of tactics, from carefully staying on an ex-husband's good side to working multiple part-time jobs or prioritizing current expenses over saving for the future.

In this chapter I argue that contrary to popular images of divorce as evidence of women's ascendance and men's enervation, the lived realities of divorce leave women worse off by many measures. Disconnected from more than just their former spouses, women are likely to lose access to steady wages, government assistance, and networks of support and sympathy. Popular expectations that divorce is controlled by, and good for, women obscure and amplify the systemic, damaging impacts on women's lives.

Dirty Failure

Images, gestures, and verbalizations of *batsu* are exceedingly common in contemporary Japan. Literally meaning "X" or "strike," *batsu* are frequently used on signs, on television programs, and in conversational gestures to convey impossibility, failure, absence, or general badness (see figure 5). For example, train stations post public service messages covered in *batsu* emphasizing behaviors that aren't acceptable. *Batsu* regularly appear on schedules and calendars, letting the reader quickly understand when a store is closed. Mizuho Bank graphically represents the days their cash machines are unavailable during a national holiday with big *batsu*, contrasting them with wide, approving circles on all the days when it is possible to access money. In person, visceral *batsu* arrive in the skinny flesh of forearms when people let you know you are wrong, or that something is not going to happen, or there are no seats, or you can't use that door. Conversational *batsu* range from the subtle, polite crossing of fingers that suggest a gentle whispered *no* to the full-body *batsu*: forearms crossed, palms stiffened flat or hands in rounded fists. Reinforced through all these daily reminders, physical gestures, and graphic representations, a *batsu* is undeniably negative. These were all the meanings Mae referenced when she crossed her forearms to make clear she didn't get the stylist job for which she'd applied.

But when a *batsu* is personalized, possessed, or used to describe a person's character—if someone says, "I have one X" or "I am one X" (*watashi wa batsu ichi*)—there is only one possible meaning: they have been divorced. To be, or perpetually possess, an X is to be divorced. Although *batsu* are used in regular conversation to suggest a range of negative things, if the term is linked with a person, the only association is with divorce. To be divorced is to embody the negative associations of the X, and the *batsu* manifests the stigma of divorce in a single label.

The link between *batsu* and divorce takes concrete form through the household registry system (*koseki*), in which a divorced spouse is literally X-ed out of their marital family's register. Upon divorce one spouse must "leave" the

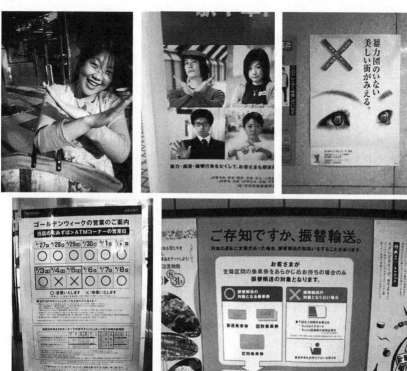

FIGURE 5. Examples of the use of *batsu* in daily life. In the upper left, a woman gestures as she tells a story and wants to signal that something didn't work out. In the upper middle, a poster in a Tokyo train station tells riders that groping is a terrible thing, using the disapproving faces of many people. Two people in this section of the poster are making *batsu*: the man crossing his wrists and the woman crossing her figures. In the upper right, a poster in a municipal office attempts to dissuade crime by saying, "A beautiful city with no gangs is visible." In the lower left, a bank represents the days its cash machines are open and closed during a holiday, with *batsu* meaning closed and circles (*maru*) meaning open. In the lower right, a poster in a Tokyo train station tells riders how to use their prepaid cards. Again, the poster is contrasting *batsu*, signaling what is incorrect or impossible, with circles signaling what is correct.

family register; usually this is the spouse who married "in" to the family and not the spouse who held the role as household head.[2] Until the *koseki* record started to be digitized in 1994—a process that was completed at different times across Japan—family membership was represented through a series of boxes and columns, including people's names and detailed notes about where and when they were born, who their parents were, and major life events (such as marriage, divorce, or adoption). Although it is still possible to request the older style, in which family information and addresses are written vertically by hand, one can now receive a typed sheet listing the same information but typed and to be read left to right. Among divorced people with whom I talked, the new computer version was rumored to be partially an attempt to remove the most obvious representations of divorce stigma: on the older version of the *koseki*, a divorce is marked with an X through the person's name.

For instance, figure 6 pseudonymously reproduces the *koseki* of Tanaka-san, a divorced woman in her fifties. She divorced her husband after years of physical and mental abuse and now lives in a small town taking care of her aging parents. When I mentioned that I was trying to understand what divorce stigma feels like, she said, "Anything is better than what I had to go through" and then offered to give me a copy of her household registration. Because of the years of abuse, she is one of the most legitimately anxious people I met in the course of this research and was constantly checking to make sure I would make everything she was telling me fully anonymous (which I have done). She was particularly worried that her husband might read something I'd written and hurt her or their children again, and almost every time I took out a notebook while we were talking, she stopped talking to check again that all the details would be changed. This background led me to be quite shocked when she said, "Sure, you can go to the city office with Daisuke [her son] and he'll get you a copy of my *koseki*."

When we first got to the local government office, Daisuke and I thoughtlessly requested Tanaka-san's own registry and were then puzzled when we didn't see any X on it.[3] A staff member explained that her record was "clean" (*kirei*) and that the implicitly "dirty" X could only be found on her ex-husband's record. She had moved into and out of *his* family, and therefore it was only there that her name would be removed with an X. We were able to request a

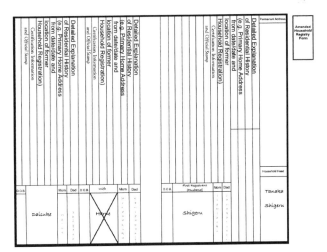

FIGURE 6. The *koseki* register from Tanaka-san's ex-husband, showing her removal upon divorce.

copy of her ex-husband's record because their son, Daisuke, remains in his father's legal family and was physically present with me in the office. On the copy of the official family record, Tanaka-san's first name was first added as the wife of the household head and then X-ed out upon their divorce. This is the dirtiness to which the staff member so casually referred. To have a divorce in your family record, or to be divorced yourself, brings stigma through figurative stains.[4]

The Stigma of Divorce

The felt presence or absence of stigma surrounding divorce is mitigated by gender, age, generation, and parenthood. Among all the people with whom I spoke, women with children, especially those in their fifties or older, were most likely to describe their worries about, and expectations for, stigma caused by divorce. That is not to say that no stigma currently exists but that those who feel it and worry about its effects tended to be older mothers. Younger men and women were less likely to feel or experience any explicit stigma caused by divorce, but many wondered about possible implicit effects. As I described in this book's introduction, Sato-san, a grandmother in Matsuyama city, refused her husband's requests for a divorce for more than twenty years. Although she wasn't particularly happy with her husband, who requested a divorce so that he could marry another woman with whom he already had children, she worried about what a legal divorce would do to her and her children. When I talked with her in 2005, she reflected on how her concern for her children prevented her from agreeing to the divorce her husband originally requested in 1975 and she finally granted in 1994, after her children were married. She contrasted her motivations to those more popular in contemporary Japan, specifically around what parents think would be most beneficial for their children.

> Generally speaking, couples should stay together because of their children, I think. Well, women shouldn't say this type of thing, especially in Japan. Japanese women have endured a lot (*shinbō ga ii*) in their marriages. Many women chose to stay in a bad marriage just for their children. However, recently, more women tend to think like Europeans or Americans. They're getting divorced not just for themselves but also for their children's benefit. I've heard that divorcing or separating would be better for the children than constantly arguing in front of them.

Given her extended efforts to protect her children from the stigma of divorce, Sato-san highlights shifts in parents' sense of risk and protection. To her, in the early 1970s, the safest move was to avoid divorce entirely. In the early 2000s, by contrast, she had heard of parents who were making precisely the opposite decision to accomplish the same goal.

A second example from earlier in the postwar period articulates the stigmatizing impact divorce could have on family members. In 1965, Mayumi's parents got divorced, at her father's request, and her mother took legal custody of Mayumi and her siblings. Although life was financially difficult for a single mother and her two children, Mayumi didn't realize the extent of her stigma until she tried to get into college. Interested in the visual arts, Mayumi had attended a strong high school and, along with her friends, applied to an elite visual arts program at a university in Tokyo. Although she had a strong application, all of her friends got in, but she didn't. She remains convinced that it was because her parents were divorced. We can't know for sure, but Mayumi is certain. As part of the application materials, the university had requested a copy of her household registry, which listed both her parents' divorce and the fact that she had moved from her father's registry to her mother's upon that divorce (i.e., that her mother held custody). In 1978, when she was applying to university, a divorce within her family either actually prevented her admission or felt stigmatizing enough that such a biased decision seemed probable.[5]

In contrast, younger people with whom I spoke were aware of a potential divorce stigma but were less likely to report feeling any explicit or obvious negative effects. For instance, when I first asked Ando-san about any stigma she's felt as a divorced woman, she laughed and said there wasn't much. Her experience, she said, has been significantly shaped by the fact that she and her ex-husband didn't have children and that they both held lucrative full-time jobs. When they got divorced in 2001, they were both in their early thirties, and she was making enough money to support herself, so getting divorced didn't really change her standard of living. But her work environment was also the location in which she faced the greatest threat of stigma. She works as a consultant in the business world and has a large client list. When she got divorced, if she changed her family name back to her natal family name, every client, not to mention the coworkers in her office, would have known, and she wanted to prevent that. So, instead, when she got divorced, she kept her married name—Ando—and told only her closest friends at work what had happened.

But it only took about a week for everyone in the office to know. She knew that everyone was aware of her divorce because, although they all remained very polite and professional with her during working hours, their behavior started to change during mandatory after-hours drinking parties. There, once everyone was drunk, people would start to tease her, patting her on the head and saying things like, "You're a thirty-year-old *batsu ichi*! It's all over now, huh?" (*Mō batsu ichi de sanjū-sai! Mō dame ne*). She says it's better now that there are other divorced women in the office, a pattern caused by the job's substantial demands and everyone's difficulties "creating a work/life balance" (*kaisha ga isogahii kara baransu ga kuzurechau*).

Ando-san gets drunken teasing from her coworkers, but she also described dating as another context in which some risk of stigma lingers. Although Ando-san hasn't had problems finding men to date, she has to decide when to tell them that she's divorced.

ALLISON: As a divorced person, are you ever embarrassed to date or have a relationship with someone again?

ANDO-SAN: Yeah, it's hard for me to make a move. If there's someone I like, it's pretty hard to tell him how I feel. But when I have a date with someone I like, I'd say to him, "Well, actually (*jitsu wa*) . . ." and confess my divorce because I don't want to be rude to him. It might be hard to start to explain why I was divorced. If he is just a friend, I won't mind. But if I have feelings for someone, it'd be hard.

In this idiom of confession, Ando-san supports one of Goffman's key descriptions of what it is like to have a stigma, what he calls "managing information about [one's] failing" (Goffman 1963, 42). Goffman echoes what Ando-san describes, saying that having a stigma prompts a constant list of internal questions: "To display or not to display; to tell or not to tell; to let on or not to let on; to lie or not to lie; and in each case, to whom, how, when, and where" (ibid.). Ando-san is far from the only divorced person I know who deployed the lingering term "actually . . ." (*jitsu wa*), with its potent and loaded ellipse, to explain their divorced status.

In recent years, groups of divorced people, primarily online, have created neologisms that make divorce seem like a potential root of identity politics. Like the appropriation of other formerly stigmatizing terms, some divorced people in Japan are reacting against the label "batsu ichi" by either embracing the term as a mark of maturity or shifting their identification toward *maru ichi*. On social media, groups have been created by people who mark their divorced status with *maru ichi*. Literally this means "one circle," but in social, emotional, and graphic terms, it is the opposite of all that a *batsu* connotes and implies. If a *batsu* is lack, wrong, forbidden, impossibility, or bad, *maru* is the opposite: approval, correct, appropriate, good. (Notice in figure 5 that posters use circles to represent positive recommendations.[6]) The symbol means all of these at once, akin to the American thumbs-up, and the generalized approval denoted by this common signal is what divorced people who self-identify as *maru ichi* are attempting to claim. Although the phrase *maru ichi* is defined in an online dictionary of slang and popular terms, I've never heard anyone using it offline except in self-conscious parody.

New Marital Losers

In 2003, Sakai Junko published a work of nonfiction, *Howl of the Loser Dogs* (*Makeinu no tōboe*), that quickly became a huge hit and colored much of the discourse about divorce, stigma, and intimate relationships. Similar in tone to *Bridget Jones' Diary*, the book presents a witty, bitter, and hilarious field guide to women who are "loser dogs"—those never married, single, or childless (Sakai 2003). Self-identifying as such a loser, Sakai articulates stated and unstated social norms that condemn women based on their intimate relationships. In her descriptions, the losers seem far more interesting. Ultimately, Sakai critiques "the stupidity of those who are swayed by the dominant ideology that divides women into winners and losers based on marital status" (Yamaguchi 2006, 111). Because of this book, the terminology it popularized, and the wave of media on similar topics that came in its wake, many people I met wanted to have conversations about what it means to "win" in life, and particularly in relation to intimate relationships.

Echoing the sardonic judgment of the book, one young, unmarried woman articulated a common description of what "winning" meant at the same time as she emphasized the absurdity of it all. She said that by standard perceptions a woman who has won (*kachigumi*, literally in "the winners' group") would have a good degree and job before marrying a successful professional like a doctor or a lawyer, who himself had gone to an elite school like Keio University. (In case it's not clear, this young woman was making fun of Keio graduates for being convinced of their own superiority.) After she has two perfect children, the winning woman wouldn't have to work but would instead become a devoted mother. This young woman highlighted the problems caused by defining winning only through marriage: as long as a woman got married, and got married to a "winning" husband, she was a winner. As Sakai's satire made clear, the quality of a marriage, or indeed its stability, did not matter in this common measure of success. In contrast, she implies that being unmarried or divorced might instead be evidence of bravery, self-confidence, or rationality. *Howl of the Loser Dogs* asked readers to critically reconsider standard hierarchies defining intimate winners and losers.

When *Howl of the Loser Dogs* was published, its sardonic appraisal of intimate hierarchies meshed well with changing perceptions of what intimate relationships said about, and did to, the people in them. If previous norms suggested that any married person had "won" compared to any unmarried person, contemporary debates were no longer so clear. Japan's growing populations of never married, divorced, or childless men and women meant that many more people were in categories previously defined as failure. Newly positive attitudes toward divorce were particularly visible in conversations about these revised hierarchies. In contrast to what I heard from older people, and the scholarly record delineating severe stigma after divorce, in the early twenty-first century middle-aged and younger people described divorce as preferable to some of the other possibilities.

The first time anyone described divorce as better than being unmarried I was so confused I thought I misunderstood. Etsuko is a lively, smart, and open woman who had unfortunately become a widow in her thirties. Five years after her husband's passing various people—myself included—were constantly trying to set Etsuko up with men. (Against all my hopes and efforts, apparently I can't translate my knowledge about divorce into successful matchmaking.) In one instance, Etsuko and I were standing in her kitchen, talking as we prepared dinner. A friend had just suggested that she go on a date with a man the friend knew—he was a lawyer! Didn't that sound good? I didn't know the man, but I knew her friend and thought that the description of the man made him seem attractive, or at least worth a first date. Etsuko wasn't so sure and described her reticence by articulating the clues she saw about his possible weirdness. He was forty-seven and unmarried. Even worse than "unmarried" he was also "never married," and, as far as Etsuko was concerned, that probably meant something was wrong with him. As she laid it out to me, if he was divorced at forty-seven, it would make him look a lot more normal—at least that would have meant that he was able to have a relationship with someone, for some period of time. But "never married" could mean that he'd never been able to sustain a relationship and, having been single for so long, he was probably curmudgeonly and stuck in his ways. She agreed to meet him but wasn't so excited about it, and they didn't hit it off. Estuko's intuition and preferences made clear how associations with divorce are shifting amidst broader discussions of stigma surrounding intimate choices.

Japan's Increasing Inequality

Howl of the Loser Dogs, with its sardonic redefinitions of winners and losers, became popular at the moment when parallel language was being used to describe Japan's increasing economic inequalities. Throughout the postwar period, Japan had been a famously middle-class society: from the 1970s to the 1990s, national surveys routinely reported that 90 percent of citizens identified as middle class (Kelly 1986, 604). Although there have always been significant differences of social class, during that period such distinctions were underemphasized in Japanese popular perceptions, media representations, government policy, and scholarship. In the early postwar era, basic demographic data make clear that there was tremendous variation within the population identifying themselves as "middle class"—from mothers who worked outside the home because of financial need to unequal educational opportunities and consumerist possibilities—but these truths did little to minimize the "folk sociology" of Japan's uniquely equal class structures (Kelly 1986, 605). Japanese media discourse invented a range of terms, for instance "100 million-person middle class" (*ichioku sōchūryū*), which further concretized perceptions of a shared middle-class-ness (Chiavacci 2008, 10).

Popular attitudes supported the feeling of a shared, mass middle-class identity, facilitated through an education system imagined to be a meritocracy. Especially in comparison with high income inequality during World War II and immediately after, in the years of the economic boom, relative inequality fell. In the 1970s, "as economic development raised average household incomes, the differences in incomes between white-collar and blue-collar workers became smaller because of the small differences in education" (Tachibanaki 2005, 75). Foreign scholarship about Japan at this time also emphasized the meritocratic outcomes of the strict education system in which where you went to school (*gakureki*) ultimately influenced the course of your life (Chiavacci 2008, 13; Tachibanaki 2006, 16). Unlike in the contemporary moment, in the 1970s and 1980s, the education system was understood to be a key mechanism supporting Japan's shared equality.

At the beginning of Japan's economic boom, when Sawyer (1976) found Japan to have extremely equal income distribution compared with other wealthy nations, his conclusions seemed to prove what everyone already knew: Japan's booming economy was strengthened through its unusually equitable shared wealth. Such rhetoric meshed perfectly with popular ideologies of *Nihonjinron*, theories identifying Japanese uniqueness as the root cause for the postwar economic miracle and subsequent economic success. In that theory, which was explicitly promoted by the conservative government, Japan's ethnic homogeneity enabled a uniquely equal, meritocratic, middle-class society (Chiavacci 2008, 13). Almost a decade later, when scholars recalculated Sawyer's figures, they found his numbers to be simply wrong. Countering his conclusions and the parallel popular understandings, Japan had substantially higher rates of inequality compared with other wealthy nations. The affective and experiential identifications with the middle class had never really translated into shared wealth (ibid., 14; d'Ercole 2006, 2; Ishizaki 1983).[7]

Even though Japan was never as uniformly middle class as popular perceptions suggested, those images continue to serve as a foil against which people view contemporary inequality. After the bursting of the economic bubble and ensuing decades of recession, Japan has become a society with much greater inequalities. Since the 1990s, both socioeconomic inequality and public consciousness about it have increased in Japan (Ishida and Slater 2010). In a 2004 survey, for instance, 64.5 percent of respondents felt that inequality was "high" or "slightly high," and in 2006 the term "unequal society" (*kakusa shakai*) was a finalist for "word of the year" (*shingo ryūkōgotaishō*) (Tachibanaki 2006, 6).[8] These perceptions reflect increased media attention to the topic, but also very real demographic shifts. Between the mid-1980s and 2000, the percentage of the population living in absolute poverty (defined as income less than one-half of the median disposable income) increased by five percentage points, putting Japan well higher than other comparable nations; in 2000, 15 percent of the Japanese population was living in relative poverty (R. Jones 2007, 16). During the same time period, many more workers were hired as "nonregular" (*hiseishain*) employees, provided lower pay, fewer benefits, and less job security than those in "regular" (*seishain*) positions. In 1984, only 15.3 percent of the labor force was in "nonregular" positions, but by 2008, that number had grown to 34.1 percent (Osawa et al. 2013, 314). On average, these "nonregular" employees make between 40 and 70 percent of the salary paid to regular workers, even though they are doing the same job, thereby increasing socioeconomic inequality (Japanese Trade Union Confederation 2006, 45; R. Jones 2007, 10; Song 2014, 97). By 2006, the income gap between the wealthiest 10 percent of the population and the poorest 10 percent had increased to have a twentyfold difference (Funabashi and Kushner 2015, xxix) When discourse about new marital "winners" and "losers" became popular in the early 2000s, it was in the midst of this broader awareness of growing inequality.

MAE: THE SURPRISE OF POVERTY

Mae, the thirty-seven-year-old woman first introduced at the beginning of this chapter, finds herself living a life she didn't expect. She is open, funny, and willing to talk with almost anyone. We first met because my friend got his hair cut at the salon where she worked. They started chatting and she mentioned her recent divorce, which prompted him to introduce us. She was equally open with me and we grew to be friends partially because she is hilarious and partially because she was looking for someone to hang out with. Lord knows the anthropologist has nothing but time, so we went to concerts, talked about TV over cake and coffee, and brainstormed together about what she wanted to do with her life. Because I have known her for more than a decade, I have witnessed what she describes as the downward trajectory of her life.

When we first met, her life wasn't exactly what she had expected, but she certainly didn't feel like a loser. Growing up in the suburbs of Tokyo, she was always interested in fashion and music. When she was still in school, she would come in to Tokyo and hang out in Harajuku, a trendy neighborhood that closed streets to cars every Sunday to make space for the large groups of teenagers who gathered. This is where she met the man who would become her husband: they were sixteen and he was thoroughly into rockabilly fashion and music, which she thought was pretty awesome. (It was the 1980s and rockabilly was a solid look.) They became best friends and stayed that way for years. When they were twenty-two, they started dating and ultimately got married eight years after that.

In hindsight, Mae sees mistakes and red flags she previously missed. The primary mistake she identifies is that she didn't live with her husband before they got married, so she didn't know what he was really like. Even though he was fun and liked to drink, she realized that his family norms set his expectations in a fundamental way: because everyone deferred to his father in a way Mae found "feudal" (hōkenteki), her husband expected that she would also behave that way once they got married. He would be goofy and fun in public but demand she act like a traditional wife. It felt like a bait and switch, and she wasn't interested in conforming to his requirements. Five years after they were married, and thirteen years after they started dating, they were divorced. Mae felt like their divorce was necessary and the right choice, although she was mad at herself for missing the clues.

After Mae graduated from high school, she followed her interest in fashion to get a hair stylist's license. She could find jobs and ended up working for years at a time in various salons. As a freelancer, she would rent a chair from the salon owner and solicit her own clients. Although she was based in a particular salon, she wasn't an employee and wasn't guaranteed any hourly wage. Instead she was responsible for finding her own clients and working enough to cover the cost of her salon space. When they got divorced in 2001, Mae didn't ask her husband for financial support for a number of reasons: they didn't have kids; they had both worked throughout their marriage; he didn't have much money; and she really just wanted to be done with the divorce. She had been making decent money for years and had every reason to imagine that she could support herself.

By the time I met her in 2003, Mae was struggling, and by 2005 things had gotten even worse in ways she never expected. A few moments of bad luck made clear how shallow her safety net was. When a salon owner had stolen some of her money and spread nasty rumors about her as a cover, Mae suddenly found herself iced out of the salons where she used to work. She would have liked to move into a Tokyo salon, but the rents there were more than she could afford. Without a steady job, she ended up cobbling together four part-time jobs in order to cover the rent for her studio apartment in Kawagoe city, ninety minutes from the center of Tokyo. First, she cut hair in her friend's barbershop, but only on a casual basis because he was kind enough not to charge her to use the space. In a good week, she had about four appointments, and charged 4,000 yen ($40) for each one. Second, she worked two or three nights a week styling hair and doing makeup for hostesses in a club. That could bring in about 20,000 yen ($200) over a week. Third, from 6 to 10 a.m. three mornings a week, she baked bread in a national chain of bakeries. Working for minimum wage (673 yen, just under $7), this earned her about 8,000 yen ($80) each week. Fourth, she sold men's toupees door-to-door but only earned money if she sold something, which was rare.

Making enough money to cover her living expenses was a daily, weekly, and monthly struggle for Mae, but it wasn't the only problem she felt. As I described in this book's introduction, Mae repeatedly told me how much she wanted a boyfriend, how she missed physical contact—not even sex, necessarily, but just being touched by someone. When we talked in 2005, it had been two years since she had dated someone. She was lonely, sad, and confused about how her life took such a turn. Describing it, she says that her "level dropped," phrasing that simultaneously refers to status, wealth, social class, dating, and friendships.

> When I got divorced, I thought, "Ok, it's done now. I'll be ok." But I've been having financial difficulties now. My life is very hard. I used to think I could do all sorts of stuff on my own. I was confident enough to think that I was able to do almost anything. For instance, when I studied English, I could speak it reasonably well. Thai, too. I travelled abroad and made some friends there. Of course, here, too. I got along with many people where I went. [. . .] I was confident. And I wasn't scared of failing. But now my level has dropped. My self-esteem is low. Everything scares me. There are so many things I couldn't handle.

As she says here, Mae was a confident, outgoing, and curious person who prioritized making friends with different kinds of people and learning languages. After steady work evaporated, and she needed to cobble together part-time work, she simply couldn't afford to do much except hustle for work. Merely working hard wasn't enough; she was hustling to get jobs in the first place and then hustling to get more hours or clients. Like the hosts Takeyama (2016) describes staying in contact with their clients, Mae was constantly texting clients to keep her in mind when they needed a haircut, or to tell them the address of the salon where she was newly based. Not having a steady job, home salon, or dependable income took a real toll and started to change her perspective on the world. Things seemed much scarier than they used to.

The challenges Mae faced coalesced when she began working a fifth part-time job, in a Tokyo bar (*izakaya*). At first, she was excited to tell me about her new job because the manager who had hired her, Suzuki-san, was twice divorced and in his third marriage. Mae represented him as a fun and interesting person, who must have amazing stories to tell, but it wasn't until I saw them together that I realized what was going on: Suzuki-san was a big flirt and Mae had a crush on him, or at least really enjoyed attention from him. She had been very clear with me about her desire for a boyfriend, and in Suzuki-san's presence I could see that playing out as I had never before. Before I first met him, Mae had tried to warn me that he was especially interesting and attractive—she described him as having an "aura"—but he just seemed like a good bartender to me, namely someone who was chatty and engaging as long as you kept buying drinks. Mae scampered around the bar, giggling with Suzuki-san, in ways that demonstrated how lonely she was and how much she craved male attention. As I discussed in the introduction, during this fieldwork I did not judge people's intimate choices. I saw my job as understanding why someone made the decisions they did, rather than questioning those choices. But this evening with Mae and Suzuki-san almost broke me because it was nauseating to see someone I cared about so besotted with a person who didn't seem genuinely interested in her. I wanted to ask, "Him?" but the answer was already so clear.

A few weeks after she began working at the bar, Mae told me that the aura was gone. Working for Suzuki-san was a totally different experience than being his friend or a customer in the bar. He treated his employees very badly, demanding they arrive early, work without breaks, and stay late. All the employees were unhappy and scared. Mae realized that Suzuki-san was manipulative and intentionally hired only people in vulnerable positions—immigrants to Japan, or divorced women—who are desperate for work and won't complain about the treatment. Moreover, and most upsettingly, she hadn't received any salary. I tried to convince Mae to make clear that she needs to be paid, or at least get a sense of when she could expect her wages, but she was reluctant to make demands. She assured me that working in a bar (*izakaya*) was adjacent to working in the "sex trades" (*mizu shōbai*) and therefore we could not expect it to operate like a normal workplace. To be clear, Mae never articulated any hint that she might want to become a sex worker, but she was using that terminology to justify and excuse behavior that would otherwise be totally unacceptable. She thought I was dumbly naive to suggest that she should demand wages, and maybe I was.

Mae was well aware of how much her life had changed since her divorce, and how far she'd fallen, but she wasn't sure exactly what she could have done differently. In a sad moment, she listed the constellation of what she lost:

> Before I got married, I was always popular. Guys always paid me attention. But now, I have none of that. I don't have a job, and I'm not popular, I don't have self-confidence, and I don't have much of anything.

Her delineation was clear and absolute: no job, attention from men, or self-confidence. She felt like she didn't have anything, losing even the self-confidence that had previously felt so fundamental to her personality. Although she grew up on the lower side of the middle class, Mae had slipped into the working poor. Once, in an offhand way, Mae described how serious a toll this trajectory had taken on her. In contrast with her earlier working years, she was no longer paying into the national pension program. Supposedly a universal benefit system, albeit one under threat by the cost of Japan's aging population, the national pension was automatic for all Japanese citizens and foreign residents of Japan. In 2005, the monthly payments were a little more than 10,000 yen ($100), and there was no way Mae could afford that. Her logical decision made it much more likely that the poverty exacerbated by her divorce will have compounding consequences far into the future.

Gender and the Poverty of Divorce

Decades of scholarship demonstrate a clear gender disparity in divorce outcomes. In many cultural contexts, divorce reduces women's wealth and standards of living at the same time that it causes men's wealth and standards of living to dip only slightly or even to increase (Smock 1994, 251). Such incongruous effects were first popularized by Wietzman (1985), in her controversial book *The Divorce Revolution*. Although later scholars demonstrated that her figures were incorrect, Wietzman initially claimed that among her research subjects in California in the late 1970s, divorce caused women's standards of living to decrease 73 percent on average and men's to *increase* 42 percent, a 115 percent gap in the gendered outcomes. Focusing specifically on the then-new "no-fault" divorce option, Wietzman concluded that "rules designed to treat men and women 'equally' have in practice served to deprive divorced women (especially older homemakers and mothers of young children) of the legal and financial protections the old law provided" (ibid., xi). A decade later, Peterson (1996), having recalculated based on as much of Wieztman's original data as still existed, roundly refuted her figures. By his calculations, in Wieztman's original sample, women's standards of living dropped by an average of 27 percent while men's increased by 10 percent. He found a similar trend—women faring worse financially after divorce—but to a much less extreme degree and with negative repercussions for some men, too. Although Wietzman's original claims were eventually discredited, because they had been so widely cited in scholarship, political contexts, and the media, they remained influential in American law, policy, and popular understandings of divorce (Abraham 1989; Braver 1999, 113; Nielsen 2014, 165).

Later scholarship exploring how divorce impacts wealth and standards of living necessarily responds to this formative controversy. Like Peterson, most scholars find that divorce causes more financial harm to women than men, although men can be hurt, too.[9] Within this broad pattern, scholars have found a range of more specific trends: In the US, childless women fare about as well as men because the expenses of having children hurt mothers (Smock 1994). Only wealthy men experience no financial decrease after divorce; middle-class and disadvantaged men see their standards of living falling (McManus and DiPrete 2001). More recently, in the United States and other places, divorce has become more tightly linked with social class. Not only does divorce lower women's relative wealth, but men and women with lower socioeconomic status have a higher likelihood of divorce in the United States (Amato and Previti 2003; Carbone and Cahn 2014, 15; Martin 2006), Korea (Park and Raymo 2013), and Japan (Raymo, Fukuda, and Iwasawa 2013).[10] Amato and Previti (2003, 622) find that while people with low socioeconomic status are more likely to get divorced, they are also more likely to explain the divorce as a result of problematic behavior (like abuse) rather than problems in the relationships (like divergent personalities). This plethora of research makes clear that negative financial outcomes for divorced women are not at all unique to Japan.

In the last twenty years, however, divorce in Japan has become very tightly correlated with women's poverty through two interrelated dynamics. First, divorce increases the risk of poverty, meaning that women who get divorced are much more likely to become impoverished. Second, poverty increases the risk of divorce, meaning that women of lower socioeconomic status are more likely to get divorced. These interwoven problems account for a staggering amount of Japan's growing social and economic inequalities, and particularly the sharp increase of children living in poverty. These dynamics, and the harm they cause, began only in the 1990s and thus represent a recent and significant change in the lived realities of divorce.

In contemporary Japan, divorce impoverishes an extraordinary number of single parents. Almost 40 percent of single mothers, and 25 percent of single fathers, live in relative poverty (Abe 2012, 64). Most significantly, divorced mothers are likely to earn less than other workers. In 2010, the average income for single-mother households was less than half that of all households with children: whereas all households with children averaged 6.58 million yen (about $65,800), single mothers earned only 2.91 million yen ($29,100), even though they were supporting the same number of children (Kyodo News 2017; Takada 2011, 106). Such low annual incomes occur even as the vast majority (85 percent) of single mothers work outside the home (Zhou 2008). Forty-six percent of single mothers are in temporary or part-time positions, and 42 percent are in permanent jobs (Takada 2011, 106). Single mothers take low-paying "marginal full-time jobs" because they desire a predictable income, even if they have to trade higher wages for employment stability (Ono 2010, 171). Higher-paying, regular positions would be less likely to allow for the flexible scheduling necessary for parenting (Ezawa 2016, 83; Murakami 2009; Raymo and Zhou 2012, 731). Although mothers are increasingly likely to negotiate child support with their ex-husbands, as discussed in the previous chapter, enforcement mechanisms remain weak enough that many mothers cannot count on those funds (MHLW 2011; Murakami 2011).

In a complementary dynamic, only since the 1980s, women's relative poverty has become a strong predictor of divorce. Using women's formal educational attainment as a measure of social class, Hayashi and Yoda (2014) find that among men and women married between 1945 and 1974, there is no difference in the divorce rate between those who ended formal education in high school and those who graduated from university or junior college. This correlation shifts dramatically for those married later, for whom less formal education predicts a much higher likelihood of divorce. For people married after 1980, those with a lower socioeconomic background are much more likely to get divorced (ibid.; Raymo, Iwasawa, and Bumpass 2004). Given this, "the risk of divorce is concentrated at the lower side of socioeconomic hierarchies" and has increased rapidly in the last thirty years (Hayashi and Yoda 2014, 52; Ono 2010, 156). Contradicting popular ideas that women divorce when they can afford it, here we see strong evidence that divorce is most likely for women who can afford it the least.

CHIHARU: MAKING IT WORK

I first met Chiharu-san at a summer picnic organized by the Kanto Family Center, a counseling group focused on family issues. Although I participated in weekly counseling groups for almost a year, and knew all the regulars, I had never met Chiharu-san until this picnic. Once she introduced herself with her online handle, as opposed to her real name, I realized how I knew her: she was an active, kind voice on the center's mailing list, posting about her own struggles and responding empathetically to other people's messages. Chiharu didn't attend the regular in-person counseling sessions because she couldn't afford them. Just being on the center's mailing list cost 5,000 yen ($50) a year, and the counseling sessions were far more expensive. As discussed in the next chapter, the "women only" group I attended met on Friday mornings during regular work hours and cost ¥6,000 ($60) for each two-hour session. Chiharu would have loved to participate but didn't have that kind of money or time, so she compromised by joining the mailing list and connecting with people there, or at the occasional party.

Chiharu-san is a woman in her early fifties, with three children ranging from eighteen to twenty-five. She wore simple clothes and carried a nice purse—both of which made it harder for me initially to see the relative poverty with which she struggled. That only became visible when she was kind enough to invite me to her home, forty-five minutes from the center of Tokyo. Her rented apartment had two small bedrooms, which she shared with the two children who still lived at home. Many people in and around Tokyo live in very small spaces, and there is a shared art of packing stuff into tiny rooms with little storage space. Chiharu's small apartment, by contrast, was practically empty. She had functional furniture but nothing extra—no accumulation of material goods, none of the piles of extra stuff to which I had become so accustomed.[11]

Chiharu had only been divorced for a few years but had lived apart from her husband for almost a decade. Their marriage had been extremely violent. Her husband was an alcoholic who abused her and their children, but Chiharu had waited as long as possible to leave him. She understood some virtue and maturity in enduring something difficult (*gaman*), and so she tried to keep her husband happy while also protecting her children. Finally, after many years of violence, and when their youngest child was nine, she moved from their family home into this small apartment. Even then, the apartment was considered old, and therefore came with a lower monthly rent. She was able to afford it—barely—by working at a bank. Her position didn't pay particularly well, and she was in an hourly position rather than a salaried one, but she was happy to have a predictable income. She was also happy, frankly, to get such a steady job because she knew it was harder for older women.

During Chiharu's long separation from her husband, the children had begun to repair their own relationship with him. Although they mostly stayed at Chiharu's apartment, sometimes the older children, especially, would go to their father's place. In this way, even though she never received child support or alimony, Chiharu was able to share some small degree of their children's expenses with her ex-husband. When I asked, she explained that she would prefer her ex and their children have some kind of relationship, but she didn't see how that would be possible for herself. He was less likely to threaten her now, but she saw no benefit in trusting him or looking to him for help. By living extremely frugally, she made enough money to facilitate a life for herself and her children. It wasn't fancy, but it worked, and her children were doing well enough in school that it seemed possible for them to get decent, middle-class jobs. The bare-bones apartment was evidence of her tremendous victory.

Is Divorce Worth the Cost?

When Japanese men and women divorce, they face lingering stigma. Even if younger people are less focused on how divorce might hurt themselves or their children, it remains a marked category requiring explanation and justification. From jokes uttered by drunken coworkers to the insulting terminology of "one strike," divorce highlights unmarked norms as people deviate from them.

One of the strongest stereotypes about divorce in contemporary Japan represents it as evidence of women's ascendance relative to men. While such common perspectives suggest that divorce manifests gendered power, the lived realities of divorce present a very different picture. Getting divorced increases a woman's likelihood of falling into poverty, especially if she has children, and furthers the widening gaps between economic "winners" and "losers."

These truths, however, make it no easier to claim divorce as inevitably good or bad for those involved; none of the women profiled in this chapter would choose to forgo divorce, given the counterfactual opportunity. They did not predict the challenges they have faced, and chose to divorce because of the freedom, stability, and possibility it could—and possibly should—bring. They met some of these goals, but stability can be much harder to reach for reasons both personal and structural. As so poignantly narrated by Mae in her reflections about how she has become more fearful, the harsh truths of divorce's reality only become visible later, hitting hard and limiting choices. Only after the fact does it become clear how many disconnections divorce can bring.

6

Bonds of Disconnection

This research has been haunted by a lonely, starving, older man. In various contexts, when I asked general questions about the overall risks and benefits of divorce, men and women worried aloud about a hypothetical man who was left all alone when his wife divorced him. In their descriptions, this older man lives alone and can't take care of himself because, conforming to models of disconnected dependence, he never learned to cook or clean. Instead of eating healthy food made by his wife, he is living off of prepared foods bought from convenience stores, and therefore almost starving. Numerous men and women mentioned that particular detail in their imaginings of divorce's worst repercussions: an older man, left behind, disconnected from everyone, and lacking basic nutrition because he was no longer cared for and could not care for himself. Most frequently, people described this specter as pitiful (*kawaiisō*); even if they could understand how he contributed to the breakdown of his marriage, or if the divorce might have been a reasonable idea, this was a sad, pitiable outcome. For people with whom I talked, divorce logically and inevitably created a swath of older men so disconnected as to be broken and nearly dead.

As highlighted in this gendered dystopia, many people imagine divorce to symbolize and enact fundamental disconnections. In their expectations, divorce isolates so completely that it leaves certain people desperately alone, almost fatally isolated. Amidst popular discourse about the new lack of "social bonds" (*muen shakai*), divorce seems to be the most obvious instantiation of these trends: people intentionally breaking bonds they had previously held. More specifically, divorce seems to be a zero-sum game in which freedom for one spouse leaves the other in an impossible, totalizing loneliness.

While divorce can bring loneliness and disconnection, however, it also enables new bonds that would have been otherwise impossible or highly unlikely. Rather than merely isolating individuals, divorce catalyzes "bonds of disconnection," opportunities for new types of connection and relationships emerging precisely because of previous separations. In therapeutic spaces, recreational contexts, or within groups of friends unified by similar experiences, divorce brings people together and enables them to create meaningful social ties. These new ties complicate common understandings of neoliberalism, within and beyond Japan, which assume "a good citizen cares for himself or herself by evading or denying social relations" (Rimke 2000, 61). Although they can be created in therapeutic spaces, the new bonds between divorced people do not automatically enact neoliberal styles of intimacy. Like a spouse considering divorce, or a noncustodial parent building a relationship with their child, in friendships after divorce we see men and women navigating the risks and benefits that come with connection.

People's lives after divorce and the new bonds they create are deeply shaped by gender, but this is not to suggest that men are categorically less connected. Instead, I argue, gender dramatically impacts postdivorce lives in two key ways. First, formal therapeutic spaces are more likely to be created intentionally for women to discuss their relational dilemmas and build new bonds. In contrast, many men create bonds in less formal venues, parrying divorce as if it was something they weren't entirely prepared to discuss. Second, experiences after divorce are significantly shaped by the gaps between the "leaver" and "left" identifications, which divide former spouses into the person who decided to end the marriage and the person who was willing to continue it (Vaughn 1990). In general terms, these oppositional identities tend to produce divergent perspectives on the former relationship and different attitudes moving forward. Although certainly not all divorces in Japan are initiated by women, my research supports the popular assumption that most contemporary divorces are the result of women deciding to leave. For that reason, the socially meaningful distinction between "leaver" and "left" strongly correlates with gender in this context.

In order to represent shifting desires, bonds, and disconnections, this chapter is organized around several extended profiles of men and women responding to divorce. Although some of these people actively requested a divorce and others worked hard to prevent one, they each have better and worse days and are equally likely to feel energized or lonely. These profiles are designed to convey the complexity of, and variety within, life after divorce and the ties that people create in response. With one key exception, each of the people represented in this chapter was included earlier in the book; their extended profiles here are intended to more richly situate those shorter descriptions, to give the reader a broader sense of how divorce shapes their daily lives. In depicting the bonds created through and after divorce, I simultaneously foreground the social ties that enabled this research in the first place. More than anywhere else in the book, I appear as a character here, as someone divorced men and women accept, reject, and include in their lives.

A Society without Bonds

Discussions in Japan debating the current lack of social bonds almost always reference a particularly disquieting death. In July 2010, a mummified corpse was found in central Tokyo. The deceased man had died thirty years before but his death was not reported by his family, who continued to live in the same house. According to official records, the man was alive at 111 years old and counted as an example of Japan's long life expectancy (Nozawa 2015b). This death challenged many popular notions, not the least of which was the possibility that official calculations of Japan's high average life expectancy might be artificially inflated.[1] In this case, at least three types of bonds or ties were suddenly demonstrated to be missing: First, the nation's official population record (the *koseki*) had spectacularly failed to track at least one citizen. Second, his family did not care enough to memorialize him, let alone report his death.[2] Third, broader social connections—with friends, neighbors, or former coworkers—had evaporated. No one seemed to miss him, or miss him enough to explore what had happened.

Two terms came to be associated with this event and broader social trends that supposedly contributed to it: "a society without bonds" (*muen shakai*) and "solitary death" (*kodokushi*). Spurred by a television documentary on the topic, *muen shakai* quickly became a shorthand for describing social disconnection (NHK 2010). However, the phrase does not immediately gloss into English because of complex meanings and associations surrounding "en," the second half of the first word. ("Mu" is absence or lack, and "shakai" is society.) *En* could be glossed as ties, bond, or connection but also can take on a distinctly Buddhist connotation, as in the social, spiritual, and emotional bonds between the living and the dead (Rowe 2011). For this reason, a lack of appropriate or necessary bonds might manifest in a socially isolated person, or a grave that has been allowed to grow filthy from inattention (ibid.; Ozawa-de Silva 2018). In Japanese media, "a society without bonds" was first associated with death, the risks of dying alone or of dying without younger relatives to care for your grave.

Broader trends have expanded the symbolic and functional meanings of the phrase, such that it has come to represent the general risks of disconnection. From people living alone, to workers untethered from full-time positions, or young people primarily communicating through technology, the new lack of social ties creates and extends social problems (Hommerich 2015; Iwama 2011; Luckacs 2013; Tachibanaki 2010; Ueno 2009). Reflecting Japanese media narratives, particularly after the triple disasters of March 2011, Allison (2013) links the restructured labor market with government (non)responses to the Fukushima nuclear meltdowns under "precarity." In precarity and *muen sha-kai*, we find the risks of neoliberalism: citizens and family members abandoned by networks that used to provide support. At the same time, other ethnographic research has found some people who feel occasional benefits in diminished ties. Older residents of Osaka, for instance, welcomed the absence of ties that had been "too close": nosy or controlling neighbors and family members with demanding requests (Kavedžija 2018). Like the divorced and divorcing people represented in this book, these retired people worked to navigate between being dangerously connected or dangerously disconnected, too close to or too removed from other people.

In my research, the most ubiquitous desire for new bonds was visible in a persistent pattern: all the time, in various contexts, people asked me to introduce them to new romantic partners. Sometimes they were joking, sometimes they were half-joking, and sometimes they knew they were seeking an unrealistic fantasy person. But they asked because they quickly intuited that someone who studies divorce must necessarily know a lot of single people. Contrary to my own expectations, I never heard a divorced person express a political frustration with heterosexual marriage broadly, or claim that their divorce represented an expansive rejection of marriage. On the contrary, people were more likely to describe their previous marriage as a failed attempt to enact an ideal they still found attractive, and as something that didn't work only because of the specific people involved. They were sure marriage could be better than what they had previously experienced, and in their requests I heard a desire for connection, a renewed search for bonds. Their requests focused on romantic partners; no one explicitly asked me if I could help them find a new friend, although I might have filled that role myself.

YOSHIDA-SAN: TOO CLOSE

My perspectives on what it's like to live as a divorced person in contemporary Japan were most significantly shaped by my friendship with a Japanese man who has not yet appeared in this book. Precisely because he is one of my closest friends in Japan—certainly my closest friend who is also divorced—his experiences simultaneously enlightened me to complex realities of divorce, involved me most organically and directly, and made me reluctant to describe his case.[3]

I first met Yoshida-san in 2002, when I spent a summer doing preliminary research in Japan. At that time, I planned research exploring how the birth control pill was being marketed in Japan. The pill had only been legalized a few years before, in 1999, and I was interested in how pharmaceutical firms would attempt to create a market for it. In the course of a summer, I made friends with Yoshida-san, a man in his early forties who worked as a bureaucrat. He was married, but his wife was teaching Japanese abroad and I never met her. Theirs had been a marriage resulting from introduction (*omiai*), and they married at slightly older ages than was typical. Yoshida-san is very social and was perpetually inviting people to join groups he'd created for fun activities—dinners, picnics, games. He had many friends who lived or worked abroad and organized gatherings where we could talk about cross-cultural experiences. As an easy extension of his natural tendency to build networks of friends, he introduced me to people who would be helpful for my research, or people who might know someone.

Flash forward a few years. Yoshida-san and I remained friends but the situation had changed. I realized that my birth control project simply wasn't viable because no one was taking the pill—at that time, less than 2 percent of Japanese women using birth control used oral contraceptives—and I listened to friends when they told me that all of a sudden it seemed like everyone they knew was getting divorced (Matsumoto et al. 2011, 888; Sandberg 2019, 59). The first time I met Yoshida-san after I switched my research topic to divorce, his face fell when I told him. He hadn't yet told me but his wife had asked for a divorce that he didn't want. Suddenly, *horribly*, my research and his life dovetailed in ways that made both of us extremely uncomfortable. In contrast to his constant help when my project had been about something unconnected to his life, now we both stayed clear of my research topic. Only when he was drinking, if someone asked how we knew each other, he'd offer a sardonic explanation: "She studies divorce and my wife wants a divorce." Most of the time, when he said this, the other person looked uncomfortable and we all laughed nervously, or pretended he hadn't said it.

Yoshida-san refused the divorce for as long as he could. He refused to sign the "mutual" paperwork, therefore pushing his divorce into formal mediation. Those mediation sessions turned out worse than he ever could have imagined. Echoing dynamics I discussed in chapter 3, he explained that he was mortified to discuss his private affairs with a bunch of judgmental strangers (i.e., the mediation team). He survived two sessions before acquiescing to the divorce that he never wanted.

Dealing with a divorce that was both heartbreaking and humiliating, Yoshida-san was mostly quiet. We would hang out a few times a month, but, as far as I could see, he didn't create any space or time to focus on his divorce.

He very clearly didn't want to talk about it and stopped asking me how my research was going. He continued to plan events, to invite big groups of people to hang out together, and to drink. Indeed, although he had enjoyed alcohol for as long as I'd known him, after the divorce his drinking seemed to take on a renewed importance in his life, and the gaps between how he would act while sober and drinking became more pronounced. Responding to his behavior, I never asked him about his divorce and tried to be a supportive friend rather than a researcher. In fact, I felt bad and worried that my mere presence reminded him of divorce.

Despite his general reticence, Yoshida-san occasionally brought up his continuing struggle with his divorce. One particularly striking moment occurred when we attended the wedding of a mutual friend. During the wedding banquet, as family members and friends shared beautiful toasts about the happy couple, Yoshida-san leaned over and said, out of nowhere, "She called me last week." Since he had told me about the end of his divorce mediation many months before, Yoshida-san had not said anything about his divorce or ex-wife. But now, as we listened to amplified voices praising the new married couple, Yoshida-san brought up this most personal and difficult topic using very simple phrasing, as if he was returning to a topic that existed just beneath the surface. Because we hadn't ever much talked about his ex-wife—and not at all since they had finalized their divorce—it took me a long moment to understand which "she" he was talking about.[4] Yoshida-san explained more details: He hadn't actually spoken with her, but the week before he had suddenly gotten three calls from an unknown number in the prefecture where her parents live. He hadn't picked up and the caller hadn't left a message, but he was absolutely sure it was her. I was less sure, but also realized it didn't really matter. He was sure something might happen between the two of them and broke his silence on the topic to tell me. It felt like a surgical strike on his part: a quick confession in a context that prohibited further discussion. Sure enough, the wedding toasts soon finished, and the people at our table included us in a conversation that ended our exchange.

Still trying to be a good friend, and convinced that Yoshida-san wanted to talk at least a little about the phone calls from his ex-wife, I brought the topic up again a few weeks later. Over dinner at an Indian restaurant, as we chatted about work and mutual friends, I tried to return to the topic he introduced so intentionally before. I asked, "So, what happened with those phone calls?" In a friendly but firm way, Yoshida-san looked up, tapped his lassi yogurt drink, and said, "Not yet" (*mada*). In that gesture, he conveyed that his ex-wife was not an appropriate topic of conversation when we were drinking something other than alcohol. Because we were planning to go to a bar after dinner, he was making clear that such talk and topics should only occur in certain contexts. I felt terrible for bringing up something he didn't want to talk about and became suddenly aware of how much Yoshida-san liked to drink.

I have no idea if he is an alcoholic, but Yoshida-san certainly enjoys drinking and seems better able to relax, be silly, and talk about difficult topics with alcohol nearby. The physical layout of bars also seemed to make it easier for Yoshida-san, and other men with whom I talked, to discuss emotionally fraught topics. By firmly postponing any discussion of his divorce until "later," Yoshida-san was also relegating the topic to a moment when we wouldn't physically be facing each other. Unlike the Indian restaurant where we had dinner, at the bar we sat next to each other—shoulder to shoulder—and didn't have to make eye contact. Perhaps more than the alcohol, this arrangement felt most comfortable to him. Looking directly at someone when he talked soberly about the divorce he hadn't wanted was simply too close for comfort.

Yoshida-san is a man processing a divorce he never wanted. Because his wife was living outside of Japan when she requested the divorce, his daily life didn't change as much as would, say, that of a father who no longer lives with his child. But the process of divorce presented Yoshida-san with a number of surprises and dilemmas, starting with his wife's sudden (to him) request, the awkward prying in court mediation, and his eventual capitulation to a separation that challenged his sense of himself. He thought of himself as a perfectly normal man, working hard, trying to maintain connections with his parents and siblings, building friendships and organizing events. Although his unwanted divorce didn't automatically change any of the other details of his life, it nevertheless felt like a bolt from the blue that changed everything, even if he didn't want to talk about it.

Leaving vs. Being Left

In her classic investigation of American breakups, sociologist Diane Vaughn discovered that major differences in the ways people respond to divorce result from the divergent identities of "initiator" and "noninitiator" (Vaughn 1990; see also Hopper 1993b). Divorce and other breakups are entirely different for the person who decides to leave the relationship, as opposed to the person who understands themselves as having been left. Vaughn hastens to emphasize that these roles are likely fluid and can switch between partners during the long course of a breakup, but by the eventual end, one person usually wants to continue "working on" the relationship and the other refuses. These choices create the roles of "leaver" and "left," which harden over time and, in Vaughn's analysis, correlate with strongly predictable responses.

In Japan, as in other places in which heterosexual marriage is an unmarked norm, any divorce necessarily requires each partner explain, to themselves and to anyone else, why the relationship ended. Vaughn found that the root of the key differences between the "leaver" and "left" roles appear in these socially required explanations about what "happened" in the relationship. Although both partners might be unhappy, she argues, one partner first begins to imagine the relationship ending. That partner might not take steps to manifest such a dissolution but begins the complicated process of psychologically imagining the breakup. They find reasons and identify unfixable problems and often link current tensions with what they see as very long-standing patterns in the relationship. So when they finally decide to leave, the "initiator" understands the breakup to reflect fundamental problems in the relationship and therefore believes it was doomed from the start. In contrast, the other partner likely also felt tensions and was unsatisfied, but they remained convinced that the problems could be solved. By virtue of the fact that this partner did not make the move to leave, they were necessarily still committed to continuing the relationship. To this partner, the person who is "left," the breakup often feels like a horrible surprise and a turn of events no one could have seen coming. Because of these dynamics, we see a strong correlation: the partner who identifies as "initiator" is much more likely to describe the relationship as fatally flawed from the beginning, whereas the partner who was left continues to see potential in the relationship and instead describes the breakup as the result of the initiator's sudden snap or unexpected change of heart.

My research found patterns very similar to those described by Vaughn, although with an added layer that reflects the deeply gendered patterns of divorce initiation in contemporary Japan. As visible in Yoshida-san's example above, as well as others presented throughout this book, many Japanese men are shocked when their wives request a divorce. They didn't see it coming, don't really know what to say, and thought any marital tensions they felt fit within the normal range for any marriage. Media representations and popular perceptions often characterize this shock as fundamentally male or as evidence of a common masculine response to divorce (Ikeuchi 2006). Men, in this thinking, are simply less prepared for divorce, less able to process intimate disconnections, less able to be alone, and therefore more likely to end up as a starving lonely specter. Understanding Vaughn's typology of American breakups allows a more complex interpretation: the trouble many Japanese men have recovering from divorce reflects not a universal masculine response, but their status as the partner who did not initiate the breakup.

For these reasons, the higher likelihood that Japanese women will initiate divorce starts a domino effect that shapes patterns of recovery after divorce.

According to Vaughn, any "initiator" has likely been thinking about a breakup much longer and therefore, when it comes to fruition, has a jump start on coming to terms with what has happened, and usually seems to get over it faster. Asymmetrically, by contrast the other partner has just begun to process the relationship's end and is "preoccupied with retrospective analysis, sorting through the relationship's history, examining past conversations, mentally reliving life with the other person" (Vaughn 1990, 136). To an outsider, the person who was "left" looks stuck in the past or unable to move past a relationship that is already over. They are, in fact, trying to process a sudden ending that shifted the ground beneath their feet.

Therapeutic Infrastructure

Compared with how they described the early 1990s and before, people struggling with marital problems in the early 2000s were increasingly likely to turn to what could be broadly defined as the counseling industry. A divorcing person seeking professional or semi-professional advice faced a range of possible fees, formats, and therapeutic spaces. The counseling options now available represent a major change to previous ways of dealing with family problems. In one of the groups I attended, a participant said that she joined because there were no such groups when she'd gotten divorced fourteen years before. Despite being more than a decade past her divorce and happily remarried, she found value in devoting one morning a month to a group discussion and she paid ¥6,000 ($60) to participate in each session.

Japan's growing counseling industry reflects neoliberal attitudes toward the self, demands for expert knowledge, and privatized systems of support (Gershon 2011; Rose 1998; Yang 2015). When I asked people over fifty if they had ever sought the help of a professional counselor, many explained that counseling has its own stigma. They suggested that only people who had major psychological problems would seek out such counseling. Tanaka-san, a working-class mother who had divorced her husband in 1993 after years of emotional and physical abuse, said that the stigma she felt being a divorced woman would have only been compounded by going to a counselor. Thus one of my most consistent findings was that the vast majority of people now facing divorce understand counseling, in any form, to be a more acceptable and available option than it was in the early 1990s and before, a pattern also reflected in scholarship (Iwakabe 2008, 104; Iwasaki 2005; Ozawa-de Silva 2006).

Marital and family counseling in Japan is available in formats in which privacy, cost, and personalizing all vary. Anyone with an internet connection can find multiple websites with generalized tips for solving common marital

problems or negotiating divorces.[5] Without too much searching, Yamada Sadako's website also appears, through which she offers free and personally tailored advice to people seeking to improve their marriages. When I met with
her, Sadako, then in her late twenties, explained that her interest and skills in
counseling stemmed from two very common sources: problems in her marriage and advice from mainstream popular magazines. By her own estimation, Yamada has communicated with almost two thousand people via email,
spending hours each day responding to messages with personalized advice.
She has never charged a fee and, before me, had never met anyone in person
who has contacted her through her website.

In contrast, Yoko Sekiguchi's regular appearance on television talk shows
has made her name well known, and she has created a higher-end counseling
center that offers a range of options for people seeking advice. In my conversations with her, Sekiguchi described how clients can pay over ¥30,000 (approximately $300) for an hour of personal counseling with her, which she happily
characterized as "more expensive than a lawyer!" Freely admitting that she
has no formal training in counseling, Sekiguchi's "Kanto Family Center" has
trained counselors on staff to help clients who want more long-term therapy.
In addition to the private advice sessions, Sekiguchi herself offers workshops
about dealing with common problems surrounding divorce such as splitting
finances, agreeing on child custody, and negotiating a divorce's terms.

Counseling opportunities can also become available through one's employer. In a small office in the middle of Tokyo, two middle-aged women sat
chatting between computers and telephones. They have both been marriage
counselors for many years and now work for a telephone counseling service
that derives most of its business from corporate clients. Large companies hire
this counseling firm to provide telephone counseling about a variety of issues,
ranging from marital problems to domestic violence and school refusal. These
counseling lines reflect not only changing family problems but also corporate
awareness of the risks of sexual harassment or power harassment claims, or
employee depression (Kitanaka 2012; Okada 2005). Because a large percentage
of the people who call in are living overseas, having been transferred by their
companies, the counselors explained that they regularly give advice about living in foreign countries and the stress that such a move can cause within families. Importantly, for these corporate clients, the callers themselves do not pay
directly—the availability of the telephone number is a benefit of employment,
and the company is charged a flat rate. When the counselors described this
as a relatively new system, something that has become more popular in the new
millennium, it seemed a major shift in the benefits some companies deem necessary to keep employees functioning and happy: if entertainment accounts

were once used to keep (male) employees involved in the company's business beyond working hours (Allison 1994), marital and family counseling has become similarly necessary to enable productive workers.

I found not only a growing opportunity for potential clients to find counselors but also an increased viability of events organized around counselor training. The structure of these events presented a slippage between potential patients and counselors. Ostensibly the audience was offered general advice that they could use to help others. But in practical terms, based on how participants introduced themselves, most people were there to address their own problems. For instance, when I joined a weekend training course run by a Kansai-based psychology center, the vast majority of participants described their interest in becoming counselors as the result of their own difficulties or those of their friends or relatives. To these ends, each of the forty-three participants paid ¥5,000 (approximately $50) for each two-hour training session once a week. One week, lessons focused on how best to perform care and affection in ways that don't make other people uncomfortable. We focused on how to tell someone you have a crush on them and how to respond if they do or don't reciprocate. Although the person holding the crush hopes for a relationship and looks forward to divulging their feelings, the counselors reminded us that such confessions can feel burdensome to the recipient, who suddenly has to deal with another person's emotions. In skits and pair work, we practiced phrases that walked a line between being honest but not threatening, while also honing our attention to our interlocutor's verbal and nonverbal responses. In these activities, we were learning behaviors to apply to our own lives or recommend to others. If someone feels any stigma surrounding counseling, perhaps this frame—as a workshop to help start a new career and/ or to help other people—might suffice as cover. All the workshop participants with whom I spoke, some of whom have been profiled elsewhere in this book, were themselves struggling to recover from challenging life events such as divorce. But they were also genuinely hoping to help other people, to learn advice so they could give advice, in a new job that might also be more flexible.[6]

No Man Wants This

In many cases, the infrastructure of therapeutic spaces was explicitly or implicitly built for women. This point was driven home during a summer gathering at Sekiguchi Yoko's "Kanto Family Center." Located in a small but elegant apartment that had been converted into offices, the party included three female counselors, as well as eight men and forty-three women who had some relationship with the center. Some had attended private counseling sessions with Sekiguchi-san, some were members of ongoing therapy groups, and others only subscribed to the newsletter. Everyone had some personal experience with family conflict, whether they were struggling to decide to end a marriage or to deal with a divorce that had already occurred.

The depths of people's ongoing pain was most visible when we were asked to introduce ourselves in small groups, to share as much of our problems as we would like. As was normal, some people were more motivated to share, and my group's discussion focused on a woman who quickly began to cry while describing her husband's unwillingness to show any affection at all. In her late thirties, this woman had been married for seven years, had no children, and made clear that she wasn't merely missing sex. Feeling no affection at all was making her go crazy, and as she quietly cried people in the group offered support and suggested that, contrary to what her husband seemed to be implying, her requests were more than reasonable. As the activity came to a close, her face was still wet but, perhaps just trying to be polite, she told us all that she felt better for having shared.

Toward the end of the gathering, Sekiguchi-san and the other counselors announced that they had prepared small door prizes, as a way to lighten the mood after some difficult conversations. Smiling, Sekiguchi-san held out three cheerful bouquets and a small gift bag with the Chanel logo on it. Immediately the mostly female audience made excited noises, wondering what expensive item could possibly be in the bag. As Sekiguchi-san smiled at our excitement, a harsh male voice rose up out of the back of the room: "What are *we* supposed to do with that?" The room's mood very quickly shifted from excitement to sudden awareness that, presumably, only women would be interested in these prizes. The man who spoke had earlier introduced himself to the group by mentioning that his marriage had ended when he'd had some extramarital affairs, and to summarize his frustrating divorce process, he'd written on his nametag "Mr. Had Enough."[7] His language now was hard, demanding, and coded with linguistic masculinity. Ever the professional, Sekiguchi-san apologized, thanked him for his point, and hoped that if a male participant won he might have someone he could share the prize with, if he wanted.

As the game got started, Sekiguchi-san decided she also wanted to play and therefore asked for a volunteer from the audience to take over as emcee. After a quick pause, she turned toward Mr. Had Enough and asked if he might be willing to take the microphone. (Like an excellent teacher or group leader, she adeptly found a way to involve someone who made it clear he wasn't motivated to participate.) Mr. Had Enough moved to the front of the room to lead the games, and the group settled back into the simple pleasure of trying to win prizes. He turned out to be a spectacular emcee and kept everyone laughing as the three bouquets were claimed. In the last round, so many people were competing for the grand prize Chanel gift bag that Mr. Had Enough tried to pester men into dropping out. "C'mon," he said, "what man wants *this* [prize]? No man wants this." Not only had the well-meaning organizers unthinkingly brought prizes that were coded feminine, but one of the men who had decided to attend the gathering was now loudly emphasizing to the other men how little they belonged there. Ultimately, a man won one of the bouquets and seemed happy with his victory; he said he'd give it to his daughter. The Chanel bag turned out to contain facial blotting paper, and the woman who won seemed pleased with her prize.

During the course of my research, one of my biggest ongoing questions concerned how gender mattered in divorce. Everyone told me that women were seeking divorces at much greater frequency, but, ever the skeptical researcher, I sought evidence for this fact and also wondered why so many people so insisted on it. I was not the only one trying to figure out how men fit into structures focused on divorce. Despite, or because of, the patriarchal society and structural sexism, the therapeutic infrastructure I encountered surrounding divorce was most explicitly set up by and for women.

The Women's Group: Learning to Listen

Sekiguchi's Kanto Family Center had a monthly workshop only open to women. Sekiguchi-san herself explained to me that a decade before they had a group just for men but now, when more women were seeking divorce, this structure fit the demand. Although the group was centered on "human relationships" (*ningen kankei*) rather than specific family issues (*kazoku mondai*), most of the topics raised by participants focused on problems with husbands or children.[8] The formal group sessions were focused on teaching participants to diagnose relationship problems and skills to improve certain situations. Informally, the group, and the center more generally, created bonds of disconnection that extended into other spaces.

In the women's group, eight participants ranged in age from late twenties to midfifties, led by a female counselor in her forties. The theme and activities for our second session were about being good communicators and being aware of all the different possible ways to communicate meaning and emotion. For example, the counselor said, it is very easy to understand what someone is feeling when they're standing with their arms crossed looking angry, even if they say, "I'm not angry." She asked us to think about how any medium of communication shapes the messages, specifically focusing on communications by phone, email, and in person.[9] The counselor suggested that one way to make it easier for listeners to accept your ideas is to surround a negative comment with positive comments on either side: say something good, then something bad (the message you really want to convey), followed by something else good.

After a tea break, the counselor asked the participants to apply the tips about good communicating to a practice conversation. We paired off and were each supposed to practice being good listeners for three minutes while our partner talked about something she'd been enjoying recently. I was paired with Nagako-san, a middle-aged woman waiting to divorce her husband, and we giggled and waffled as we decided who should go first. The leader had told us that good listeners make eye contact, don't sit with arms crossed over their body, and ask open-ended, engaged questions. I talked about enjoying a friend's open mic performances while Nagako-san was a good listener. Then we switched and I tried my hardest to be a good listener as she talked about enjoying some opera performances recently. After everyone had a chance to practice listening, the group came together again and talked about the experience. The general consensus was that the conversations felt good and that active, engaged listening was a real pleasure to experience. Everyone agreed that the time had gone very quickly. Women mentioned having problems talking about their daily lives with their husbands, saying they had no idea what their husbands did each day at work, or even how to ask them. The counselor suggested that the phrase "by the way" (*tokorode*) could be a powerful tool in conversation with their husbands. The women agreed that this phrase would be a good way to bring up subjects that they had problems talking about and the session drew to a close. We packed up our handouts, and the notes we had taken, and thanked the counselor.

Walking out of the counseling center together as a group, the participants fell into step with each other. Nishimura-san, one of the quieter participants, kindly asked me questions about my research and shared that she had briefly lived in New York, as the others chatted. When we got to a main street, Nagako-san, my "listening" partner, said goodbye while the rest of us continued to walk to the nearest subway station. A few minutes later she came rushing back, slightly out of breath, to share an idea that had just occurred to her: Would anyone be interested in having lunch together? Not everyone could stay, but five of us were happy to continue the conversation and walked to a nearby restaurant.

Over lunch, Nagako-san's impromptu invitation quickly came to resemble a full blown "afterparty" (*nijikai*), a more casual gathering that follows the main event. In this case, we spent almost three hours talking about ourselves, our relationships, the problems we were worried about, and the goals that motivated us to join the counseling group. We were all practicing engaged listening, but conversation was quicker, louder, and bawdier than it had been in the counseling session. Nishimura-san, a quiet woman in her fifties with adult children, talked about discovering her husband's infidelity, and Nagako-san described her own relationship with a man other than her husband. After many cups of coffee, we finally separated, exchanging phone numbers and emails so we could keep in touch between the group sessions.

This group of women quickly became a core group of new friends. In addition to joining our regular group at the center, we met up for meals and movies, travelled together on weekend getaways, and even attended a weekend workshop at another counseling center. The group was big enough that not everyone could attend every event, but we shared powerful experiences and talked through deeply personal topics both in therapeutic group sessions and in the casual gatherings that came to follow each event. The counseling group had first introduced us, but a real friendship and shared empathy—if dissimilar experiences—kept us together.

NAGAKO-SAN: VERY FIRM PLANS

Long before she became my "listening" partner, the first time I met Nagako-san she announced very clearly that she wasn't divorced but she would be a year later. As I described in the book's introduction, Nagako-san was a woman in her fifties who was then waiting for the new pension law to take effect, so she would be able to access up to half of her husband's national pension after she divorced him. She was extremely sure that she wanted a divorce and offered horrifying and hilarious stories about how awful her husband was. In and out of the support group we attended together, she had a wealth of stories to share about her husband's actions, his affair, and his coldness toward her. Years before, she had caught her husband cheating—and not just a couple of one-night stands. He had a deep emotional relationship with a woman he had been meeting in secret and with whom he exchanged intimate emails. It was these messages that Nagako-san found one day by accident, when she put the wrong disk in the computer. As can be imagined, she was livid, and immediately upon finding the messages printed them all out—to the tune of hundreds of pages—so that she would have them as proof if something should happen to the disk. When we met once to record a conversation about her experiences, she began by showing me the printed emails (which she had bound together) and offering to let me read them. Weeks later, when I returned the binder in a paper bag at the beginning of a support group meeting, she openly explained what it was to the other members and offered to let anyone else read it, too. She was angry at her husband and still smarting from both the depth of his betrayal and his sense that what he did wasn't that bad. He wasn't contrite or apologetic enough, and it made her feel better when other people with whom Nagako-san shared the emails confirmed his terribleness of his actions.

As far as she was concerned her marriage was entirely over and she was merely waiting out the clock to be able to receive a part of his national pension.[10] The two years before the pension law change would go into effect seemingly gave Nagako-san time to live the life she had been wanting. Unlike many other women I knew who wished for a sensitive and loving partner, Nagako-san had actually found one. In diametric opposition to her husband, who was cold, distant, and noncommunicative, her boyfriend was fun, smart, and energizing. Among the group of counseling participants, her story was something of a fairy tale: an older woman leaves a husband who takes her for granted only to begin a relationship with a charming, and seemingly perfect, younger man. Nagako-san was living the dream of connected independence.

They had met at a museum and shared a deep interest in film. This shared hobby enabled Nagako-san and her boyfriend to travel occasionally to screenings, with much more in the way of overlapping interests than she had with her husband. The boyfriend knew about her marital situation and empathized, but they didn't talk about it a lot. Nagako-san had moved out of the house she shared with her husband, but not in with her boyfriend. She was enjoying the new relationship, and the new style of intimacy it brought, but was also enjoying living alone. Although she described her relationship with this younger man as a truly intimate relationship—and she made it clear they were having sex—I could never tell how much of this intimacy was a result of her feelings of betrayal resulting from her husband's actions. There was no need to pick apart her relationships with her husband and with her boyfriend because they were inexorably related. As she described it in 2005, she had fully and firmly decided to divorce and was merely waiting until the legal situation was more to her benefit. In the course of my research, I never talked with anyone with a clearer conviction that divorce was in their future.

Her future turned out differently than anyone expected. By September 2006, just months before the pension law that Nagako-san had been waiting for would go into effect, she was uncharacteristically quiet during a group dinner. As the "women's group" participants chatted with each other and caught up, Nagako-san struggled to bring up a new topic. She didn't know how to tell us, but her husband—the one who had cheated on her and whose intimate emails she had found—had just been diagnosed with cancer. She'd found out that week and didn't know what to do. The details started to spill out of her, shocking not only because of her husband's diagnosis but also because of her new, unexpected reluctance to leave him. Despite all her firm plans to divorce and pursue a new romantic life with her younger boyfriend, suddenly she was reconsidering. She didn't want to leave him with no support. She didn't want him to die. If she didn't help him, who would? Everything became more complicated. Although she had been saying for months that getting divorced was really what she wanted, this diagnosis made that option far more complicated and unclear.

Despite her concrete plans, ultimately Nagako-san decided not to divorce her husband. She couldn't imagine him facing cancer alone. She was still incredibly angry at him and felt sure their relationship would never be a happy partnership. But the bonds they had built through years of marriage, as problematic as it might have been, compelled her sense of responsibility. She seemed surprised by her choice, almost embarrassed by the gap between the very firm plans she had made (and been genuinely excited about) and her eventual decision to stay with her husband. His illness changed the situation and her calculations in response. She couldn't imagine him entirely alone, sick and possibly dying. Divorce might have been nice, but she couldn't leave him so utterly disconnected.

YOSHIDA-SAN AND AKIHOSHI-SAN: I AIN'T MISSING YOU AT ALL

It was just starting to rain when I met my old friend, Yoshida-san, on a corner of a neighborhood full of bars in Shinjuku, Tokyo. Without any details, he had tantalized me by saying that there had been an "incident" (*jiken*) at his regular bar, so he didn't want to go there this evening and had, instead, made other plans. Soon after I showed up, Akihoshi-san walked around the corner. I was happy to see him for the first time since, months before, his former co-workers used my research topic to tease him about his marital problems. The three of us were the entire group, apparently, and Yoshida-san announced with fanfare that tonight's theme was . . . eighties music! We would be singing *karaoke*! But we were only allowed to choose non-Japanese eighties music. He began teasing me almost immediately: "Oh, Ally, you might be able to pronounce all the English words easily, but can you sing?" (I cannot.) Akihoshi-san smiled and, ducking under his umbrella, started leading the way to the karaoke spot Yoshida-san had picked. Yoshida-san walked next to him, and I fell into step behind on the slick sidewalk overcrowded by open umbrellas.

Our little huddle had just turned a corner when Yoshida-san, half a step in front of me, yelled "Whaaat!?!" (*eeehhhh?*) and turned back to ask me, "Did you know that?" (*Shiteru desu ka?*). Over the city noise and rain, I hadn't heard what they were talking about, and I answered, "No, I didn't know.

What's going on?" Yoshida-san looked frantically between me and Akihoshi-san, who continued to look down as he walked down a slight slope. "I got divorced" (*Rikon shita*), he said very simply and quietly, and in obvious opposition to Yoshida-san's boisterous agitation. Without waiting for our reactions, Akihoshi-san kept walking, and Yoshida-san stopped and gave me an open-mouthed surprised face. He was certainly surprised but also looked more than a little happy, perhaps because now there was another divorced man within his extended group of friends.

Despite all the questions I had asked of divorced people, I really didn't know what to say to Akihoshi-san. If he had sounded even a little bit more matter-of-fact or happy about his divorce, I might have tried out a new line I'd been using: "Congratulations!" For some people, mostly younger women who really had to struggle to complete their divorces, congratulations were really in order. But here, that certainly wasn't right, and I was quiet for a full five seconds before I came up with a possible reaction. In a somber tone, I said, "Ah, so, how does it feel?" (*Ah, dou desu ka?*).

Yoshida-san, who had fallen into step with us, seemingly didn't know what to say either and waited quietly as Akihoshi-san explained that the divorce only happened the previous week. Nothing in his tone gave me a sense of how to interpret what he was saying, and there were no hints about whether he was happy or sad about it. Many people say they've been divorced and, in the same breath, give their audience some suggestion about how to interpret it, intimating whether their divorce was a good or bad thing. Akihoshi-san did nothing like this, and by asking how he felt I had been trying to get such clues out of him. Still walking, and looking down, Akihoshi-san answered by first saying only "free" (*furii*) with an English-derived pronunciation, and then extending it to say "free feeling" (*furii fiiringu*). He didn't elaborate. Although he might have felt free, the tone in which he said these words didn't sound positive at all, and it seemed like he was trying to make the best of a bad situation. I didn't want to ask any more questions, but Akihoshi-san continued by saying that his experience was perfect for my research and that maybe hearing about my project the last time we'd met had influenced him. The last comment was meant as a joke, particularly becuase his wife had requested the divorce, and he laughed a little as Yoshida-san stepped forward into the karaoke bar to arrange a singing room for us. After a moment of heavy silence, I asked Akihoshi-san how he had spent the Golden Week holiday, and we chatted while Yoshida-san got us a place to sing. In the elevator up to our room and as we got settled, we talked about previous karaoke outings while everyone studiously avoided mentioning divorce.

As beer and appetizers were delivered to our singing room, Yoshida-san turned on the karaoke machine, handed out microphones, and reminded us, again, of the evening's theme. Only eighties, no Japanese songs. I was still sad and surprised about Akihoshi-san's divorce, so when the two men started singing, every lyric felt like a comment on failed marriages and the divorces to which both of these men were forced to agree. I was almost in tears as Yoshida-san sang Chicago's "Hard to Say I'm Sorry" and then Akihoshi-san followed with "I Ain't Missing You at All" by John Waite. Those lyrics narrate the singer's insistent refusal to admit his longing for a former partner, to whom the song is directed. As the singer's list of all the precise ways he is not missing "you" becomes longer and more detailed throughout the song, his declaration becomes so fervent that it cannot be true. The depth and feeling of these lyrics hit me hard, and the songs had never sounded so somber and free of cheesy schmaltz.

Both men speak English reasonably well but didn't seem to be registering the brutal appropriateness of the lyrics they were belting out. When my turns came around, I repeatedly sang stupid, upbeat songs by Belinda Carlisle or Cheap Trick (not really the eighties, but I was given a break). For the first twenty minutes, I thought I was the only one who noticed the contrast until, having just finished The Police's "Every Breath You Take," Akihoshi-san turned to me and asked exactly what the song was about. I explained that, as much as I like the song, the lyrics are kind of romantic but also creepy because the narrator sounds like a stalker. Akihoshi-san looked up and burst out laughing. "So it's perfect for a divorced husband, then, huh?!" The floodgates opened. As the karaoke machine played videos of young couples on dates and standing on windswept bridges, Akihoshi-san and Yoshida-san sang the lyrics superimposed over the images. In the midst of singing about how lonely he is, Akihoshi-san would stop and explain that these lyrics were the perfect articulation of what he was feeling. I wasn't sure if he knew the songs well enough to anticipate, and therefore choose, lyrics that felt appropriate for a recently divorced man, or if he was picking the songs he remembered and they all happened to have lyrics to which he could relate.

Our singing session quickly came to include the personal confessionals that I was more used to hearing in support groups, albeit, in this case, literally embedded in the middle of karaoke songs. Without explaining many details or providing a narrative of how his divorce came to be inevitable, Akihoshi-san sang and talked about how he felt like a failure, was lonely, and didn't know what to do now. Most of the lyrics he sung were directed at an unnamed "you," but the words he spoke in the middle of songs were more about himself and how he was feeling. Yoshida-san continued to sing when his turn came up but didn't add soliloquies in the middle of the songs. He listened to Akihoshi-san but, in contrast to my dampened mood, made jokes and cheered. Yoshida-san did his best to keep the mood light while Akihoshi-san talked and sang about very personal things.

No conclusions were reached. In contrast to support groups, there was no allotted time for wrapping-up or feedback—or even verbal recognition of what was going on. About two hours after we got there, a staff member called the phone in our room and reminded us that the time we had signed up for was ending. Did we want to add more? After a quick consultation, we realized we did not. Akihoshi-san lived far away, so to catch his last train, he had to leave Tokyo well before 11:30. He pulled out his cell phone to check the train schedules and suddenly everything started to move more quickly. Akihoshi-san scarfed down another slice of bad pizza as Yoshida-san finished up his song. We headed down to the front desk to pay the bill and almost ran to the nearest train station. With a few quick goodbyes and thank yous, Akihoshi-san was gone. With a little more time to spare, Yoshida-san and I walked more leisurely to our trains, but we didn't talk about what had happened beyond simple pleasantries like "That was fun. We should do it again sometime." Weeks later, when I brought the evening up to share my surprise that men were so willing to share such personal reflections, Yoshida-san dimissed the basic premise of my comment. "That would never have happened if you weren't there," he insisted. "Men don't talk like that."

I had spent more than a year trying to let Yoshida-san talk about his divorce, making clear that I would be happy to listen if he ever wanted to bring it up. I can easily imagine that a female friend who also researches divorce might be the last person with whom he'd want to discuss his relationship and therefore I don't expect that the silence he maintained around me characterizes all his friendships. Although he knew Akihoshi-san was having marital difficulties, Yoshida-san was truly surprised to learn the divorce had already happened and was visibly giddy to have another man with whom to share any mention of divorce. That the discussion happened in between verses of loud music, while drinking, in a darkened casual space that is already socially marked for emotionality seemed to make it that much easier.

Can Coming Apart Bring People Together?

After decades of research on Japanese masculinities during the economic bubble and after, Itō (2018) identified the early 2000s as a period of the "masculinization of deprivation" (*hakudatsukan no danseika*). Amidst gender scholarship focused on women and their structural impediments, Itō reminds us that men are similarly, though not identically, burdened by the weight of restrictive gender norms. In his analysis, men in the early 2000s face interlocking but largely invisible problems, culminating as "a sense of deprivation of unknown cause" (*gen'in fumei no hakudatsukan*) (ibid., 63), a reworking of the "problem with no name" (Friedan 1963). Although restructured job opportunities might be the most visible, men face deprivation in various forms, including diminished family bonds, confused sense of purpose, and decreased access to previously inviolable markers of masculinity. Itō holds normative masculinity and men themselves accountable for these dynamics, suggesting that the problems stem partially from men who are unable to acknowledge their need for, and dependence on, other people, particularly women. Men's tenacious investment in their own "illusions of independence" (*jiritsu gensō*) pulls them into angry cycles of relying on others while refusing to acknowledge those very dependencies (ibid., 75).

As I've argued throughout this book, in the early 2000s, many people in Japan struggled with determining what makes a relationship worth sustaining and how to create ideal relationships with other people. Popular discourse and media representations of Japan's society without bonds (*muen shakai*) comment on the domino effects of neoliberal policies in action. From young people uncomfortable leaving their rooms to those forced into homelessness when unable to find secure work to men and women unable to find marriage partners, Japan is awash in images of the disconnections that neoliberalism brings (Allison 2013; Arai 2016; Horiguchi 2011; Mathews 2017; Miyazaki 2010; Ueno 2009). Without false optimism, this chapter has traced the tentative work of new connections built after divorce. In these new bonds, I saw substantially different patterns for men and women, partially reflecting my own positionality and how people reacted to me. Many more therapeutic spaces were explicitly or implicitly designed for women, and more women I met were interested in utilizing them or creating their own. Although some spaces were free or inexpensive, much counseling infrastructure is quite expensive, in terms of money but also time spent during normal working hours, and therefore accessible to only a few. The men with whom I did research felt, on average, less comfortable in or prepared to utilize formal therapeutic spaces and instead created their own moments of exchange. Although not all were harboring illusions of their own independence, they were navigating the risks and benefits that come with social bonds.

Divorce is not a singular path to complete disconnection, nor an isolating choice that leaves social ties shattered in its wake. The disconnections divorce creates present no total, clear-cut closure. Instead, as demonstrated in these profiles, we see the sheer range of potential interactions, coping tactics, and affinities that surface once divorce enters the scene. Amidst popular discourse that emphasizes the risk of decreased, or shifting, social bonds, divorce came to stand for the worst results of decisions to separate. Although divorce can certainly shift family bonds or prioritize new friendships over former marital relationships, for many people it is not only an end, but also a beginning.

Endings and New Beginnings

Divorce is not entropic. Marriages do not end in an automatic disintegration, coming apart as soon as partners stop working to hold relationships together. Popular media and private discourse in Japan and other places tend to emphasize the work of starting or sustaining intimate relationships, rather than the work necessary to end them. This book has attempted to represent the personal, social, legal, and economic work required to end a marriage in contemporary Japan, as well as demonstrate the analytical value gained by paying attention to such endings.

In Japan and other cultural contexts, divorce connotes personal failure, social collapse, family breakdown, or gender disparities playing out in real time. Any person going through a divorce must navigate through a gauntlet of such symbolism and figure out how to respond to (or ignore) people who hint that their divorce necessarily says something bigger, either about their personal capacities or about the fate of society. In Japan at the turn of the millennium, divorce was overdetermined as a symptom of gender shifts, taken by many to be a clear indication that women now held more power and control than men did. This book has tried to take such claims seriously, while examining actual experiences of divorce occurring in relation to such discourse.

I have argued that decisions to divorce, choices made within the process, and efforts at recovery after divorce are fundamentally shaped by people's efforts to reconcile tensions they perceive between intimacy, connection, and dependence. On a spectrum from disconnected dependence to connected independence, people consider the best ways to build intimate relationships and the forms those relationships should take. These frameworks reflect Japanese cultural norms suggesting that certain forms of dependence (*amae*) are beneficial to relationships, companionate norms that prioritize emotional interdependence, and neoliberal ethics emphasizing independent self-responsibility. In practice, men and women are trying to decide how to be close in ways that don't cause harm, as well as how to disconnect without being too isolated or self-centered. From navigating marital tensions to debating a child's ongoing relationship with a noncustodial parent or building friendships in therapeutic spaces, connections between people bring hope but also potential risks. And even after they spend the time necessary to determine what style of intimacy feels best to them, men and women face the burdensome gap between that imagined ideal and the logistics of building such relationships in the real world.

Reconsidering Relationality

Anthropologists have made clear that, in practice, neoliberal policies often drive people into tighter and more dependent family relationships. When the government reduces support and removes structures of social welfare, many people turn to family networks for care and assistance. In Japan neoliberal ethics are being used to challenge the social contracts that previously held families together. In this way, neoliberal ethics are simultaneously restructuring labor markets, pushing individuals to be responsible for themselves, and offering vocabulary to those who want to describe family relationships as inherently damaging. Rather than a set of policies that pull family members tighter together, neoliberal recommendations for independence can here become a wedge that forces families apart.

In this research, I found men and women seeking relationships at the same time that some of them were suspicious about the side effects that relationality can bring. With me, with each other, and on their own, men and women questioned what they want and need from intimate relationships. As Japan's intimate political economy shifts, marriage no longer offers the security and benefits it had for previous generations. Likewise, for some parents, divorce no longer immediately connotes a definitive "clean break" between spouses, or between parents and their children. At stake and under debate are the impacts of intimate relationships and relationality more generally.

Divorce in contemporary Japan offers unique perspective on the ideologies, methods, and practices people implement when they try to situate themselves in relationship to other people. As a legal process not only defined by law, divorce is a social and personal transition made more complicated because of the crosscutting differences it can include. Divorce looks very different for someone who is excited to leave their spouse versus someone who is working hard not to be left—the gap between freedom and anxiety. Similarly, spouses with children are well aware that divorce would require disconnecting or reconfiguring more than just their marital bonds. This book has traced the process by which men and women draw on competing ideologies of dependence and connection to construct their own meaningful models of ideal intimacy. Their choices reflect deep ambiguities and confusions about how to judge the risks and possibilities that relationships bring.

The End

"What do you think? Isn't it exciting?" Midori-san met me at her apartment door with questions. It was the final week before I was scheduled to leave Japan, and Midori-san had invited me over to her Tokyo apartment for a final dinner with some of the women who had met through our participation in support groups. For this evening, she had invited Nagako-san, Nishimura-san, and Shoda-san. All four of them were women in their mid- to late fifties, and all were thinking about getting divorced or had already.

Among the dinner guests, Nishimura-san was the person I knew least well. Although we had participated in many group activities together, I had no real sense of the problems that drove her to participate. In group meetings, it was always perfectly possible to sit quietly and reveal relatively little about one's own experiences. Although other people talked in great detail about their family lives, plans, and concerns, Nishimura-san was much more likely to stay silent. She was certainly listening to what other people said, and made supportive comments, but she shared almost nothing about herself. Even when Nishimura-san and I roomed together during a weekend retreat, she didn't share any more of a sense of why she was there.

When Midori-san answered her door with questions for me—"What do you think? Isn't it exciting?"—I had no idea what she was talking about. I was the first guest to make it to her apartment and she started to make tea as she continued to pepper me with questions. It took me a little while to realize that there had been some announcement that I clearly must have missed. "Didn't you read the listserv today?!" she asked incredulously. I thought about it. Uh, no, I hadn't. In the final week before I was to leave, I spent more time packing or visiting with people than I did reading my email. I had no idea what she was talking about. Luckily for me, Midori-san was more than happy to fill me in.

In her first-ever contribution, that morning Nishimura-san had posted a long message to the listserv. The previous day her husband had come home. She explained the problems in their relationship—which had been going on for years—but mostly pinpointed it to a long-term relationship that her husband had been having with another woman. Rather than hiding the relationship, Nishimura-san's husband literally brought the woman back to their house on a regular basis, and Nishimura-san found herself cooking for her husband's girlfriend. She felt like a servant. As occurred in other stories I have related in this book, Nishimura-san's husband didn't believe that she would ever leave him and had taunted her for years. Apparently, he liked to tell her that if she thought she was so strong and capable, she should just get the locks changed.

This day, she'd finally done it. Although she wasn't able to explain what had changed, she'd finally had enough and decided that she needed to act. She called a locksmith and changed the house locks, and then called her husband to tell him, before emailing the counseling center listserv to relay the events. Then she had to go to work.

By the time Midori-san finished the story, Shoda-san and Nagako-san arrived and contributed details to the telling. They were all very happy that we had scheduled this dinner so that we could see Nishimura-san on what turned out to be an important day for her. She had sent a message saying that work might go late so that she wouldn't make it to Midori-san's apartment until well after dinner, but she was definitely coming.

As the four of us sat around and waited for her arrival, splitting a huge order of take-out sushi, the topics of conversation naturally drifted to similar turning points for the other women. Midori-san told a story that resonated with Nishimura-san's changing of the house locks. After years of physical and emotional abuse directed at her and their children, Midori-san couldn't take it anymore and changed the locks to their house. But she didn't know how to tell her husband, so she didn't and hid in the house waiting for him to come home. As she described, when he returned it was like a suspense movie—he tried his key in the front door's lock, and then tried it again, jiggling and jiggling, until it finally occurred to him what happened. There was a moment of silence as he took it all in and then a large rock came breaking through the glass that surrounded their door. He couldn't get in, but he continued to terrorize Midori-san and ran around the house screaming threats at her and the children. Midori-san's story knocked the air out of all of us. We were excited for Nishimura-san and looking forward to seeing her, but everyone suddenly understood the weight of her choices in a new light. We sat talking and picking at food, waiting for Nishimura-san to arrive.

Contrary to many fieldworkers, I had a very firm sense of when I was leaving the field. My visa was expiring so I had to go. This pragmatic motivation made me no less interested in looking for a "natural" end to my project. Were there any signs that would enable me to know I was "finished," that this project was not complete but at least settled? When I had arrived at Midori-san's apartment door for our goodbye dinner, when she peppered me with questions about events I hadn't known about, this is what I had been thinking. How could I be sure this was the proper end? Was I right in thinking that this was the best time to go? Had I tried my hardest and done my best? Surely, readers are more aware than I was in that moment of the ways in which my own thoughts about endings mirrored my interlocutors' about their marriages and divorces. Even Midori-san, who had been divorced for almost a decade and ended a marriage that was violent and problematic by anyone's definition, continued to wonder if she had done the right thing in leaving, especially when she considered the difficult relationship she was having with her adult children.

When I arrived at Midori-san's door thinking about endings, I was met by an overwhelming wave of hope and excitement about the new beginnings that endings bring. The women were thrilled that Nishimura-san had finally decided to end her terrible marriage, indeed only telling us about its real terror as she ended it. When she finally arrived for a very late dinner, Nishimura-san looked very tired but was also more talkative and energized than I'd ever seen her before. Maybe she should have ended this marriage years before, but she was never sure before that morning, and now that she had begun to construct an ending, she was visibly excited. There was plenty more to discuss and much more to do.

Acknowledgments

Anyone who knows me—arguably anyone who has *met* me—knows that I think best in conversation. Talking with people, putting pieces together, and sharing ideas and energy bring me real joy but also are basically required for me to figure anything out. This book, then, is the result of literally thousands of conversations and time and energy many wonderful people shared with me.

My first and deepest thanks go to the many generous people who were willing to let me into their lives, to share their stories and experiences with me, and to help me understand what they know to be important. I am continually amazed by how open, welcoming, patient, and generous people were to me. I learned so much from the people whose stories are represented here and will always be grateful. Thank you all for putting up with my questions, presence, and confusion. I hope you recognize yourselves in this book and I look forward to our future conversations.

The research on which this book is based was funded by the Fulbright IIE, the Japan Foundation, Yale University, and the Light Fellowship. I thank the University of Michigan's ADVANCE program for funds to improve the manuscript and the Center for Japanese Studies for a Scholarly Leave Grant that permitted me time to finish the manuscript. Funding from TOME (Toward an Open Monograph Ecosystem) provided the opportunity to create an Open Access version of this book. The book was significantly improved by Masayo Sodeyama's careful research assistance and transcriptions. At the University of Chicago Press, it has been a joy to work with Priya Nelson, and I am grateful to her thoughtful stewardship of this project. My thanks also go to Dylan Montanari and Caterina MacLean for their hard work improving the manuscript. Two anonymous reviewers provided the most constructive and helpful reader reports I've ever seen, and I thank them for manifesting the best of the academy.

In ways that I think might embarrass him, Joe Hopper first planted the seed of this project. Taking his courses at the University of Chicago literally changed my life and certainly changed the way I look at the world. His own brilliant research on divorce in the United States served as a model for me when, many years later, I began to put this project together. I know it was a long time coming, but I am deeply indebted to Joe for teaching me so much and setting me on a path that was otherwise inconceivable.

In Bill Kelly I have truly the best mentor anyone could ask for. His commitment to thinking critically, to making connections across fields, to supporting a wide range of exploration, to teaching, and to being patient as students figure things out will always be the primary model for me. Whenever I'm faced with a difficult professional question, trying to imagine what Bill would do provides me the right path forward. I am forever grateful to be part of the generations of students he trained in anthropology and Japanese studies.

Glenda Roberts has always provided the most generous of home bases and has repeatedly allowed me to join her *zemi* group at Waseda University. She has built a truly extraordinary network of committed scholars to whom she imparts her unwavering (and inexhaustible) energy for thinking, research, and teaching. I know my voice is only one in her enormous *deshi* group, but I am truly grateful for her guidance, support, and energy.

Throughout the creation of this book, a group of smart and generous readers gave me comments that have vastly improved the manuscript. In its earliest iteration, Susan McKinnon, Len Schoppa, and Christine Yano were incredibly generous in suggesting improvements and, indeed, chapter 4 was written in direct response to their questions about how children factor into divorce. I thank them for their hard work and the University of Virginia for the funding to make possible their feedback. Chapter 3 was significantly improved with comments from UVA Law School's Law and Humanities workshop. Sungyun Lim was a positive and honest cowriter, giving me a boost when I needed it the most. Emma Cook modeled how to write a book and then read every word of this manuscript multiple times, vastly improving it with her suggestions. Adria LaViolette is a far smarter reader and editor than any one person should be and has shared brilliant comments on topics well beyond her fields. Jeff Hantman has been planning our podcast on his own while I focused on this writing, and I thank him for both his patience and his support. Hopefully, Molly Margaretten already knows how amazing she is, but let me take this opportunity to thank her for being the smartest, funniest, most level-headed friend I could ask for.

In the final months of writing, I was lucky enough to receive deeply engaged and thoughtful feedback in a workshop supported by the University of Michigan. Ilana Gershon, Akiko Takeyama, and Caren Freeman gave numerous suggestions that have vastly improved the book. I am truly forever in their debt. Liz Wingrove, Abby Stewart, and Sue Juster were equally generous readers who shared thoughtful recommendations for improvement. All of these people have demonstrated through words and actions their efforts to improve the academy generally and my work specifically.

Many thanks go to my teachers and colleagues, who listened to me talk about this project for many years, offered thoughtful suggestions, and asked questions that prompted me to head in new directions. For my training at Yale, I thank Hal Scheffler, Helen Siu, Karen Nakamura, Linda-Anne Rebhun, John Szwed, and Kathy Rupp. Barney Bate was an exemplary mentor and I miss his joyful engagement with ideas. For stimulating conversations in Japan, I thank Hiroko Yako-Suketomo, David Slater, Joseph Hankins, Satsuki Takahashi, David Leheny, Mayumi Ono, Karl Jakob Krogness, Azusa Nishimoto, Takeshi Hamano, and Chie Yoshiya. As wonderful colleagues, I thank Sherine Hamdy, Andrea Smith, Kira Lawrence, Paul Barclay, Ira Bashkow, Lise Doborn, Ellen Contini-Morava, Fred Damon, Eve Danziger, Richard Handler, Pati Wattenmaker, Jim Igoe, Dan Lefkowitz, China Scherz, John Shepherd, Kath Weston, Kerry Abrams, Molly Bishop Shadel, Anne Coughlin, and Allison Pugh. In my current position, I am lucky to have received extraordinary support from Victor Mendoza, Pardip Bolina, Kiyoteru Tsutsui, Jatin Dua, Abby Dumes, Shinobu Kitayama, Mark West, Rosie Ceballo, Yasmin Moll, Michael Lempert, Yeidy Rivera, Yuri Fukazawa, Brad Hammond, Peggy Rudberg, Amy Myers, Ruby Tapia, Atsushi Kinami, Anna Kirkland, Keiko Yokota-Carter, Meredith Kahn, Justin Bonfiglio, Mike McGovern, Peggy McCracken, Gayle Rubin, Maria Cotera, Amal Hassan Faddalla, Wang Zhong, Sara McClelland, Petra Kuppers, Valerie Traub, Dean Hubbs, Jennifer Jones, Scotti Parrish, Ava Purkiss, Emily Peterson, Kira Thurman, and Lisa Young Larance. I have had the honor of being inspired and energized by wonderful students including Macario Garcia, Dannah Dennis, Kunisuke Hirano, Chelsea Jack, Xinyan Peng, and Alice Register. I could fill another book detailing all the ways you have helped me.

Throughout the writing of this book, my life has been dramatically improved by awesome friends who listened to me and laughed at me in appropriate proportions. When the ideas in this book were first coming together Satomi Kusano, Raj Nayak, Kalanit Baumhaft, Susanna Fioratta, Joe Hill, Richard Payne, Gavin Whitelaw, Tanya Saunders, Adam Chapin, Margaret Chatfield, Diley Hernández, and Osvaldo Cleger gave me incredibly helpful suggestions.

I thank Amanda Alexander, Vanessa Quimpo Obrachta, Katie Selenski, Mark Rowe, Noriko Imai, Yoko Kageyama, Hoyt Long, Ron Brunette, Allen Finkel, Alana Brunette, Pat Herbst, Vilma Mesa, Bruno Herbst, Emma Cook, Brandon Taylor, Maryse Richards, Heather Richards, Niara Richards, Stephanie Lovelace, and Chiaki Nojiri for being amazing, inspiring, and generous. I promise I will be more fun moving forward.

This book is about families, and I'm blessed to be a member of some wonderful families. The hilarious Alexy/Wood branch continues to invite me to the beach and then quietly swallow their shame about my inability to tan. The Jackson/Roland families have been more welcoming and generous than I could have ever imagined, and the 2018 family reunion will likely be the best party I will ever go to. The Gorhams have supported and sustained me, giving me space to do my work and love whenever I need it. Lynn and Mo Smith have been beautiful rays of sunshine, helping me remember what is really important. Eunice Jackson is full of love, generosity, and wisdom on which I've been lucky enough to rely.

While writing an early draft of the introduction, I was trying to come up with a quick shorthand to describe "companionate love," and my first thought was "when your husband reads your drafts." Particularly for someone who writes about divorce, I have been extremely lucky to have such an extraordinarily smart, kind, and patient partner in Reginald Jackson. He has read, edited, and improved every word of this book, but he also makes me a lot of nutritious meals, lets me jabber about nonsense, and is the best teammate imaginable for wading through swamps. I thank him for being such a joyful light in the world. Not today, Satan.

This book is dedicated to my mom, Alice Gorham, as the smallest token of my gratitude for what she has enabled me to do. In the course of this research, people naturally asked about my own family and were shocked that my mom allowed me to spend so much time away from home. Not only has my mom let me follow my interests, but she has worked incredibly hard to make those opportunities possible in the first place. I thank her for the decades of hard work that paid for my education and other adventures, a lifetime of great advice, and her willingness to let me be myself. It brings me great pleasure to know that this book will arrive during her retirement, when she has more time to read and relax. Mom, I don't imagine this book will jump the line before whatever mystery is next scheduled, but please know it would not have been even remotely possible without you.

Appendix A: Profile Summaries

This chart includes short descriptions of all the people whose experiences I explicitly represent in this book. It is designed to help readers keep track of the "characters" they encounter and to compare and contrast across examples. The names are listed in order they appear. I designate social class based on the person's own description of their identity, but also my knowledge of their relative wealth. Such classifications are necessarily subjective (both on my part and theirs), particularly in a society where most people identify as middle class (Ishida and Slater 2009; Kelly 1991). All these details were correct as of 2005–6, when I conducted the majority of this research.

	Chapter in which represented	Gender	Age	Marital history	Children	Social class	Occupation	Residence
Yamaguchi-san	Introduction, chapter 1	Male	mid-60s	Married	Two adult children	Middle class	Retired salaryman	Tokyo
Nagako-san	Introduction, chapter 6, conclusion	Female	mid-50s	Planning for a divorce, still married	Two adult children	Middle class	Housewife, then part-time tour guide	Tokyo suburbs
Sato-san	Introduction, chapter 5	Female	mid-80s	Husband requested a divorce in 1975, but she refused until 1994	Three adult children, multiple grandchildren	Lower-middle class	Housewife, then office worker	Matsuyama, Shikoku
Mae	Introduction, chapter 5	Female	late-30s	Divorced after five years of marriage, dating	None	Working class	Hairdresser	Tokyo suburbs
Mariko Ando	Chapters 1, 2, 5	Female	Early 30s	Divorced after three years of marriage	None	Upper class	Finance	Tokyo
Nomura-san	Chapter 1	Female	early 80s	Married	Three adult children, multiple grandchildren	Upper class	Housewife	Tokyo
Aoyma-san	Chapter 1	Female	Late 30s	Divorced, at her request	Two children; her ex-husband has custody	Middle class	Office worker	Matsuyama
Yamada Sadako	Chapters 2, 6	Female	mid-30s	Married	One young child	Middle class	Housewife and online marriage counselor	Tokyo suburbs
Fujita-san	Chapter 2	Male	mid-30s	Married	One young child	Lower-middle class	Barber	Tokyo suburbs
Osada-san	Chapter 2	Female	mid-40s	Divorced	None	Middle class	Office worker	Tokyo suburbs
Etsuko	Chapters 2, 5	Female	early 40s	Widowed, dating	None	Middle class	Teacher	Tokyo
Yano-san	Chapter 2	Male	mid-50s	Unhappily married, dating	Three	Upper-middle class	Designer	Tokyo

Name	Chapter	Gender	Age	Marital status	Children	Class	Occupation	Location
Taiji	Chapter 2	Male	mid-40s	Single, never married	None	Middle class	Salaryman	Tokyo
Midori-san	Chapter 2, conclusion	Female	late 50s	Divorced	Two adult children	Upper-middle class	Shop owner	Tokyo
Wada-san	Chapters 3, 4	Female	early 50s	Divorced, living with new partner (Okada-san) but not remarried	Adult child, de facto shared custody	Upper-middle class	Consultant	Tokyo
Noriko	Chapter 3	Female	mid-30s	Seeking divorce	None	Middle class	Office worker	Tokyo suburbs
Sakurai-san	Chapter 3	Female	mid-50s	Divorced	None	Middle class	Teacher	Tokyo
Tanaka-san	Chapter 3	Female	late 50s	Divorced	Two adult children	Working class	Housewife, retired from part-time office work	Tokyo suburbs
Okada-san	Chapter 4	Male	mid-50s	Divorced, living with new partner (Wada-san) but not remarried	Two adult children, de facto shared custody	Upper-middle class	Salaryman	Tokyo
Miho	Chapter 4	Female	mid-20s	Single, parents are divorced	None	Middle class	Student	Tokyo
Endo-san	Chapter 4	Male	mid-50s	Divorced twice	One daughter; his ex-wife has custody	Middle class	Salaryman	Tokyo
Mayumi	Chapter 5	Female	mid-50s	Married, parents are divorced	Two adult children	Middle class	Housewife	Tokyo
Chiharu-san	Chapter 5	Female	early 50s	Divorced	Three adult children	Working class	Office worker	Tokyo suburbs
Yoshida-san	Chapter 6	Male	early 40s	Divorced	None	Middle class	Salaryman	Tokyo
Sekiguchi Yoko	Chapter 6	Female	mid-50s	Divorced, remarried	Two adult children	Upper-middle Class	Marriage and divorce counselor	Tokyo
Nishimura-san	Chapter 6, conclusion	Female	early 50s	Thinking about divorce	Two adult children	Middle class	Housewife, now working part-time	Tokyo suburbs
Akihoshi-san	Chapter 6	Male	mid-40s	Divorced	None	Middle class	Salaryman	Yokohama
Shoda-san	Conclusion	Female	early 50s	Thinking about divorce	None	Middle class	Office worker	Tokyo

Appendix B: All Quotes in Original Japanese

This appendix includes the original Japanese language shared in quotes in each chapter.

Chapter 1—Japan's Intimate Political Economy

Page 56—Aoyama-san discusses her frustrations with a common term for "husband":

> もともとは、旦那さんというのは、多分、おきやってわかります？女の人を買う所。吉原とか、昔江戸時代とかにそういう女の人を買うところがあって、自分のスポンサーになってくれる男の人を旦那さんと呼んでいたのですよ。だから、自分の旦那さんというのはそれから来ている言葉らしいのですけど、旦那さんというのは自分のスポンサーなのですよ。[. . .] 旦那さんというのは、私の中でスポンサー的なイメージがすごく濃いと思う。

Chapter 2—Two Tips to Avoid Divorce

Page 64—A "communication advisor" online offers tips to improve a marriage:

> 言葉のコミュニケーションは、まさに会話。ご夫婦でキャッチボールは出来ていますか？ボール（パートナーにかける言葉）すら持っていない、というご夫婦もあると思います。[. . .]そこで、私がもっとも大切に思っているのは、心のコミュニケーション。『以心伝心』とよく言われますが、これはかなりハイレベル。「わかってると思ってた」なんて、喧嘩の種にしかなりません。

Page 65—The National Chauvinistic Husbands Association's list of how husbands can recover from chauvinism:

初段 3年以上たって「妻を愛している」人
二段　家事手伝いが上手な人
三段　浮気をしたことがない人、ばれていない人
四段　レディーファーストを実践している人
五段　愛妻と手をつないで散歩ができる人
六段　愛妻の話を真剣に聞くことができる人
七段　嫁・姑問題を一夜にして解決できる人
八段　「ありがとう」をためらわずに言える人
九段　「ごめんなさい」を恐れずに言える人
十段　「愛している」を照れずに言える人
プラチナ・マスター段　妻にプラチナをプレゼントして「プロポーズ・
　アゲイン。」した

Page 67—Sadako, a semi-professional marriage counselor, explains previous problems in her own marriage:

あの頃はあの頃で普通だなって思ったんだけど。今思うともう冷め
切っていて会話もないし、毎日仕事で帰りが遅くて、子供がいなか
った時。で帰ってきて、ご飯を出して、「いただきます」も言わな
いで食べて。終わったらそのままで、お風呂入って寝ちゃうってい
う。私がもうイライラしちゃって。イライラしちゃうから強く当た
っちゃうんですよ。そしたらやっぱり、そういう夫婦が多いんです
よね。だからこのままじゃマズイと思って穏やかにして自分を。毎
日笑顔を忘れずに「お帰り」とか「ただいま」とか、挨拶を自分か
ら多くするようになって。で、少しづつだんなもそれに答えてくれ
るようになって。一杯私が話しかけるの。会話が一番大事だと思う
から、夫婦にとって。

Page 67—The author speaks with Fujita-san, who refers to "love like air" to describe his marriage:

アリー：プロポーズはしましたか？
藤田さん：一応しましたよ。したけど、そんな「結婚してください」
　とかそういうんじゃなくて。でもうちの奥さんも多分全然結婚す
　る気だったんだと思うんで。自然に。どうする？　　いつ来る？
　みたいな。じゃあ今度の3月でいいかなみたいな。そういう
　ノリ...でした。そんなテレビとか映画のような「アイ・ラーブ・
　ユー」みたいなのはなかった。自分もうちの奥さん。もよく言っ
　ているのは、2人とも空気みたいな人。

アリー：どういう意味ですか？

藤田さん：要は、なきゃ困る。空気だから、なきゃ困る。でもあっ
　　ても邪魔じゃない。

Page 68—Fujita-san explains that absurdly high phone bills also contributed
to his decision to get married:

> 結婚したきっかけは、やっぱり経済的なこと。自分が千葉まで車で
> 奥さんを送迎していたけど、高速代やガソリン代がかかって。あと
> は電話代。今みたいに携帯も無いし、電話料金が八万円にもなっ
> た。毎日話していたから。うちの奥さんが年下だから電話代ぐらい
> は自分が持とうと思って、かかってくると一回切って、こっちから
> かけ直した。なるべくうちの奥さんに負担をかけないようにね。で
> も八万円を超えた時はね。だって家賃より高かったから。

Page 71—The author talks with Osada-san about her husband's problematic
reaction when they considered having children:

アリー：子どもが欲しかったんですか？

長田さん：欲しかった。

アリー：彼は？

長田さん：そうそう。。。でも彼は、子供が生まれるまで、僕が赤
　　ちゃんになってあげるって言ってて。こんなおっきい赤ちゃんい
　　らないって思ってましたね。甘えっ子。日本の男の人そういう人
　　多いよね。奥さんに、お母さん代わりにしちゃう。奥さんをお母
　　さんみたいにしちゃう。だから、母ちゃん呼ばれてましたよ、結
　　婚してから。母ちゃん、母ちゃんって言われて、オカーチャンジ
　　ャナイヨ！

Page 77—Midori-san describes the kind of relationship she would like:

> 私は女で、相手は男で、ちゃんとこう自転車をこぎ合う関係をね？
> 私の人生でやり残したことをやりたい、もう一度。あ、もう一度じ
> ゃないわね。一度でいいからやってみたい。結婚中やれなかったこ
> とだった。セクシュアリティはね、子どもを作るってこと、私は無
> 理かもしれない、セクスの部分とか。ちょっとほど遠いかなと思
> う。それがね、今の私の夢かな。恋人募集中です。よろしく。紹介
> して。(笑う)

Chapter 3—Constructing Mutuality

Page 98—Mariko explains how she and her ex-husband began the legal process of divorce:

> あとは、私たちってわりとすんなり問題なくできたほうだと思っていて、出たあとに3〜4回2人で会って御飯食べて話したりして、私はもう絶対戻る気はないからって言ったら彼もわかってくれたみたいで、最終的には弁護士とか調停とかなく、二人で離婚しました。もともと2人で一緒の貯金とかってしてなくて、口座も二人で別々にあって、生活費も、彼が...何か忘れちゃったけど、家賃は折半で、食費は私で、っていうふうに別々に結婚してるときは払ってたから、ふたりで一緒にしてたものを分けるとか、そういうお金の面では面倒くさいことは無かった。そうだったらまた違ってたと思うんだけれど。

Page 99—Wada-san describes her reasons for seeking a divorce:

> それも私はすごい怒る、夫に怒る。すごい大ゲンカ。で、子どもは泣く。最悪ですよね。でも、日本の男の人は月曜から金曜までずっと会社に行っていて、遅くまで会社にいて、まあお酒を飲んだり、付き合いだって言って。本当に大変な時に全然手伝ってくれないんですよ。一日ぐらい早く帰って買い物してくれるとか、助けてくれることは全くない。休みの日は自分だけ出かけちゃったりするんですよ。意地悪ですね、最後はね。自分だけ靴とか洋服も買っちゃうし。自分は働いているから必要なんだって言うんですよ。で、買っちゃうのね。ちょっと私は面白くなかった。[...] 女が我慢するっていうのは仕方ないのかなっていう感じはありましたね。おかしいわよね? まるでね、お手伝いさんみたいなの。メイドみたいなの

Page 100—Wada-san narrates signing divorce forms and waiting a year for her husband to sign them:

> 別居中に私が離婚届に自分でサインして印鑑も押して、彼に預けておいたんです。郵便で送って預けておいたんです。そしたら彼が1年経ったぐらいから...あの、電話が来て、「僕もハンコを押して出しておいたよ」って。これはすごく彼もすっきりしていた。お互い新しいスタートをもう切るんだなっていう事が分かったみたい。私はもう...元の家庭はもう元に戻らないから、彼の新しいスタートを切んなきゃいけないのね。それが分かったみたいで、とてもね、明るかった。だから今も、まあ、友達というか。友達になっていますね。

Page 101—Noriko describes how upset she is when her husband delayed their divorce by refusing to sign the forms:

年末に帰って話したの。「もうちょっと別れることにしたい」って、「まぁおまえの決めたことだから、わかった」って。まぁそれで終わったんだけど、彼がぁ、彼のご両親に、まだ話してなかった。彼が、私の両親に話さないのはまだいいんだけど、彼は、彼の両親に話してなかったの。[. . .] だから一、彼に、それは私も言っとくけど、私もその方が良いと思うから、あの、伝えてねって言う風に、あーん、言っとくけど、話をしてたの。「言っとくね」って話をした。それで、じゃぁ今年の、それじゃぁ1月25日に出そうと思って。もう会社も休んで、一日休んで、ずっと準備してたの。準備は、会社を休んで、書類を出して、免許証の、名前とか変えて、あと銀行に行いかなきゃとか。午前中にあそこに行って、もう戸籍を取って変えたら、これをもらって、あそこへ行って免許証を変えて、一生懸命考えてたの。まずお父さんに電話して、あの、「明日出すから」やっぱね、報告で、電話したの。

Page 103—Sakurai-san describes the lingering affection she and her ex-husband had for each other:

離婚もしない、それでこのまま別居したまま離婚もしないで何年もいるのは私の将来も考えていかなくちゃならないですよね。それじゃ弁護士を立てましょうってことで母の友達の息子さんが弁護士をしていたのでちょっと頼んだんですね、まあ調停という形で彼も来て、別れるんだったら慰謝料はいくらかっていう話をしたんです。でもその間も、本当にお互い嫌いだ！っていったのとちょっと違うので、で、私とも別れるっていうことを決めてね、はっきりすればこちらも、私もなんていうかな、離婚したくない、彼のことがまだ好きだという気持ちがあったので、もし戻れるんだったら戻りたい、でも女の人と付き合うならもう無理だ、っていうようなことで、私も相手次第って言うところがあったんですよね。

Page 103—Sakurai-san narrates the long process of waiting for her husband to sign the divorce forms and the confusing gifts he brought her after they were divorced:

彼も、離婚届、私が印鑑押して彼のところに残して、で、私は東京に戻ったんですね、でも、それでも彼は押さないでずっと持ってたんです。で、結局一年後に彼はおして手続きをしたんですね。でも、そんなことしてるのに、なんか誕生日にコーチ、コーチって分かる？誕生日にはもう離婚届だしてるんですよね。だしたあとに、メロンを出張に行ったからっていって送ってきたり、まあ、優柔不断、はっきり決められないっていう、すごい、今から思えばほんとに腹が立つんだけどそうゆうことが、でもそのときはそのやさしさに私も引っ張られてまあ、彼もいい面はすごくあったので、でもいい面にひ

きずられ、ひきずられじゃないですね、まあやっぱりぐじゅぐじゅ
ぐじゅぐじゅしたってところがありますね。

Page 105—Tanaka-san remembers her husband's violent threats about sign-ing the divorce forms:

あれだけ、早くもってこいもってこいって言っときながら目が真っ
赤なのよ。で、結局自分が、お金、お給料とってまあまあの暮らし
してたわけじゃない、私は働かないで、だから別れればお金もない
し、生活できるわけがないから、わかられるはずがないと思ったん
じゃないの、相手は。でもあれだけ、自分の方から何度も何度も離
婚用紙もってこいって言ったんだから、それで、いざ持ってきたと
きに、真っ赤に泣きはらして。

Chapter 4—Families Together and Apart

Page 114—Wada-san describes how she and her ex-husband shared custody of their daughter:

彼と娘は会っている。でも私と彼は会わない。電話で「今度の日曜
日、会いたいんだけど」って言うと、「ああ、いいですよ。じゃ、
ちゃんと送ってきてね。」って。で、どこか遊びに行って、遊園地
に遊びに行って。で、時間になるとちゃんと家まで、駅まで送って
くれて。一緒に駅まで来てくれて。改札口でバイバイして。「楽し
かった？」って言って。そうするとね、「なんでお父さん、帰っち
ゃうの？」とかって言って、困らせる。

Page 115—Wada-san further narrates how she made a point to tell her daugh-ter about her father's contributions:

だんなも、うちも全部賃貸だったので、慰謝料は、私はもらいませ
んでした。請求しませんでした。なぜかというと、私の方から離婚
したいという風に彼にお願いをしたから。そんなに2人ともお金はな
かったです。本当にお金は全然何にもなくて。彼は彼1人で生きてい
く、私は私で娘と一緒に生きていく。彼は自分のお給料の中から養
育費をずっとくれてます。それはもう一回も休まずにくれてます。
私は銀行に行ってキャッシュ・ディスペンサーでお金を出して、それ
を子供に見せて「これはお父さんがくれたお金で、これからこれで
買い物に行くよ」って。ちゃんとお金をもらって、そのおかげで修
学旅行の新しい洋服とか、欲しいものをね、買うことができるって
いうのをね、言ってます。

Page 116—Wada-san explains the challenges that came with new stepparents:

子供はまだいないみたいだけど。前の主人の新しい奥さんの家に娘が遊びに行っているんです。すごい可愛がってくれて。でもうちの娘はちょっと意地が悪いから、新しい奥さんの前で「パパを取らないで」ってやってるんだと思う。

Page 116—Okada-san reflects on his inability to become a "former parent" or "ex-father":

奥さんとは離婚して別れたら、まあ、気にはなるけど、もう他人でしょ？でも子供は絶対他人にはならないでしょ？だから子供のことはいつでも気になる。それは普通かな。どこでも。私はそうです。

Page 118—As quoted in a newspaper article, Hasegawa Kyoko delineates potential problems if parents are forced to share custody:

もし、別居親が同居親の子育て方針に反対を乱発したら、子育ては行き詰まり、子どもの福祉を損ねます。対立するたびに裁判所の判断を仰ぐなら、生活と子育てを1人で担う同居親の負担は、時間、金銭、心理的ストレスの面で途方もなく大きくなります。それは経済的、社会的、時間的に追い詰められがちなひとり親から、子育てに必要なゆとりを奪います。そういう影響は司法の体制改善などで乗り越えられるものではありません。

Chapter 5—The Cost of Divorce

Page 140—Sato-san reflects on her sense of changing attitudes about how divorce might hurt children:

大筋は大体いっしょなんでしょうね。子供の事とか色々あると思いますよ。大体はいっしょじゃろう思うけど、女の人がそんなん言うたらいかんけど。また日本の女の人言うたら辛抱がいい、言うたらちょっと語弊があるかもしれんけどね。子供のために辛抱するような人が昔は多かったですからね。それが段々と欧米風に似て自分の人生じゃないんだから子供のためだけに離婚するゆうね。。。そやけど子供のためにこういさかいばっかりしよるよりは別れた方が子供の為にはいいいう説も聞いた事はありますよね。

Page 142—Ando-san describes when and how she feels the potential stigma of divorce:

アリー：離婚した人がデートしたいとかお付き合いをしたいというのは恥ずかしいことですか？

安藤さん：ちょっと言えない。だからやっぱり素敵だなって思う人がいても、なかなか言い出せないかもしれない。でも付き合うときにはやっぱり失礼だから、実はって。やっぱり最初は言いつらいよね。恋愛感情がない普通の友達だったら言えるかもしれないけれど、この人いいなって思う人には言いづらいかも。

Page 148—Mae reflects on how much harder divorce has been than she expected:

離婚したときはそうなんだけど、そう思ったから、「もうそれはいい、オッケー」と思ったけど、今、私の生活がすごく大変なので。今は彼も私も、私もうちょっと自分でいろんなことができることと思ったし、しっかりしていると思ったし、いろんなことをなんでも割りとできた。例えば、英語を勉強するのも、適度に英語が喋れた、タイ語もすれば適度に喋れる、外国に行けば、外国人の友達が適度にすぐ出来る、日本にいても、いろんな人とうまくすぐできる。[. . .] 怖いものがなかった。失敗も怖くないし。だけど、今、レベルが下がったら、怖いものもいっぱいだし、上手くいかない事の方が多いし。

Page 150—Mae describes her losses after divorce:

結婚する前、いつもモテてた。いつも男の人からの人気はあったけど、今は全然ないし、仕事もないし、人気もないし、自信もないし、何もない。

Notes

Introduction

1. Significant anthropological attention has been paid to intimacy and companionate romance, including work in Japan (Ryang 2006), Hong Kong (Adrian 2003), China (Rofel 2007; Santos and Harrell 2016; Yan 2003), Nepal (Ahearn 2001), India (Reddy 2006), Papua New Guinea (Wardlow 2006), Spain (Collier 1997), Mexico (Hirsch 2003), and Brazil (Rebhun 2002). Scholars in other fields have explored how intimacy impacts society and social relationships (Beck and Beck-Gernsheim 1995; Illouz 2012; Jamieson 1988; Rubin 1983).

2. For instance, Japan Airlines (JAL) was privatized in 1985, Japan's National Railway (JR) was privatized in 1987, and regulations for taxis in Tokyo and Osaka were relaxed in 1994 (La Croix and Mak 2001). As I discuss in greater detail in chapter 1, Prime Minister Koizumi made privatizing the Japanese Postal Bank his legislative priority in 2005, and his successful campaign clearly linked corporate privatization with personal (self) responsibility (Porges and Leong 2006).

3. In Japanese, these words all begin with the same character, *ji* (自), which is the first character in the term for "self" (*jibun*, 自分). As I describe later in chapter 2, scholars have long argued that Japanese understandings of selfhood are particularly connected and relational, a point Senko Maynard connects with the etymology of "*jibun*." She says that "*Jibun* literally means 'portion given to the self,' that is, a portion appropriately distributed to a person out of a larger whole, a piece of the pie, so to speak. At the level of etymology, *jibun* implies that the self is not an autonomous entity entirely disconnected from society" (Maynard 1997, 38). Because these newer, neoliberal buzzwords all use "self" (自) but not "part" (分), the same logic implies that the neoliberal terminology is less interested in seeing the self as part of anything larger.

4. In a telling, if extreme, example of "self-responsibility" rhetoric put into practice, three Japanese citizens taken hostage in Iraq were publicly shamed and made to repay the government for part of the costs of their rescue. When two freelance journalists and one aid worker were first taken hostage in April 2004, media and popular sentiment seemed very much on their side. But after they were released, media coverage viciously attacked the former hostages as selfish and naive, suggesting they wasted taxpayers' money by being so irresponsible as to require rescue. Ultimately, after receiving hate mail, they were billed about $21,000 for their rescue (Inoue 2007).

5. For instance, scholars have examined discourse about romance and intimacy in Japan (Ryang 2006; McLelland 2012) and China (Lee 2007; Rofel 2007).

6. For instance, see Malik and Courtney (2011); Zuhur (2003); Reniers (2003).

7. Revealing that people around me spontaneously create reading groups feels like evidence of some deep truth about my personality. In this case the group was created by Kimura-san, who, after his painful divorce and happy remarriage, had retired to focus on learning things he hadn't had time for when he was working.

8. Scholars in other fields also found it hard, if not impossible, to interview pairs of divorced spouses (Hiller and Philliber 1985; Maccoby and Mnookin 1992, 14).

9. Other scholars have used the term "retrospective reimaginings" but have not linked it to families, intimate relationships, or divorce (Cunneen 2011; Fuchs et al. 2011; Shahani 2008).

10. Of course, gay, lesbian, and queer people can legally participate in marriage, as long as they marry a person of a different gender. Scholarship within and beyond Japan demonstrates that some queer people decide to participate in heterosexual marriage in order to satisfy familial requests, demonstrate filial piety, or balance personal desires with what they see as their responsibilities (Brainer 2017; Cho 2009; Engbretsen 2014, 57; Lunsing 1995; McClelland 2000, 464). In my research, no person leaving a heterosexual marriage told me that their marriage had been a "paper" marriage nor, to my knowledge, subsequently began a relationship with someone of the same sex.

11. That said, a number of people were invested in "proving" things to me, and thus I was inundated with many gigabits of evidence demonstrating extramarital affairs and other marital problems. I always appreciated people sharing such personal information with me and categorically took them at their word. Rather than trying to confirm anything, I recognize such gestures as attempts to solidify and confirm wounding betrayals. Precisely because divorce can seem to come out of nowhere, and forces a reassessment of a relationship that had seemed clear and predictable, people sought confirmation that they reacted rationally and reasonably.

12. In order to protect the privacy of people who contributed to this project, all names and some identifying details have been changed.

Chapter One

1. Before they got married, Mariko and her boyfriend hadn't lived together, and therefore Mariko wasn't able to experience her husband's domestic expectations in practice until after they were married. Cohabitation before marriage is not particularly common in Japan, with between 10 and 20 percent of couples doing so (Raymo, Iwasawa, and Bumpass 2009, 787).

2. For analysis of how housewives felt engaged with, and fundamental to, the national economic project see Goldstein-Gidoni (2012); Imamura (1987); LeBlanc (1999); Vogel with Vogel (2013). For parallel research about male white-collar workers linking their labor with the national project, see Rohlen (1974) and Vogel (1971). Cole (1971) and Roberts (1994) focus on blue-collar workers, and Bernstein (1983), Kelly (1990), and Mulgan (2000) explore attitudes among farmers and agricultural workers.

3. The term in Japanese is pronounced as a loan word from English and written in the katakana characters that explicitly mark it as a "foreign" word, although it probably won't make sense to any English speakers who don't also speak Japanese. The term can be glossed as *sarariiman*, *sarariman*, or *salaryman*. In this chapter, I choose to use the latter, and I pluralize it to *salarymen*, which doesn't happen in Japanese.

4. Scholarship examining salarymen during the economic boom and bubble includes Allison (1994); Bestor (1989); Kumazawa (1996); Ogasawara (1998); Vogel (1971). More recent scholarship, which is also analyzed in the next chapter, explores how salarymen responded to the

Heisei recessions and economic restructuring from roughly 1991 until 2010 (Dasgupta 2013; Hidaka 2010).

5. For more on the complex relationship between masculinity and militarism in a nation with a constitutional prohibition against any military other than self-defense forces, see Frühstück (2007). As of this writing, the Japanese Diet is beginning to make changes to military policy that might allow Japanese forces to participate in more than just self-defense.

6. For instance, the series *Salaryman Kintaro* tells the story of a reformed hooligan (*bōsōzoku*) who becomes a tough, nonconformist salaryman. Many foreign films also represent Japan through salarymen, often using them to signal the weird, dysfunctional, or illegal effects of collectivist groupthink, for example *Lost in Translation* (Coppola 2003), *Rising Sun* (Kaufman 1993), and *Die Hard* (McTeirnan 1988).

7. The lifetime employment system itself has been used as evidence in culturalist arguments about Japan. In that logic, the seemingly irrational decision to guarantee employment must be evidence of inherent Japanese preferences for collectivism or group orientation (Johnson 1982; Sugimoto and Mouer 1980, 8). In fact, the lifetime employment promise was developed in the early twentieth century in response to a labor shortage and as an effort to retain employees who moved between jobs with great frequency (Gordon 1985; Schregle 1993).

8. Despite the lack of explicit contractual guarantee, in the 1970s and 1980s, Japanese employees were less likely to switch jobs, compared with Americans and Europeans (Tachibanaki 1987). During that period, longer job tenure and lower job mobility were more likely to occur in larger firms (Clark and Ogawa 1992).

9. These figures trace the likelihood that a woman is working in any type of paid labor, not only full-time work. Although women are increasingly likely to work for pay, that labor is also likely to be in part-time, nonregular work (Nakamatsu 1994).

10. The 1966 case that ended this practice was brought by a female employee of Sumitomo Cement who had been fired upon her marriage. The standard work contract she had signed stipulated that she would voluntarily "retire" upon marriage, or at age thirty-five. The Tokyo District Court ruled that this contract was "unreasonable discrimination based on sex," and ultimately the parties reached a settlement (Knapp 1995, 104; Upham 187, 127).

11. This policy was challenged in 1983, in a case brought by four female employees of Nissan Motor Corporation who were breadwinners in their families. Nissan had refused to pay them any "family allowance," which would have been an additional 10 percent of their salaries. At first, Nissan only paid male employees this allowance, and then created a new policy saying that the money would only go to people who were the legal household head (*setai nushi*), a designation in the household registry (*koseki*). As I explain more in chapter 3, it is possible but extremely unusual and frankly stigmatizing for a married woman to be the household head. In 1989 the Tokyo District Court ruled that this policy could be put in place at the company's discretion. After the plaintiffs appealed to the Supreme Court, but before that judgment was reached, Nissan changed its policy to pay "family allowance" to any female employee who was supporting her family, regardless of her role in the household registry (Knapp 1995, 105).

12. Akabayashi (2006, 354) includes a concise description of how deductions are calculated, explaining that dependent spouses who make between 700,000 and 1.35 million yen ($7,000 and $13,500) will have their deduction reduced in almost a linear fashion in segments of 50,000 yen ($500). Although specific thresholds have changed, the overall pattern remains (Takahashi et al. 2009; Yokoyama and Kodama 2018).

13. Women who make between ¥1.03 million and ¥1.41 million face a particularly high marginal tax rate. For instance, because any worker who makes more than ¥1.3 million must begin to

pay their own social security contribution, a woman who makes over that threshold must earn ¥1.44 million just to break even (Takahashi et al. 2009).

14. In the national pension system, since 1986, if a wife earns less than ¥1.1 million ($11,000) in a year, her required pension contributions are covered by her husband's employer. The pension system, therefore, "treats women differently depending on to whom they are married" (Estevez-Abe 2008, 27). Such a model only makes sense if this wife is imagined to be so fundamental to her husband's labor that she should be rewarded with her own pension (Shimada 1993, cited in Nakamatsu 1994, 92).

15. This tension between Mr. Yamaguchi and his wife reflects commonly felt tensions caused by too close a connection between spouses, especially after the husband retires. One guidebook suggests to husbands "keep a degree of distance from your wife. [. . .] If you don't want to be deserted by your wife, leave her her own space and respect her as a human being" (Hirokane 2014, 160–61, cited in Mathews 2017, 236).

16. In the 1980s, one pattern compared annoying husbands to garbage (*sodai gomi*, literally: garbage so large you have to pay to get rid of it) or wet leaves (*nure ochiba*), which are clingy and hard to clean up. Taking such rhetorical patterns seriously, we also need to be aware of the ways in which these highly gendered performances of complaining might reflect the social norms of female talk about (annoying) husbands, rather than actual annoying husbands (Lebra 1984, 124; Salamon 1975). Sometimes it's true, sometimes it's just fun to complain, and sometimes the truth is somewhere in between.

17. *Chōnan* (長男) literally means "eldest son" but immediately connotes a broad set of structural burdens and benefits. Imagined as the child most responsible for continuing the family line, eldest sons are typically expected to take care of their aging parents and any family business. Domestic responsibilities usually fall to the eldest son's wife, and the ethnographic record is full of women discussing the extra burdens of marrying a *chōnan*, particularly one in a farming family (Bernstein 1983, 44; Lebra 1984, 151; Rosenberger 2001, 55, 154). These attitudes persist despite the relative frequency of someone other than the oldest son inheriting (Bachnik 1983, 163). Women with whom I spoke in the early 2000s used "*chōnan*" as a shorthand for self-absorbed sons who were raised in conditions of indulgence, and therefore might make difficult husbands. In Mrs. Nomura's case, her husband was particularly spoiled because he was the only male born in *two* generations (i.e., his maternal grandfather's only male offspring). His mother's husband had married into their family as an adopted son-in-law (*muko yoshi*).

18. For instance, a 2004 survey found that most non-regular workers were assigned the same tasks as regular workers but were paid between 58.9 and 69.8 percent of that wage (Japanese Trade Union Confederation 2006, 45; Song 2014, 97).

19. Dispatch labor, i.e., temporary employees dispatched by an agency, has been shaped by a series of laws that mostly expanded the opportunities for this kind of work. In 1986, the Manpower Dispatching Worker Act (Rōdōsha hakenhō) restricted dispatch workers to twenty-six specialized and specific jobs. A 1999 revision greatly expanded the list of jobs open to dispatch workers. The 2003 revision, detailed above, further expanded the opportunities to hire dispatch workers and permitted contracts lasting three years, increased from one year. In 2012, the most recent legal revision attempted to create protections for dispatch workers, including prohibiting work contracts that are less than thirty days (Japan Institute for Labour Policy and Training 2016, 41).

20. Japanese language doesn't have space between words as does English, so "Train Man" is written with three characters together: 電車男. Various people have translated the term with slightly different punctuation, and TrainMan or Train-Man could both be accurate. I use

"train_man" because it is the gloss used in the film version (Murakami 2005), which includes impressive techniques for visually representing digital text on screen.

21. Indeed if the story was fictional—if the initial narration of what happened on the train doesn't reflect real events—the creator/author nevertheless did a fantastic job of guessing a topic and creating characters that many people would find compelling. The significance of the story doesn't hinge on its veracity but on its popularity as an interactive exchange (people posting on a bulletin board) and a narrative successful across various media forms.

22. The film *Tokyo Sonata* (Kurosawa 2008) similarly represents a salaryman removed from his previous position of social authority and security (Arai 2016, 31–32; Dasgupta 2011).

23. Aoyama-san's husband brings us back to earlier discussions of extramarital affairs and their efficacy as a measure of the quality of a marriage. The ethnographic record shows that marriages built on disconnected dependence often included sexuality as realm in which spouses might be disconnected, and therefore male extramarital affairs did not immediately present as a reason to end the marriage (Allison 1994, 106; Dore 1999 [1958], 180; Lin 2012). Moore (2010, 65) found a common distinction between two terms for extramarital affairs: *uwaki* describes only men's affairs and is imagined not to be so serious, while *furin* describes all affairs by women and "serious" affairs by men. Elaborating on this distinction in a potentially self-serving way, one sixty-eight-year-old man says "Unless one's heart is in it, it doesn't count as an affair" (ibid.).

24. *-katsu* is appended to other terms to indicate a concerted search or intentional preparation, including *shūkatsu* (終活), elderly people preparing for the end of their lives; *ninkatsu* (妊活), a dedicated effort to getting pregnant; *tomokatsu* (友活), a search for new friends; and even *rikatsu* (離活), preparing for a divorce. I have not heard these terms used as popularly as *konkatsu* (婚活).

25. Examining how female earning potential impacts the likelihood of marriage, Fukuda (2013) demonstrates that attitudes toward women's paid labor shifted between generations. In the generation born in the 1960s and coming of age in the 1980s, during the height of Japan's bubble economy, a woman with high earnings was less likely to be married. By contrast, for the generation born in the 1970s and coming of age during the 1990s recession, the inverse was true. This captures a shift in understandings about what makes a marriage secure, from "traditional" gender roles to collective earning potential.

Chapter Two

1. Scholarship and surveys make clear that violence and abuse are among the most common reasons for divorce, particularly for women (Kozu 1999; Yoshihama and Sorenson 1994, 64). The (jokey) guidebook I cite in this chapter's opening lists the top reasons for later-life divorce in order as: no help with housework, verbal abuse, husband is generally useless (*kaishō ga nai*), husband had an affair, alcohol (*sakeguse ga warui*), husband's violence, and debt (*shakkin*) (TBS Program Staff 2006, 9). Popular websites make similar claims, with one suggesting that as of 2018, the first reason for both men and women is a mismatch of personalities (*seikaku no fuicchi*). For women, the second most popular reason is violence (*bōryoku*). For men, the second most popular reason is an extramarital affair (*uwaki nado no isei kankei*), and violence is the ninth most popular (https://ricon-pro.com/columns/10/#toc_anchor-1-1).

2. This practice is no longer as prevalent as it once was but was built from the premise that if a person knew he or she was dying, the experience would be even more stressful and difficult. Therefore, especially for patients with cancer, Japanese medical professionals regularly did not

inform a patient of a terminal diagnosis and relied on family members to decide if the patient should be told. Although this system might seem distasteful or patronizing, it meshed with doctors' paternalistic attitudes and a sense that the doctors were trained and able to bear the burden of terminal diagnoses (Annas and Miller 1994; Higuchi 1992). I thank China Scherz for pointing out that such strategic silences by doctors surrounding terminal diagnoses are not limited to Japan (Harris, Shao, and Sugarman 2003).

3. For instance, this advice appears in a wide range of marital and divorce guidebooks, from those directed at "saving" marriages (Ikeuchi 2002, 2005; Okano 2005; Waki 2009), to attempts to diagnose problems particular among middle-aged couples (Ikeuchi 2006), to advice specifically for men (Muroi et al. 2006; Watanabe 2004). Commenting on the overlap between violence and verbalized affection, Kuwajima (2019, 120) found that advisors at domestic violence shelters emphasize that "there are many men who hit women while saying 'I love you.'"

4. This quote came originally from a webpage offering advice about marriages and divorce, particularly for older couples during the lead-up to the 2007 pension law change. Although it is no longer at the original address, it can be found searching the Internet Archive (www.web .archive.org) for http://www.jukunen-rikon.com/2007/03/post_37.html.

5. This list was originally published on the organization's website: http://www.zenteikyou .com/.

6. At the same time that the benefits of air-like relationships are being questioned in intimate relationships, a relatively new insult derides people who "can't read the air" (kūki ga yomenai; often shortened to KY)—that is, those who are socially oblivious or clueless. The insult derived from this idea is not limited to intimate relationships and is instead a general term to describe a socially awkward person. I thank Laura Miller for bringing up this point. Moreover, Roquet claims discourse about KY actively ignores how social and structural contexts are built, instead imagining them as naturally occurring (Roquet 2016, 15).

7. Like "Thank you for this meal," an expression Sadako used above in this quote, the phrases she uses here are everyday greetings that are very typically used to demonstrate the kind of "polite speech" that should occur within healthy families. These are aisatsu phrases, which are commonly recognized greetings and responses. Elsewhere I have written about Japanese marital guidebooks suggesting the regular use of aisatsu as a way to improve one's marriage (Alexy 2011b, 896).

8. In Japan, only the person placing a call is charged; someone receiving a call isn't charged at all. In this situation, Fujita-san was being generous and bearing the cost of all the phone calls between himself and his future wife, even when she initiated many calls.

9. At the height of Japan's global economic power, "Japanese trade negotiators used to make maximum use of the alleged cultural uniqueness of Japanese society and benefited by mystifying Japan's social practices" (Sugimoto 1999, 88). For instance, in 1987, Former Agriculture Minister Hata Tsutomo asserted Japan could not import more beef because Japanese stomachs are different and could only digest local meat (Krauss and Naoi 2010; Robinson 1987; Sugimoto 2003, 184).

10. Although Doi clearly states that amae tendencies likely exist in all humans (before they are emphasized or reduced through socialization), he also makes clear his investment in Japan's "national character" (Doi 1973, 65). Because a national character is necessarily totalizing—assuming similarity and minimizing difference—this move pulls Doi theories more directly into Nihonjinron.

11. Working with American white-collar workers who had been laid off, Lane (2011, 45) found that some eschewed dependence to such an extent that they characterized desire for any secure employment as an act of weakness.

12. In this case, Smith is referring to how Japanese speakers will use different first-person pronouns depending on the context and the person to whom they are speaking. There are different pronouns for "I," including those which index masculinity, femininity, formality, and informality, all in relative terms (Abe 2004; Miyazaki 2004).

13. Anthropologists' theorization of Japanese selfhood has extended over multiple decades, including Bachnik and Quinn (1994), Lebra (2004), Ohnuki-Tierney (1993), Ozawa-de Silva (2006), Rosenberger (1992, 2001), and Smith (1983). Cave (2007, 31–43) provides a particularly trenchant timeline and analysis of scholarship about this topic.

Chapter Three

1. Name stamps (*inkan* or *hanko*) are commonly requested for formal notifications. Every adult has a name stamp—the cheapest cost only a few hundred yen (approximately $5)—and is accustomed to using it to fill out paperwork. In many ways, *inkan* function as signatures do in the United States: as formal proof of a person's identity.

2. Only lawyers or legal scholars mentioned this phrase directly to me, but, as demonstrated throughout this chapter, many nonspecialists voiced similar preferences and/or organized their lives to reflect this idea.

3. During the Tokugawa era (1603–1868), there were four regular categories of social status—warriors, farmers, artisans, and merchants—in addition to the "untouchable" status of "filth" (*eta*) or "nonpersons" (*hinin*). Registering citizens in social classes influenced the later creation of the mandatory "household registration" (*koseki*) system, discussed later in this chapter.

4. Books I, II, and III of the Civil Code, pertaining to general rights, property rights, and torts, respectively, were promulgated in 1896, but the two books pertaining to family law and inheritance were promulgated in 1898 (Hatoyama 1902, 300; Oda 2009, 113). The promulgation of the new Civil Code in 1898 prompted a sudden drop in the divorce rate, from a high of 3.39 in 1883 (Fuess 2004, 3).

5. Although laws required all members of a family to obey the household head, in court, they could accuse the household head of abuse of power (Akiba and Ishikawa 1995, 589). Burns (2009) includes compelling examples of cases brought to family courts in the early Meiji period.

6. Examples of the daily, lived realities of structural positions within an *ie* are demonstrated in greater detail in many ethnographies of Japanese family life, including Alexy (2011a); Bernstein (1983); Hamabata (1991); Hidaka (2010); Lebra (1976); Vogel with Vogel (2013); and White (2002). See also Nomura-san's case, in chapter 1.

7. Proto-*koseki* existed in Japan as early as 654 CE, but the immediate antecedent to the system operationalized during the Meiji period was the Tokugawa-era requirement that every household formally register membership in a Buddhist temple (Chapman and Krogness 2014; Krogness 2011, 65–66). This system was designed to verify that no citizens were Christian, a religion that had been outlawed by the Tokugawa government (Cornell and Hayami 1986; Jansen 2000, 57).

8. Krogness (2014) describes specifics of how the *koseki* system has changed over time. For parallel discussion of changes in the law and practices pertaining to the *ie* system, see Tanaka (1980); Toshitani (1994); and Watanabe (1963).

9. Divorce is recorded by removing one spouse (and any children whose custody they hold) from their marital *koseki*. This removal remains visible and, as I discuss in chapter 5, contributes to stigma.

10. *Koseki* documents were effective tools for discrimination and were regularly used by potential employers, schools, and marriage partners to check on "appropriate" family history (Tsubuku and Brasor 1996, 83). In 1969, after activism from Buraku organizations, a law was passed to close these records to public view precisely because they offered, and continue to offer, fodder for discrimination (Hah and Lapp 1978).

11. In contemporary cases, there are examples of one staffer refusing a notification or *koseki* change that is eventually accepted by a different staffer, perhaps in a different office (Mackie 2014, 206). Chen reports that an effective tactic for people trying to accomplish a controversial registration can be to simply try different offices until they find a friendly staffer who complies (Chen 2014, 235). My own experiences lead me to believe that, like any bureaucratic system run by humans, the finely tuned *koseki* registration system includes more variations based on idiosyncrasies than might first be visible.

12. In this course of my research, this was the only instance I heard directly from someone who used a "divorce nonacceptance" form, although such stories are occasionally reported in the media (Yomiuri 1992, 1996), especially in advice columns (Yoshihiko 1996). Ninomiya (2005, 92) estimates that in 2002, about 40,000 such forms were submitted in Japan.

13. In one example of gender difference encoded in law, until 2015, women were required to wait six months before they were allowed to remarry (Japanese Civil Code, Article 733). After a Supreme Court decision in 2015, women now have to wait 100 days. Men can register a new marriage at any time and, as I discuss in chapter 4, one person with whom I spoke said her husband remarried the very day after their divorce. This legal difference was originally intended to verify paternity. By restricting women from remarrying immediately, any unknown pregnancy will become apparent before the woman remarries, allowing the "real" father to be legally designated. The Japanese Civil Code, Article 772, delineates the presumptions associated with paternity: any child born to a married woman is assumed to be her husband's child, and any child born within 300 days of a divorce is assumed to be her ex-husband's child. This logic, of course, ignores the possibility of a woman's extramarital affairs or genetic paternity testing. Like separate surnames for spouses, this law has been a target of many activists who argue that there are now much more accurate ways to judge paternity (Matsushima 1997; White 2018). As suggested by Burns (2009) and Goldfarb (2019), "genetics" as an *idea* is extremely important in Japanese family law and is given precedence over testable genetic relationships. When women are not allowed to remarry immediately, legally defined paternity is being preferred over genetically defined paternity.

14. The "negotiation" to which Sakurai-san refers are meetings conducted by their lawyer in his office, as opposed to the mediation ordered and conducted by the family court.

15. See, for instance, Dewar (2000); Halley (2011a, 2011b); Hasday (2014); and Nicola (2010).

16. This disinterest in using law to solve problems might reflect more general attitudes toward law, what has been called "Japanese legal consciousness" (*hō ishiki*) and specifically seeks to explain relatively low per capita litigation rates, as well as people's preference for informal mediation rather than formal court cases (Kawashima 1967). On the surface, when the vast majority of Japanese people settle family conflicts without directly engaging the formal legal system, it might appear to confirm the simplest images of Japanese legal consciousness. Elsewhere I argue that people are deciding to settle conflicts in this manner because they are socially cognizant of the many benefits available from it, including substantial restrictions that come within the formal family law system, court-appointed mediators who might espouse deeply conservative views on family norms, and the sheer amount of time it would take to reach an agreement working within the system (Alexy forthcoming).

Chapter Four

1. According to news reports, their divorce was of the "mutual" (*kyōgi*) type. As described in the previous chapter, this type of divorce is accomplished when spouses both agree to the divorce. Supposedly Koizumi's female family members—including his mother and sisters—and political advisors convinced him to ask for a divorce and pressured Kayoko to sign the papers (Reitman 2001). Koizumi also sought custody of the youngest son, who was then not yet born, but it was not granted.

2. Legally married spouses in Japan hold a privileged position in comparison with unmarried partners, getting tax breaks, inheriting property, and being allowed to make medical decisions for their spouse (Mackie 2009). Such privileged status extends to children of married couples, who have more legal rights and better social status than children of nonmarried parents (Hertog 2009, 81). Until 2004, children born to unmarried parents were entered into their *koseki* household registry in ways that made their "illegitimate" status immediately apparent (Mackie 2014, 206; White 2014, 240), and until 2013 these children were legally entitled to only half the inheritance designated for "legitimate" offspring in a family (Jones 2015, 151). That policy was changed partially in response to the UN Convention on Children's Rights, to which Japan acceded in 1994. Although that particular legal difference was removed, a child's parents' marital status still remains visible in their *koseki* record and can therefore be used for discrimination even in the current moment (Goodman 1996, 109; Krogness 2011, 75; Mackie 2009, 150).

3. During parental separation but before a legal divorce is completed, *kangoken* can be granted to only one parent. Jones (2007b, 217) argues that the parent granted *kangoken* while separated will be most likely awarded all custody (both *kangoken* and *shinken*) upon divorce. If a parent is aware of this pattern, or advised about it by their lawyer, it can induce them to restrict their child's contact with the other parent during divorce negotiations, thereby increasing the likelihood that they will "win" the final custody decision. Jones describes the difficulty of legally awarding visitation when parents are estranged but not yet divorced and therefore both have de jure, if not de facto, access to their children (ibid.).

4. In all legal categories of divorce, it is unusual for parents or the courts to grant the two different types of custody to different people (Saito 2016, 945). For example, in 1993, the Supreme Court reversed such a shared custody agreement, "because the court felt cooperation between the parents was no longer possible" (T. Tanase 2010, 17).

5. The *sankin kotai* system became regularized as Tokugawa policy between 1635 and 1642 as a way of forcing loyalty from local leaders who might otherwise be able to gather power in their regional homelands. Although the Tokugawa shogun stayed in Edo (Tokyo), he needed support from lords (*daimyo*) who lived in distant prefectures atop their own structures of power and authority. In order to make sure that these *daimyo* wouldn't foment revolution as soon as they left Edo, the Tokugawa shogun required that *daimyo* alternate residence with their wives and heirs. When the *daimyo* was residing in Edo, his family members could live in his regional home, but when he was doing the work of leadership in his regional home, those family members must be in Edo under the shogun's watchful eye. See Gordon (2003, 13); Maruyama (2007); Vaporis (2008).

6. Although the *koseki* system is "pervasive and entrentched," citizens are also recorded in the concurrent "residency registration system" (*jūminhyō*) (Chapman 2008, 425). This latter record is the responsibility of municipalities and tracks people's current addresses for electorial and other purposes (ibid.). People recorded in the same legal household (according to their *koseki*) need not live in the same residence (accourding to their *jūminhyō*).

7. A total of 13,196 people called in to this poll. Another unscientific survey conducted on Yahoo News in the same year found that of 13,721 respondents, 57 percent favored a joint custody option, 29 percent opposed it, and 14 percent weren't sure (Yahoo News 2009).

8. Of course, people have different associations with these terms, and the debates about what terms are best echo debates about how marriages should be organized. For instance, in chapter 1, Aoyama-san linked the common term "husband" (*danna*, literally master) to the problems she felt in a marriage built on disconnected dependence. For more analysis of the loaded terms for "husband" and "wife," see Mizumoto (2010).

9. Tanase (2004, 28) suggests that noncustodial parents who are flexible about time with their children—for instance, responding positively when a child doesn't want to keep a visitation appointment—create better outcomes.

10. Instead of using the term "stepmother," here Wada-san literally says "my former husband's new wife" (*mae no shujin no atarashii okusan*). This likely reflects the lack of common terminology to describe a stepparent relationship (Nozawa 2008, 79). Although she could have used the term *mama haha*, literally meaning "stepmother," that would have a colder, more legalistic tone and is almost never used in everyday speech. In this English gloss, I have tried to capture a friendly, casual tone equivalent to Wada-san's use in Japanese.

11. In these debates about which family members should maintain connections with each other, I see an inverse parallel to Weston's concept of "families we choose" (Weston 1991). In her analysis, American same-sex partners created families that were, at the time, unrecognized by law or mainstream society. In contrast, some divorced parents in Japan are choosing to end relationships with their children, at times choosing a new "second" family over the children from their first marriage, as if these relationships were zero sum. Japanese courts have made similar determinations, for instance in a 2003 order reducing a noncustodial mother's time with her son because the father had remarried and his new wife (the son's stepmother) had legally adopted the boy. In that opinion, the Osaka High Court said, "exposing the child to different lifestyles and methods of discipline [in two households] can have adverse effects on the feelings and emotional stability of the child" (Tanase 2011, 569).

12. One survey of divorced parents and children found that 28 percent of parents never explained the divorce to their children. In this group, parents of younger children felt that their children would not be able to understand. Parents of older children felt they didn't need to explain because the children already knew of the divorce through custody disputes, or because the parent felt it was impossible to explain the reasons for divorce (Family Problems Information Center, 2005; see also Saito 2016, 959).

13. In the Embrees' account of Suye village, a divorced mother who remarried would have to leave her children with her natal family if her new husband didn't want those children around. Their account includes multiple examples of stepparents mistreating their stepchildren (Smith and Wiswell 1982, 169). Almost a century later, Ono (2010, 168) used data from the Japanese General Social Survey to find that custodial fathers are much more likely to remarry than custodial mothers.

14. Films and television shows represent the "clean break" as the unmarked norm, even in stories that narrate the problems it can cause (Kore-eda 2011, 2015; NHK 2005; Takita 2008).

15. In these statistics, it is, of course, impossible to tell if both parents agreed to the clean break. As explained later in this chapter, it is also quite possible that these figures include many noncustodial parents who would like to have contact with children but do not.

16. Later she learned that her father had, indeed, remarried the "other" woman, supposedly a day after his divorce from Miho's mother was registered. As described in the previous chapter, it

is legally possible for men to remarry immediately after a divorce, but women were, at that time, legally required to wait six months. In 2015, the required waiting period was reduced to 100 days.

17. In a newspaper forum discussing child custody and financial support, Professor Shimoebisu Miyuki describes this by evoking the risks of neoliberal self-responsibility: "Secure child support at your own risk (*Yōiku-hi wa jiko sekinin de kakuho seyo*)" (Ushida 2016). Similarly, in a news story on tensions within the visitation system, reporter Baba Hayato is quoted as saying that "In Japan, settling a divorce and visitation schedule is still the problem of the family members themselves (*tōjisha no mondai*)" (NHK 2017).

18. In American discourse, the term "visitation" has been replaced with "parenting time" in an effort to symbolize the ways noncustodial parents are doing more than merely *visiting* their children (Fabricius et al. 2010). However, in Japan, "visitation" (*menkai*) remains the most common term and is therefore what I use here. Moreover, contact between children and their noncustodial parents in Japan, especially as facilitated through the court system, are much more literally visits: short interactions that rarely include overnights. Therefore, in the Japanese context, "visitation" seems like the most appropriate term, and I use "co-parenting" when I'm describing more integrated and mutual parenting style. In Japan, the terminology has shifted from "mensetsu kōshō" (面接交渉), which literally means "interview negotiation" and sounds legalistic, to "menkai kōryū" (面会交流), which suggests a face-to-face exchange (Kaba 2014).

19. Although it is helpful to see these statistical comparisons between divorces settled through "mutual" (*kyōgi*) agreements and all other types, the sustained frequency of "mutual" divorces skews the ratios of these figures and the conclusions we can draw from them. "Mutual" divorces are such a strong norm that families that fall outside the category are likely unusual in other ways as well.

20. This report divides responses into those for single-mother and single-father households; single-mother households are far more common, accounting for almost three times as many households in this survey. Of single-mother households, 27.7 percent are currently doing visitation, 17.6 percent once did but aren't currently, and 50.8 percent never have (MHLW 2011, 57). The rates of visitation with their mothers for children living with single fathers are slightly higher: 37.4 percent are currently doing visitation, 16.5 percent once did, and 41 percent never have (ibid., 58). This survey makes clear that most children in these single-parent households have no regularly scheduled contact with their noncustodial parents.

21. Examples of these charts are available online at http://www.courts.go.jp/tokyo-f/saiban/tetuzuki/youikuhi_santei_hyou/. For more on these charts, and how they need updating, see Miyasaka (2015).

22. There is some debate in the scholarship about legal contempt power in Japanese courts. Although many scholars suggest there is no legal contempt, or that such power is extremely limited (Ginsburg and Hoetker 2006, 34; Haley 1991; Jones 2007a, 177). Ramseyer and Nakazato (1999, 148) urge an expanded definition of "contempt" to include a judge fining a noncompliant parent in a custody dispute. As of this writing, there are multiple legislative proposals to fine parents who do not conform to promised visitation schedules (Kaneko 2016).

23. For instance, a recent exception proves the pattern, if not the rule: in 2015, Fukuoka Family Court awarded legal custody to a previously noncustodial father because his ex-wife had been refusing visitation to which she previously agreed. A prominent scholar of family law, Tanamura Masayuki, emphasized the uniqueness of this ruling, saying: "This is the first time legal custody has been shifted because a parent prevented scheduled visitations" (Asahi Newspaper 2015).

24. Language of entrance and exit are quite commonly used to describe family membership, but these verbs refer not to the family specifically but to the household register. For instance, a typical shorthand for "getting married" is "entering the registry" (*nyūseki*), i.e., a woman entering her husband's household register (*koseki*) as his wife. For more on the spatial and gendered language referencing the *koseki* to describe family membership, see Alexy (2011a, 247) and T. Tanase (2010, 18).

25. These patterns run parallel to shifts in American custody law. In the broadest terms, through the end of the nineteenth century, American courts understood children to be the property of their fathers, and thus overwhelmingly granted custody to men. In the twentieth century, courts began to imagine young children, especially, as needing their mother's care, the so-called "tender years doctrine." Since the 1960s, courts are more likely to decide custody based on the "child's best interest," an idea that can be interpreted widely (Mason 1996).

26. Although recent custody preferences are another example of the many unfair and unbalanced elements of the family law system, many laws and legal norms remain deeply and consistently discriminatory against women—including the code that prohibits only women from remarrying less than 100 days after a divorce, the requirement that all family members have the same last name, and the court's inability to guarantee child support payments that have been pledged. To be clear, the existence of other unfair practices doesn't make these truths any more acceptable, but it is possible for the family court system to overwhelmingly award child custody to mothers and still not be uniformly prowoman, as some activists claim.

27. There are many examples of noncustodial parents, especially fathers, writing about being granted extremely limited contact with their children—for instance, one hour every three months, or less than twice a year (Nishimuta 2017; Sakuda 2017; Tanase 2011).

28. The father pictured in the first poster was Maruyama Masaharu, the husband of hugely famous pop star Amuro Namie. Three years after the poster featuring Maruyama as an ideal father, the couple divorced (Nakatani 2006, 95). Gossip media suggest that Mr. Maruyama received legal custody of their son, but both parents lived in the same apartment building to co-parent. In 2005, after Maruyama remarried, Ms. Amuro appealed to Family Court and was granted legal custody of their son (Anon. 2015b). The literal poster boy of the *ikumen* movement initially shared custody after divorce, conforming to my expectations that a more involved father would work to maintain connections after divorce. After his remarriage, however, and the birth of his daughter with his new spouse, legal custody and their de facto practices seem to shift. This mirrors the idea mentioned above that "new" families are threatened by continued connections with "old" families.

29. In Japanese, the police say: "Mōshiwakenain desu kedo, kono ken ni tsukimashite wa, maa, yuukai no keijijiken wa taranain desu yo. Myūcharu toraburu to iutta mon de, miuchikan no mondai, de sasuga kairi dekiru you na mondai jya nain de . . ."

30. In this instance, I am thinking of an American counterexample: Alan Diaz's infamous image of Elián González screaming while being confronted by an Immigration and Naturalization Services Officer pointing a submachine gun at him. Japanese family court officials work to never get to such a point and often leave children with the parent (or relative) who simply refuses to give them up, no matter the legal agreements at play.

31. As the current system is set up, one technique to reduce the likelihood of parental abduction is for a custodial parent *not* to allow visitation with a noncustodial parent. Given the legal responses to parental abduction, this unequivocal refusal is a reasonable and logical way for parents to reduce the risk that the other parent could take the child.

32. Naoi (1996), citing Iwanaga (1990), finds that a mother's education background, rather than a father's, is more likely to influence a child's educational aspirations. Because women's educational attainment often correlates with social class status, this dynamic is a mechanism for class reproduction.

33. For overviews of these long-lasting debates in the United States see Amato and Booth (1997); Hetherington (1999); Kelly (2002); Stewart et al. (1997); Wallerstein, Lewis, and Blakeslee (2000). Reinventing the Japanese "clean break" in the American context, Goldstein, Freud, and Solnit (1973) argue that sole custody should be the only option because children face "loyalty conflicts" between parents who can't get along.

Chapter Five

1. In this case, the survey distinguishes between women who live with children and those who do not, as opposed to those who are or are not mothers. In my phrasing, "divorced women" are women who do not live with children in the same residence, although they could be non-custodial mothers.

2. *Demodori* (出戻り, literally someone who has left and returned) is a highly stigmatizing term to describe a divorcee. Although it might seem gender neutral, because women are expected to marry "out" of their natal family "into" their husband's family, and then "return" upon divorce, this term is only ever used to disparagingly describe a divorced woman. It connotes something akin to "crawling back." Because no man would be described as failing in this way, Takemaru (2005) found that women understand this to be a particularly sexist phrase. It is possible to create one's own independent household registry, but this is rarely done (Krogness 2011).

3. Legally speaking, we probably shouldn't have been able to get this because Daisuke was not requesting his own registry. After a revision to the Civil Code went into effect in 1976, citizens could only get access to their own records, no one else's (Bryant 1991, 149; Chapman 2014, 98). The legal changes were put into effect because people, particularly private investigators, were using these family records to discriminate against those with stigmatized family histories. Daisuke shouldn't have been allowed to request his mother's record (as opposed to his own), but she wasn't feeling well and didn't want to come with us to the city office, so she gave him her name stamp (*inkan*) and the staffers were willing to accept that with his honest explanation.

4. Other scholars have found rhetoric of "dirt" and "stains" used to describe household registries, and families themselves, that deviate from normative ideals (Bryant 1992, 407; Krogness 2011, 82). A conservative father from Kyūshū used the term "batsu ichi" to express tremendous shame and embarrassment about his daughter's divorce from an abuser (Bloch 2017, 27).

5. Mayumi's interpretation of these events is reasonable given other explicit and implicit discrimination at the time. In 1983, for example, the Kinokuniya bookstore chain had a secret policy against hiring divorced women, among other categories (Fan 1999, 109).

6. Reflecting their Japanese origins, the standard set of emoji on American cell phones includes multiple uses of both *batsu* and *maru*. For instance, there are male and female versions, each giving the *batsu* sign (forearms crossed in front of the body) and the *maru* sign (arms making a circle above one's head, like a ballerina). In a Japanese context, the former is the equivalent of a "thumbs down" and the latter is a "thumbs up." When I asked, my American friends variously interpreted them instead as cheerleaders making poses, a referee's gesture for "goal!," and as a signal for "get away" or "I don't play," which makes me long for a paper about cross-cultural emoji translation.

7. In this case, Sawyer and Ishizaki used the Gini coefficient, a standard measure of any society's income or wealth distribution. A higher Gini coefficient signals a higher degree of inequality. Sawyer (1976) originally calculated Japan's Gini as 0.316, but Ishizaki (1983) found it to be 0.400. That difference moved Japan from being quite equal to very unequal, compared with other OECD nations (Chiavacci 2008, 14). Tachibanaki (2005, 67) suggests that these differences might also reflect the differences between the two most prominent longitudinal surveys on income inequality in Japan.

8. A 2011 online survey returned similar results, with 74.3 percent of the respondents saying they thought the disparity between rich and poor had grown in the last five years in Japan (Oshio and Urakawa 2014, 762).

9. Scholars have found a gender gap in economic well-being after divorce that disadvantages women in the United Kingdom (Brewer and Nandi 2014; Jarvis and Jenkins 1999), Europe (Uunk 2004), the Netherlands (Manting and Bouman 2006), Canada (Finnie 1993; Gadalla 2008), and the United States (Avellar and Smock 2005; Bianchi, Subaiya, and Kahn 1999; Espenshade 1979; Newman 1986; Smock 1993; Smock, Manning, and Gupta 1999), among other places. Some scholarships finds that women "bounce back" after a relatively short period of time, especially if they remarry (Dewilde and Uunk 2008; Hao 1996; Morrison and Ritualo 2000).

10. In many countries, including Japan, South Korea, and the United States, people are decreasingly likely to get married, which necessarily impacts the divorce rate.

11. Ezawa (2016, 85) similarly describes the relatively sparse homes in which single mothers live and their intense budgeting.

Chapter Six

1. Officials found the man's body when they arrived to congratulate him on his old age (Tamaki 2014, 203).

2. His daughter, her husband, and their children explained that they were not allowed to enter the man's room and therefore had never opened the door when he failed to emerge. They continued to receive his pension, though, and were eventually prosecuted for fraud (Tamaki 2014).

3. Sandberg and Goldfarb both evocatively describe how some (social) distance between an anthropologist and the people with whom she's conducting research can make them more comfortable and willing to talk, particularly about intimate topics. See Alexy and Cook (2019, 240, 251).

4. Nonnative speakers of Japanese might recognize my confusion in this moment. In regular speech, it is not uncommon for Japanese speakers to drop the actor or subject of a sentence, assuming the listener can understand from context. That is what Yoshida-san did here, saying something closer to ". . . called me last week," leaving me to ask "Wait, what? Who called you?" There was no obvious context because we hadn't been talking about his ex-wife before his statement. I think he introduced the difficult topic this way partially because he thought I should have been able to figure out who he meant, but also because being at a wedding might have made him especially reflective. Or maybe he assumed I was always thinking about divorce as much as he was.

5. For instance, www.heartclinic.co.jp, www.rikon-web.com, www.newgyosei.com/info, and www.rikonsodan.com.

6. Counseling could, in theory, be a job flexible enough to provide a salary. Older, divorced women in particular understood that there is something of a market for such advice and support and that they might be uniquely positioned to provide it. Sekiguchi Yoko, for instance, was

able to make a considerable salary as a relationship counselor. Others were either still in train-ing (like Osada-san, profiled in chapter 2) or were offering entirely free services (like Yamada Sadako, profiled earlier in this chapter and in chapter 2).

7. This is also likely the handle he used in online interactions facilitated through the center's website and email listserv. Many people at this gathering were active on the listserv and there-fore identified themselves with their handles.

8. Outside of formal group discussions, participants sometimes told me about problems with their mothers-in-law—a classic point of tension—but they represented those conflicts as less substantial, and no one brought it up in the group sessions.

9. In a different cultural context but also discussing intimate relationships, Gershon (2012) elaborates on this point.

10. As I explained in the introduction, a pension law change was passed in 2004 but did not go into effect until April 2007. In 2005, just as I started this research, people like Nagako-san be-gan to talk publicly about their plans to divorce after 2007, which became something of a sword of Damocles hanging over men (Alexy 2007; Curtin 2002).

Bibliography

Abe, Aya K. 2012. "Poverty and Social Exclusion of Women in Japan." *Japanese Journal of Social Security Policy* 9(1): 61–82.

Abe, Hideko. 2004. "Lesbian Bar Talk in Shinjuku, Tokyo." In Okamoto and Shibamoto Smith, *Japanese Language, Gender, and Ideology*, 205–21.

Abe, Yukiko. 2011. "Danjo koyō kikai kintōhō no chōkiteki kōka" [The Long-Term Effects of the Equal Employment Opportunity Law]. *Nihon rōdō kenkyū zasshi* 53(10): 12–24.

Abegglen, James. 1958. *The Japanese Factory: Aspects of Its Social Organization*. Glencoe, IL: The Free Press.

Abegglen, James. 1970. "The Economic Growth of Japan." *Scientific American* 222(3): 31–37.

Abraham, Jed H. 1989. "The Divorce Revolution Revisited: A Counter-Revolutionary Critique." *Northern Illinois University Law Review* 9(2): 251–98.

Adachi, Yoshimi. 2018. *The Economics of Tax and Social Security in Japan*. Singapore: Springer.

Adrian, Bonnie. 2003. *Framing the Bride: Globalizing Beauty and Romance in Taiwan's Bridal Industry*. Berkeley: University of California Press.

Ahearn, Laura M. 2001. *Invitations to Love: Literacy, Love Letters, and Social Change in Nepal*. Ann Arbor: University of Michigan Press.

Akabayashi, Hideo. 2006. "The Labor Supply of Married Women and Spousal Tax Deductions in Japan: A Structural Estimation." *Review of Economics of the Household* 4(4): 349–78.

Akiba, Jun'ichi, and Minoru Ishikawa. 1995. "Marriage and Divorce Regulation and Recognition in Japan." *Family Law Quarterly* 29(3): 589–601.

Alexander, Arthur J. 2002. *In the Shadow of the Miracle: The Japanese Economy since the End of High-Speed Growth*. Lanham, MD: Lexington Books.

Alexy, Allison. 2007. "Deferred Benefits, Romance, and the Specter of Later-life Divorce." *Contemporary Japan* 19:169–88.

Alexy, Allison. 2008. "Intimate Separations: Divorce and its Reverberations in Contemporary Japan." PhD dissertation, Yale University.

Alexy, Allison. 2011a. "The Door My Wife Closed: Houses, Families, and Divorce in Contemporary Japan." In Ronald and Alexy, *Home and Family in Japan*, 236–53.

Alexy, Allison. 2011b. "Intimate Dependence and Its Risks in Neoliberal Japan." *Anthropological Quarterly* 84(4): 895–917.

Alexy, Allison. Forthcoming. "Children and Law in the Shadows: Responses to Parental Abduction in Japan." *Positions: Asian Critique.*

Alexy, Allison, and Emma E. Cook, eds. 2019. *Intimate Japan: Ethnographies of Closeness and Conflict.* Honolulu: University of Hawai'i Press.

Alexy, Allison, and Emma E. Cook. 2019. "Reflections on Fieldwork: Exploring Intimacy." In Alexy and Cook, *Intimate Japan,* 236–59.

Allison, Anne. 1994. *Nightwork: Sexuality, Pleasure, and Corporate Masculinity in a Tokyo Hostess Club.* Chicago: University of Chicago Press.

Allison, Anne. 2000. *Permitted and Prohibited Desires: Mothers, Comics, and Censorship in Japan.* Berkeley: University of California Press.

Allison, Anne. 2013. *Precarious Japan.* Durham: Duke University Press.

Amato, Paul R. 2003. "Reconciling Divergent Perspectives: Judith Wallerstein, Quantitative Family Research, and Children of Divorce." *Family Relations* 52(4): 332–39.

Amato, Paul R. 2010. "Research on Divorce: Continuing Trends and New Developments." *Journal of Marriage and Family* 72(3): 650–66.

Amato, Paul R., and Alan Booth. 1997. *A Generation at Risk: Growing Up in an Era of Family Upheaval.* Cambridge: Harvard University Press.

Amato, Paul R., and Denise Previti. 2003. "People's Reasons for Divorcing: Gender, Social Class, the Life Course, and Adjustment." *Journal of Family Issues* 24(5): 602–26.

Annas, George, and Frances Miller. 1994. "The Empire of Death: How Culture and Economics Affect Informed Consent in the US, the UK, and Japan." *American Journal of Law and Medicine* 20(4): 357–94.

Antell, Matt, and David Hearn, dir. 2013. *From the Shadows.* Los Angeles: International Documentary Association.

Applbaum, Kalman. 1995. "Marriage with the Proper Stranger: Arranged Marriage in Metropolitan Japan." *Ethnology* 34(1): 37–51.

Arai, Andrea Gevurtz. 2016. *The Strange Child: Education and the Psychology of Patriotism in Recessionary Japan.* Stanford: Stanford University Press.

Araki, Takashi. 2007. "Changing Employment Practices, Corporate Governance, and the Role of Labor Law in Japan." *Comparative Labor Law and Policy Journal* 28(2): 251–81.

Asagei Plus. 2016. "'Rikon 33-nen' hatsu shuki happyō mo Koizumi Jun'ichirō moto tsuma ga sore demo akasanu 'wakareta riyū'" [33 Years after Their Divorce, Ex-wife of Jun'ichirō Koizumi Published Note without Revealing "Reasons for Divorce"]. http://www.asagei.com /excerpt/54654.

Asahi Newspaper. 2015. "Menkai kyohi de chichi ni shinken henkō Fukuoka kasai 'haha no gendō, chōnan ni eikyō'" [Fukuoka Court Gives Custody to Father, Citing Mother for Breaking Visitation Promise]. February 24, 2015.

Asahi TV. 2005. *Jukunen rikon* [*Later-Life Divorce*].

Assmann, Stephanie. 2014. "Gender Equality in Japan: The Equal Employment Opportunity Law Revisited." *Asia-Pacific Journal-Japan Focus* 12(45): 1–24.

Atsumi, Reiko. 1988. "Dilemmas and Accommodations of Married Japanese Women in White-Collar Employment." *Bulletin of Concerned Asian Scholars* 20(3): 54–62.

Avellar, Sarah, and Pamela J. Smock. 2005. "The Economic Consequences of the Dissolution of Cohabiting Unions." *Journal of Marriage and Family* 67(2): 315–27.

Bachnik, Jane, and Charles Quinn, Jr., eds. 1994. *Situated Meaning: Inside and Outside in Japanese Self, Society, and Language.* Princeton: Princeton University Press.

Bachnik, Jane. 1983. "Recruitment Strategies for Household Succession: Rethinking Japanese Household Organization." *Man* 18(1): 160–82.

Beardsley, Richard, John Hall, and Robert Ward. 1959. *Village Japan*. Chicago: University of Chicago Press.

Beck, Ulrich, and Elisabeth Beck-Gernsheim. 1995. *The Normal Chaos of Love*. Cambridge: Polity Press.

Befu, Harumi. 2001. *Hegemony of Homogeneity: An Anthropological Analysis of "Nihonjinron."* Melbourne: Trans Pacific Press.

Berlant, Lauren, ed. 2000. *Intimacy*. Chicago: University of Chicago Press.

Bernstein, Elizabeth. 2007. *Temporarily Yours: Intimacy, Authenticity, and the Commerce of Sex*. Chicago: University of Chicago Press.

Bernstein, Gail Lee. 1983. *Haruko's World: A Japanese Farm Woman and Her Community*. Stanford: Stanford University Press.

Bestor, Theodore C. 1989. *Neighborhood Tokyo*. Stanford: Stanford University Press.

Bianchi, Suzanne M., Lekha Subaiya, and Joan R. Kahn. 1999. "The Gender Gap in the Economic Well-Being of Nonresident Fathers and Custodial Mothers." *Demography* 36(2): 195–203.

Bloch, Dalit. 2017. "More than Just *Nakayoshi*: Marital Intimacy as a Key to Personal Happiness." In Manzenreiter and Holtus, *Happiness and the Good Life in Japan*, 25–40.

Blomström, Magnus, Byron Gangnes, and Sumner La Croix, eds. 2001. *Japan's New Economy: Continuity and Change in the Twenty-First Century*. Oxford: Oxford University Press.

Blomström, Magnus, and Sumner La Croix, eds. 2006. *Institutional Change in Japan*. Abingdon, UK: Routledge.

Boling, Patricia. 2008. "State Feminism in Japan?" *US-Japan Women's Journal* 34:68–89.

Boris, Eileen, and Rhacel Salazar Parreñas, eds. 2010. *Intimate Labors: Cultures, Technologies, and the Politics of Care*. Stanford: Stanford University Press.

Borovoy, Amy. 2001. "Not a Doll's House: Public Uses of Domesticity in Japan." *US-Japan Women's Journal* 20–21: 83–124.

Borovoy, Amy. 2005. *The Too-Good Wife: Alcohol, Codependency, and the Politics of Nurturance in Postwar Japan*. Berkeley: University of California Press.

Borovoy, Amy. 2010. "Japan as Mirror: Neoliberalism's Promise and Costs." In Greenhouse, *Ethnographies of Neoliberalism*, 60–74.

Borovoy, Amy. 2012. "Doi Takeo and the Rehabilitation of Particularism in Postwar Japan." *Journal of Japanese Studies* 38(2): 263–95.

Bradshaw, Carla. 1990. "A Japanese View of Dependency: What Can *Amae* Psychology Contribute to Feminist Theory and Therapy?" In *Diversity and Complexity in Feminist Therapy*, edited by L. Brown and M. Root, 67–86. Abingdon, UK: Routledge.

Brainer, Amy. 2017. "Materializing 'Family Pressure' among Taiwanese Queer Women." *Feminist Formations* 29(3): 1–24.

Braver, Sanford L. 1999. "The Gender Gap in Standard of Living after Divorce: Vanishingly Small." *Family Law Quarterly* 33(1): 111–34.

Brewer, Mike, and Alita Nandi. 2014. "Partnership Dissolution: How Does It Affect Income, Employment, and Well-Being?" *Institute for Social and Economic Research Working Paper Series* 30:1–135.

Brinton, Mary C. 1988. "The Social-Institutional Bases of Gender Stratification: Japan as an Illustrative Case." *American Journal of Sociology* 94(2): 300–334.

Brinton, Mary. 1993. *Women and the Economic Miracle: Gender and Work in Postwar Japan.* Berkeley: University of California Press.

Brinton, Mary. 2010. *Lost in Transition: Youth, Work, and Instability in Postindustrial Japan.* Cambridge: Cambridge University Press.

Bryant, Taimie. 1991. "For the Sake of the Country, For the Sake of the Family: The Oppressive Impact of Family Registration on Women and Minorities in Japan." *UCLA Law Review* 39(1): 109–68.

Bryant, Taimie. 1992. "'Reponsible' Husbands, 'Recalcitrant' Wives, Retributive Judges: Judicial Management of Contested Divorce in Japan." *Journal of Japanese Studies* 18(2): 407–43.

Bryant, Taimie. 1995. "Family Models, Family Dispute Resolution, and Family Law in Japan." *UCLA Pacific Basin Law Journal* 14:1–27.

Burns, Catherine. 2005. *Sexual Violence and the Law in Japan.* Abingdon, UK: Routledge.

Burns, Susan. 2009. "Local Courts, National Laws, and the Problem of Patriarchy in Meiji Japan: Reading 'Records of Civil Rulings' from the Perspective of Gender History." In *Interdisciplinary Studies on the Taiwan Colonial Court Records Archives*, 285–309. Taibei: Angle Publishing Company.

Cahill, Damien, and Martijn Konings. 2017. *Neoliberalism.* Cambridge: Polity Press.

Campbell, John Creighton, and Naoki Ikegami. 2000. "Long-Term Care Insurance Comes to Japan." *Health Affairs* 19(3): 26–39.

Carbone, June, and Naomi Cahn. 2014. *Marriage Markets: How Inequality Is Remaking the American Family.* Oxford: Oxford University Press.

Cave, Peter. 2007. *Primary School in Japan: Self, Individuality, and Learning in Elementary Education.* Abingdon, UK: Routledge.

Cave, Peter. 2016. *Schooling Selves: Autonomy, Interdependence, and Reform in Japanese Junior High Education.* Chicago: University of Chicago Press.

Chapman, David. 2008. "Tama-chan and Sealing Japanese Identity." *Critical Asian Studies* 40: 423–43.

Chapman, David. 2011. "Geographies of Self and Other: Mapping Japan through the Koseki." *Asia-Pacific Journal: Japan Focus* 9(29): 1–10.

Chapman, David. 2014. "Managing 'Strangers' and 'Undecidables:' Population Registration in Meiji Japan." In Chapman and Krogness, *Japan's Household Registration System*, 93–110.

Chapman, David, and Karl Jakob Krogness, eds. 2014. *Japan's Household Registration System and Citizenship: Koseki, Identification, and Documentation.* Abingdon, UK: Routledge.

Charlebois, Justin. 2013. *Japanese Feminities.* Abingdon, UK: Routledge.

Chen, Tien-shi (Lara). 2014. "Officially Invisible: The Stateless (*mukokusekisha*) and the Unregistered (*mukosekisha*)." In Chapman and Krogness, *Japan's Household Registration System and Citizenship*, 221–38. Abingdon, UK: Routledge.

Chiavacci, David. 2008. "From Class Struggle to General Middle-Class Society to Divided Society: Societal Models of Inequality in Postwar Japan." *Social Science Japan Journal* 11(1): 5–27.

Cho, John Song Pae. 2009. "The Wedding Banquet Revisited: 'Contract Marriages' between Korean Gays and Lesbians." *Anthropological Quarterly* 82(2): 401–22.

Clark, Robert L., and Naohiro Ogawa. 1992. "Employment Tenure and Earnings Profiles in Japan and the United States: Comment." *American Economic Review* 82(1): 336–45.

Clarke-Stewart, K. Alison, Deborah L. Vandell, Kathleen McCartney, Margaret T. Owen, and Cathryn Booth. 2000. "Effects of Parental Separation and Divorce on Very Young Children." *Journal of Family Psychology* 14(2): 304–26.

Cockburn, Patrick J. L. 2018. *The Politics of Dependence: Economic Parasites and Vulnerable Lives.* New York: Palgrave Macmillan.

Cole, Jennifer, and Lynne M. Thomas, eds. 2009. *Love in Africa*. Chicago: University of Chicago Press.

Cole, Robert E. 1971. *Japanese Blue Collar: The Changing Tradition*. Berkeley: University of California Press.

Cole, Robert E. 1979. *Work, Mobility, and Participation: A Comparative Study of American and Japanese Industry*. Berkeley: University of California Press.

Collier, Jane. 1997. *From Duty to Desire: Remaking Families in a Spanish Village*. Princeton: Princeton University Press.

Coltrane, Scott, and Michele Adams. 2003. "The Social Construction of the Divorce 'Problem': Morality, Child Victims, and the Politics of Gender." *Family Relations* 52(4): 363–72.

Cook, Emma E. 2016. *Reconstructing Adult Masculinities: Part-Time Work in Contemporary Japan*. Abingdon, UK: Routledge.

Cooper, Melinda. 2017. *Family Values: Between Neoliberalism and the New Social Conservatism*. New York: Zone Books.

Coppola, Sofia, dir. 2003. *Lost in Translation*. Universal City, California: Focus Features.

Cornell, L. L., and Akira Hayami. 1986. "The Shūmon Aratame Chō: Japan's Population Registers." *Journal of Family History* 11(4): 311–28.

Crawcour, Sydney. 1978. "The Japanese Employment System." *Journal of Japanese Studies* 4(2): 225–45.

Cunneen, Chris. 2011. "Indigeneity, Sovereignty, and the Law: Challenging the Processes of Criminalization." *South Atlantic Quarterly* 110(2): 309–27.

Curtin, Sean. 2002. "Living Longer, Divorcing Later: The Japanese Silver Divorce Phenomenon." Glocom.org.

Dales, Laura, and Beverly Yamamoto. 2019. "Romantic and Sexual Intimacy before and beyond Marriage." In Alexy and Cook, *Intimate Japan*, 73–90.

Dasgupta, Romit. 2005. "Salarymen Doing Straight: Heterosexual Men and the Dynamics of Gender Conformity." In McLelland and Dasgupta, *Genders, Transgenders, and Sexualities in Japan*, 168–82.

Dasgupta, Romit. 2011. "Emotional Spaces and Places of Salaryman Anxiety in *Tokyo Sonata*." *Japanese Studies* 31(3): 373–86.

Dasgupta, Romit. 2013. *Re-reading the Salaryman in Japan: Crafting Masculinities*. Abingdon, UK: Routledge.

d'Ercole, Marco Mira. 2006. "Income Inequality and Poverty in OECD Countries: How Does Japan Compare?" *Japanese Journal of Social Security Policy* 5(1): 1–15.

De Vos, George, and Hiroshi Wagatsuma. 1961. "Value Attitudes toward Role Behavior of Women in Two Japanese Villages." *American Anthropologist* 63(6): 1204–30.

Dewar, John. 2000. "Family Law and Its Discontents." *International Journal of Law, Policy and the Family* 14(1): 59–85.

Dewilde, Caroline, and Wilfred Uunk. 2008. "Remarriage as a Way to Overcome the Financial Consequences of Divorce: A Test of the Economic Need Hypothesis for European Women." *European Sociological Review* 24(3): 393–407.

Doi, Takeo. 1971. *Amae no kōzō*. Tokyo: Kobundō.

Doi, Takeo. 1973. *The Anatomy of Dependence*. Tokyo: Kodansha.

Dore, Ronald. 1983. "Goodwill and the Spirit of Market Capitalism." *British Journal of Sociology* 34:459–82.

Dore, Ronald P. 1999 [1958]. *City Life in Japan: A Study of a Tokyo Ward*. Berkeley: University of California Press.

Dower, John W. 1999. *Embracing Defeat: Japan in the Wake of World War II*. New York: W. W. Norton & Co.

Driscoll, Mark. 2009. "Kobayashi Yoshinori Is Dead: Imperial War / Sick Liberal Peace / Neoliberal Class War." *Mechademia* 4: 290–303.

Edwards, Walter. 1989. *Modern Japan through Its Weddings: Gender, Person, and Society in Ritual Portrayal*. Stanford: Stanford University Press.

Embree, John. 1967 [1939]. *Suye Mura: A Japanese Village*. Chicago: University of Chicago Press.

Eng, David L. 2010. *The Feeling of Kinship: Queer Liberalism and the Racialization of Intimacy*. Durham: Duke University Press.

Engbretsen, Elisabeth. 2014. *Queer Women in Urban China: An Ethnography*. Abingdon, UK: Routledge.

Epp, Robert. 1967. "The Challenge from Tradition: Attempts to Compile a Civil Code in Japan, 1866–78." *Monumenta Nipponica* 22(1/2): 15–48.

Espenshade, Thomas J. 1979. "The Economic Consequences of Divorce." *Journal of Marriage and Family* 41(3): 615–25.

Estevez-Abe, Margarita. 2008. *Welfare and Capitalism in Postwar Japan*. Cambridge: Cambridge University Press.

Evans, Harriet. 2012. "The Intimate Individual: Perspectives from the Mother-Daughter Relationship in Urban China." In *Chinese Modernity and the Individual Pysche*, edited by Andrew Kipnis, 119–47. New York: Palgrave McMillan.

Ezawa, Aya. 2016. *Single Mothers in Contemporary Japan: Motherhood, Class, and Reproductive Practice*. Lanham, MD: Lexington Books.

Fabricius, William V., Sanford L. Braver, Priscila Diaz, and Clorinda E. Velez. 2010. "Custody and Parenting Time: Links to Family Relationships and Well-Being after Divorce." In *The Role of the Father in Child Development*, 5th ed., edited by Michael E. Lamb, 201–40. Hoboken, NJ: Wiley.

Faier, Lieba. 2009. *Intimate Encounters: Filipina Women and the Remaking of Rural Japan*. Berkeley: University of California Press.

Family Problems Information Center. 2005. *Rikon shita oya to kodomo no koe o kiku* [*Listening to the Voices of Divorced Parents and Children*]. http://www1.odn.ne.jp/fpic/enquete/report.html.

Fan, Jennifer S. 1999. "From Office Ladies to Women Warriors? The Effect of the EEOL on Japanese Women." *UCLA Women's Law Journal* 10(1): 103–40.

Fernandes, Leela, ed. 2018. *Feminists Rethink the Neoliberal State: Inequality, Exclusion, and Change*. New York: New York University Press.

Fineman, Martha. 2004. *The Autonomy Myth: A Theory of Dependency*. New York: W. W. Norton.

Finnie, Ross. 1993. "Women, Men, and the Economic Consequences of Divorce: Evidence from Canadian Longitudinal Data." *Canadian Review of Sociology and Anthropology* 30(2): 205–41.

Foote, Daniel H. 1996. "Judicial Creation of Norms in Japanese Labor Law: Activism in the Service of—Stability?" *UCLA Law Review* 43:635–709.

Frank, Katherine. 2002. *G-Strings and Sympathy: Strip Club Regulars and Male Desire*. Durham: Duke University Press.

Fraser, Nancy, and Linda Gordon. 1994. "A Genealogy of Dependency: Tracing a Keyword of the US Welfare State." *Signs* 19(2): 309–36.

Friedan, Betty. 1963. *The Feminine Mystique*. New York: Norton.

Fromm, Erich. 1956. *The Art of Loving*. New York: Harper and Row.

Frühstück, Sabine. 2007. *Uneasy Warriors: Gender, Memory, and Popular Culture in the Japanese Army*. Berkeley: University of California Press.

Frühstück, Sabine, and Anne Walthall, eds. 2011. *Recreating Japanese Men*. Berkeley: University of California Press.

Fuchs, Anne, Kathleen James-Chakraborty, and Linda Shortt, eds. 2011. *Debating German Cultural Identity Since 1989*. Rochester, NY: Camden House.

Fuess, Harald. 2004. *Divorce in Japan: Family, Gender, and the State 1600–2000*. Stanford: Stanford University Press.

Fuji, Toyoko. 1993. "Butsukaruto itai 100 man en no kabe" [The Painful Threshold of One Million Yen]. *Fifty Fifty*: 18–20.

Fuji TV. 2004. *Boku to kanojo to kanojo no ikirumichi* [*Me and Her and Her Life Path*]. TV program.

Fuji TV. 2009. *Konkatsu!*. TV program.

Fujita, Noriko. 2016. "*Tenkin*, New Marital Relationships, and Women's Challenges in Employment and Family." *US-Japan Women's Journal* 50:115–35.

Fukuda, Hikarada. 2009. "Haigūsha to no wakare to futatabi no deai—ribetsu to shibetsu, saikon" [Saying Goodbye to One's Spouse: Divorce, Death, and Remarriage]. In *Gendai nihonjin no kazoku* [*Modern Japanese Families*], edited by Junko Fujimi and Riko Nishino, 72–84. Tokyo: Yūhikaku.

Fukuda, Setsuya. 2009. "Leaving the Parental Home in Postwar Japan: Demographic Changes, Stem-Family Norms and the Transition to Adulthood." *Demographic Research* 20:731–816.

Fukuda, Setsuya. 2013. "The Changing Role of Women's Earnings in Marriage Formation in Japan." *Annals of the American Academy of Political and Social Science* 646(1): 107–28.

Fukushima, Mizuho. 1997. *Saiban no joseigaku* [*Women and the Trial System*]. Tokyo: Yūhikaku.

Funabashi, Yoichi, and Barak Kushner, eds. 2015. *Examining Japan's Lost Decades*. Abingdon, UK: Routledge.

Fuwa, Makiko. 2004. "Macro-level Gender Inequality and the Division of Household Labor in 22 Countries." *American Sociological Review* 69(6): 751–67.

Gadalla, Tahany M. 2008. "Gender Differences in Poverty Rates after Marital Dissolution: A Longitudinal Study." *Journal of Divorce and Remarriage* 49(3–4): 225–38.

Ganti, Tejaswini. 2014. "Neoliberalism." *Annual Review of Anthropology* 43:89–104.

Garon, Sheldon. 2002. "Saving for 'My Own Good and the Good of the Nation': Economic Nationalism in Modern Japan." In *Nation and Nationalism in Japan*, edited by Sandra Wilson, 97–114. Abingdon, UK: Routledge.

Gelb, Joyce. 2000. "The Equal Employment Opportunity Law: A Decade of Change for Japanese Women?" *Law & Policy* 22(3–4): 385–407.

Gershon, Ilana. 2011. "Neoliberal Agency." *Current Anthropology* 52(4): 537–55.

Gershon, Ilana. 2012. *The Break-Up 2.0: Disconnecting over New Media*. Ithaca: Cornell University Press.

Gershon, Ilana. 2017. *Down and Out in the New Economy: How People Find (or Don't Find) Work Today*. Chicago: University of Chicago Press.

Gershon, Ilana. 2018. "Employing the CEO of Me, Inc.: US Corporate Hiring in a Neoliberal Age." *American Ethnologist* 45(2): 173–85.

Giddens, Anthony. 1992. *The Transformation of Intimacy: Sexuality, Love, and Eroticism in Modern Societies*. Stanford: Stanford University Press.

Ginsburg, Tom, and Glenn Hoetker. 2006. "The Unreluctant Litigant? An Empirical Analysis of Japan's Turn to Litigation." *Journal of Legal Studies* 35(1): 31–59.

Gluck, Carol. 1985. *Japan's Modern Myths: Ideology in the Late Meiji Period*. Princeton: Princeton University Press.

Goffman, Erving. 1963. *Stigma: Notes on the Management of Spoiled Identity*. New York: Simon and Schuster.

Goldfarb, Kathryn E. 2016. "Coming to Look Alike: Materializing Affinity in Japanese Foster and Adoptive Care." *Social Analysis* 60(2): 47–64.

Goldfarb, Kathryn E. 2019. "Beyond Blood Ties: Intimate Kinship in Japanese Foster and Adoptive Care." In Alexy and Cook, *Intimate Japan*, 181–98.

Goldstein, Joseph, Anna Freud, and Andrew J. Solnit. 1973. *Beyond the Best Interests of the Child*. New York: Free Press.

Goldstein-Gidoni, Ofra. 2012. *Housewives of Japan: An Ethnography of Real Lives and Consumerized Domesticity*. New York: Palgrave McMillan.

Goodman, Roger. 1996. "On Introducing the UN Convention on the Rights of the Child into Japan." In *Case Studies on Human Rights in Japan*, edited by Roger Goodman and Ian Neary, 109–40. Abingdon, UK: Routledge.

Gordon, Andrew. 1985. *The Evolution of Labor Relations in Japan: Heavy Industry, 1853–1955*. Cambridge: Harvard University Press.

Gordon, Andrew. 1997. "Managing the Japanese Household: The New Life Movement in Postwar Japan." *Social Politics* 4(2): 245–83.

Gordon, Andrew. 2003. *A Modern History of Japan*. Oxford: Oxford University Press.

Greenhouse, Carol J., ed. 2010. *Ethnographies of Neoliberalism*. Philadelphia: University of Pennsylvania Press.

Gregg, Jessica. 2006. "'He Can Be Sad Like That': *Liberdade* and the Absence of Romantic Love in a Brazilian Shantytown." In Hirsch and Wardlow, *Modern Loves*, 157–73.

Grimes, William W. 2001. *Unmaking the Japanese Miracle: Macroeconomic Politics, 1985–2000*. Ithaca: Cornell University Press.

Hah, Chung-do, and Christopher C. Lapp. 1978. "Japanese Politics of Equality in Transition: The Case of the Burakumin." *Asian Survey* 18(5): 487–504.

Haley, John Owen. 1991. *Authority without Power: Law and the Japanese Paradox*. Oxford: Oxford University Press.

Halley, Janet, and Kerry Rittich. 2010. "Critical Directions in Comparative Family Law: Genealogies and Contemporary Studies of Family Law Exceptionalism." *American Journal of Comparative Law* 58(4): 753–75.

Halley, Janet. 2011a. "What is Family Law? A Genealogy, Part I." *Yale Journal of Law and Humanities* 23(2): 1–109.

Halley, Janet. 2011b. "What is Family Law? A Genealogy, Part II." *Yale Journal of Law and Humanities* 23(2): 189–293.

Han, Clara. 2012. *Life in Debt: Times of Care and Violence in Neoliberal Chile*. Berkeley: University of California Press.

Hankins, Joseph. 2014. *Working Skin: Making Leather, Making a Multicultural Japan*. Berkeley: University of California Press.

Hao, Lingxin. 1996. "Family Structure, Private Transfers, and the Economic Well-Being of Families with Children." *Social Forces* 75(1): 269–92.

Hardacre, Helen. 1984. *Lay Buddhism in Contemporary Japan: Reiyukai Kyodan*. Princeton: Princeton University Press.

Harris, Julian, John Shao, and Jeremy Sugarman. 2003. "Disclosure of Cancer Diagnosis and Prognosis in Northern Tanzania." *Social Science & Medicine* 56(5): 905–13.

Hasday, Jill Elaine. 2014. *Family Law Reimagined*. Cambridge: Harvard University Press.

Hatoyama, Kazuo. 1902. "The Civil Code of Japan Compared with the French Civil Code." *Yale Law Journal* 11(8): 403–19.

Hayami, Akira. 1983. "The Myth of Primogeniture and Impartible Inheritance in Tokugawa Japan." *Journal of Family History* 8(1): 3–29.

Hayashi, Yūsuke, and Shōhei Yoda. 2014. "Rikon kōdō to shakai kaisō to no kankei ni kansuru jisshō-teki kenkyū" [Research on the Relationship between Divorce and Social Class]. *Kikan kakei keizai kenkyū* 101:51–62.

Hertog, Ekaterina. 2009. *Tough Choices: Bearing an Illegitimate Child in Japan.* Stanford: Stanford University Press.

Hetherington, E. Mavis, ed. 1999. *Coping with Divorce, Single Parenting, and Remarriage: A Risk and Resiliency Perspective.* New York: Psychology Press.

Hetherington, E. Mavis, and Anne Mitchell Elmore. 2003. "Risk and Resilience in Children Coping with Their Parents' Divorce and Remarriage." In *Resilience and Vulnerability: Adaptation in the Context of Childhood Adversities*, edited by Suniya S. Luthar, 182–212. Cambridge: Cambridge University Press.

Hidaka, Tomoko. 2010. *Salaryman Masculinity: The Continuity of and Change in the Hegemonic Masculinity in Japan.* Leiden: Brill.

Hidaka, Tomoko. 2011. "Masculinity and the Family System: The Ideology of the 'Salaryman' across Three Generations." In Ronald and Alexy, *Home and Family in Japan*, 112–30.

Higuchi, Norio. 1992. "The Patient's Right to Know of a Cancer Diagnosis: A Comparison of Japanese Paternalism and American Self-Determination." *Washburn Law Journal* 31(3): 455–73.

Hiller, Dana, and William Philliber. 1985. "Maximizing Confidence in Married Couple Samples." *Journal of Marriage and Family* 47(3): 729–32.

Himuro, Kanna. 2005. *Rikongo no oyako-tachi* [*Parents and Children after Divorce*]. Tokyo: Tarōjirōsha editasu.

Hinokidani, Mieko. 2007. "Housing, Family and Gender." In *Housing and Social Transition in Japan,* edited by Yosuke Hirayama and Richard Ronald, 114–39. Abingdon, UK: Routledge.

Hirokane, Kenshi. 2014. *50 sai kara no "shinikata": nokori 30 nen no ikikata* [*"How to Die" from Aged Fifty On: How to Live for Your Remaining Thirty Years*]. Tokyo: Kōsaidō.

Hirsch, Jennifer, 2003. *A Courtship after Marriage: Sexuality and Love in Mexican Transnational Families.* Berkeley: University of California Press.

Hirsch, Jennifer, and Holly Wardlow, eds. 2006. *Modern Loves: The Anthropology of Romantic Courtship and Companionate Marriage.* Ann Arbor: University of Michigan Press.

Hirsch, Susan. 1998. *Pronouncing and Persevering: Gender and the Discourses of Disputing in an African Islamic Court.* Chicago: University of Chicago Press.

Holden, Livia. 2016. *Hindu Divorce: A Legal Anthropology.* Abingdon, UK: Routledge.

Hommerich, Carola. 2015. "Feeling Disconnected: Exploring the Relationship between Different Forms of Social Capital and Civic Engagement in Japan." *Voluntas* 26:45–68.

Hook, Glenn D., and Hiroko Takeda. 2007. " 'Self-responsibility' and the Nature of the Postwar Japanese State: Risk through the Looking Glass." *Journal of Japanese Studies* 33(1): 93–123.

Hopper, Joseph. 1993a. "Oppositional Identities and Rhetoric in Divorce." *Qualitative Sociology* 16(2): 133–56.

Hopper, Joseph. 1993b. "The Rhetoric of Motives in Divorce." *Journal of Marriage and Family* 55(4): 801–13.

Hopper, Joseph. 2001. "The Symbolic Origins of Conflict in Divorce." *Journal of Marriage and Family* 63(2): 430–45.

Horiguchi, Sachiko. 2011. "Coping with Hikikomori: Socially Withdrawn Youth and the Japanese Family." In Ronald and Alexy, *Home and Family in Japan*, 216–35.

Hutchinson, Sharon. 1990. "Rising Divorce Among the Nuer, 1936–1983." *Man* 25(3): 393–411.

Ikeda, Satoshi. 2002. *The Trifurcating Miracle: Corporations, Workers, Bureaucrats, and the Erosion of Japan's National Economy*. Abingdon, UK: Routledge.

Ikegami, Eiko. 1995. *The Taming of the Samurai: Honorific Individualism and the Making of Modern Japan*. Cambridge: Harvard University Press.

Ikeuchi, Hiromi. 2002. *Koware kake fūfu no toraburu, kaiketsu shimasu* [*Couple's Troubles and Their Resolutions*]. Tokyo: Magajin housu.

Ikeuchi, Hiromi. 2005. *"Ii fūfu" ni naru shinpuru na 30 hinto* [*Thirty Simple Hints for Becoming a "Good Couple"*]. Tokyo: Seishun shinso.

Ikeuchi, Hiromi. 2006. *Jukunen rikon no son to hodoku: suteru tsuma, suterareru otto* [*Unpacking the Costs of Later-life Divorce: Women Leaving, Men Being Left*]. Tokyo: Wanibukkusu.

Illouz, Eva. 2012. *Why Love Hurts: A Sociological Explanation*. New York: Polity Press.

Imai, Masami. 2009. "Ideologies, Vested Interest Groups, and Postal Saving Privatization in Japan." *Public Choice* 138(1–2): 137–60.

Imamura, Anne. 1987. *Urban Japanese Housewives: At Home and in the Community*. Honolulu: University of Hawai'i Press.

Inaba, Akihide. 2009. "Fūfu kankei no hyōka" [Examining Relationships between Husbands and Wives]. In *Gendai nihonjin no kazoku: NFRJ kara mita sono sugata* [*Modern Japanese Families: Perspectives from National Family Research of Japan*], edited by Sumiko Fujimi and Michiko Nishino, 122–30. Tokyo: Yūhikaku.

Inoue, Miyako. 2007. "Language and Gender in an Age of Neoliberalism." *Language and Gender* 1(1): 79–91.

Ishida, Hiroshi, and David Slater, eds. 2010. *Social Class in Contemporary Japan: Structures, Sorting and Strategies*. Abingdon, UK: Routledge.

Ishii-Kuntz, Masako. 1992. "Are Japanese Families Fatherless?" *Sociology and Social Research* 76: 105–10.

Ishii-Kuntz, Masako. 1994. "Paternal Involvement and Perception Toward Fathers' Roles: A Comparison Between Japan and the United States." *Journal of Family Issues* 15(1): 30–48.

Ishii-Kuntz, Masako. 2013. *"Iku men" genshō no shakaigaku: ikuji kosodate sanka e no kibō o kanaeru tame ni* [*Sociological Perspectives on "Involved Fathers": Hope for Their Participation in Child Care*]. Tokyo: Mineruvua shobō.

Ishii-Kuntz, Masako. 2015. "Fatherhood in Asian Contexts." In Qush, *Routledge Handbook of Families in Asia*, 161–74.

Ishii-Kuntz, Masko, Katsuko Makino, Kuniko Kato, and Michiko Tsuchiya. 2004. "Japanese Fathers of Preschoolers and Their Involvement in Child Care." *Journal of Marriage and the Family* 66(3): 779–91.

Ishii-Kuntz, Masako, and A. R. Maryanski. 2003. "Conjugal Roles and Social Networks in Japanese Families." *Journal of Family Issues* 24(3): 352–80.

Ishizaki, Tadao. 1983. *Nihon no shotoku to tomi no bunpai* [*The Distribution of Income and Wealth in Japan*]. Tokyo: Tōyō keizai shinpōsha.

Isono, Fujiko. 1988. "The Evolution of Modern Family Law in Japan." *International Journal of Law, Policy and the Family* 2(2): 183–202.

Itō, Kimio. 2018. "Hakudatsu (kan) no dansei-ka Masculinization of deprivation o megutte: sangyō kōzō to rōdō keitai no hen'yō no tadanaka de" [Masculinization of Deprivation: In the Middle of a Changing Industrial Structure and Labor Forms]. *Nihon rōdō kenkyū zasshi* 60(10): 63–76.

Itō, Takehiko. 2006. "Jukunen rikon shitai no wa ore da" [Men Who Want to Divorce in Later Life]. *Aera* 2(6): 34–36.

Iwakabe, Shigeru. 2008. "Psychotherapy Integration in Japan." *Journal of Psychotherapy Integration* 18(1): 103–25.

Iwama, Nobuyuki. 2011. *Fūdodezāto mondai: muen shakai ga umu 'shokunosabaku'* [*The Problem of Food Deserts: A Society without Bonds Creating Places without Food*]. Tokyo: Nōrin tōkei kyōkai.

Iwanaga, Masaya. 1990. "Asupirēshyon to sono jitsugen" [Aspiration and Its Realization]. In *Josei to shakai kaisō* [*Women and Social Class*], edited by Hideo Okamoto and Michiko Naoi, 91–118. Tokyo: Tōkyōdaigaku shuppankai.

Iwasaki, Michiko 2005. "Mental Health and Counseling in Japan: A Path toward Societal Transformation." *Journal of Mental Health Counseling* 27(2): 129–41.

Jamieson, Lynn. 1998. *Intimacy: Personal Relationships in Modern Societies*. Cambridge, UK: Polity.

Jansen, Marius B. 2000. *The Making of Modern Japan*. Cambridge: Harvard University Press.

Japanese Trade Union Confederation. 2006. *Rengō hakusho* [*White Paper from the Japanese Trade Union Confederation*]. Tokyo: Japanese Trade Union Confederation.

Japan Institute for Labour Policy and Training. 2014. *Labor Situation in Japan and Its Analysis: General Overview 2013/2014*. http://www.jil.go.jp/english/lsj/general/2013-2014/all.pdf.

Japan Institute for Labour Policy and Training. 2016. *Labor Situation in Japan and Its Analysis: General Overview 2015/2016*. http://www.jil.go.jp/english/lsj/general/2015-2016/2015-2016.pdf.

Jarvis, Sarah, and Stephen P. Jenkins. 1999. "Marital Splits and Income Changes: Evidence from the British Household Panel Survey." *Population Studies* 53(2): 237–54.

Johnson, Cedric, Chris Russill, Chad Lavin, and Eric Ishiwata. 2011. *The Neoliberal Deluge: Hurricane Katrina, Late Capitalism, and the Remaking of New Orleans*. Minneapolis: University of Minnesota Press.

Johnson, Chalmers. 1982. *MITI and the Japanese Miracle: The Growth of Industrial Policy, 1925–1975*. Stanford: Stanford University Press.

Jones, Colin P. A. 2007a. "In the Best Interests of the Court: What American Lawyers Need to Know about Child Custody and Visitation in Japan." *Asian-Pacific Law and Policy Journal* 8(2): 166–269.

Jones, Colin P. A. 2007b. "No More Excuses: Why Recent Penal Code Amendments Should (but Probably Won't) Stop International Parental Child Abduction to Japan." *Whittier Journal of Child and Family Advocacy* 6(2): 351–59.

Jones, Colin P. A. 2015. "Nineteenth Century Rules Over Twenty-First Century Reality: Legal Parentage Under Japanese Law." *Family Law Quarterly* 49(1): 149–77.

Jones, Randall S. 2007. "Income Inequality, Poverty, and Social Spending in Japan" *OECD Economics Department Working Papers* 556:1–38.

Kaba, Toshirō. 2014. "Tsuma to rikon shite mo kodomo to aeru? Shinken wa?" [If I Divorce My Wife, Can I Still See My Child? What about Custody?]. *Yomiuri Newspaper*, February 26, 2014.

Kaneko, Maki. 2016. "Kodomo hikiwatashi, rūru o meibunka Hōseishin kentō e" [Child Handover Rules to be Clarified in Review of Legal Process]. *Asahi Newspaper*, September 13, 2016.

Kaufman, Philip, dir. 1993. *Rising Sun*. Century City: 20th Century Fox.

Kavedžija, Iza. 2018. "Of Manners and Hedgehogs: Building Closeness by Maintaining Distance." *Australian Journal of Anthropology* 29:146–57.

Kawarada, Shin'ichi. 2016. "Rikon, 'ko ni awa sete' kyūzō menkai chōtei, nen 1 man-ken 7-wari ga chichi" [Rapid Increase of Divorced Parents Requesting Mediation for Visitation; 10,000 in One Year, 70 Percent Fathers]. *Asahi Newspaper*, February 3, 2016.

Kawashima, Takeyoshi. 1967. *Nihonjin no hōishiki.* Tokyo: Iwanami Shoten.

Kawashima, Takeyoshi, and Kurt Steiner. 1960. "Modernization and Divorce Rate Trends in Japan." *Economic Development and Cultural Change* 9(1): 213–39.

Keizer, Arjan B. 2008. "Non-regular Employment in Japan: Continued and Renewed Dualities." *Work, Employment, and Society* 22(3): 407–25.

Kelly, Joan B. 2002. "Psychological and Legal Interventions for Parents and Children in Custody and Access Disputes: Current Research and Practice." *Virginia Journal of Social Policy and the Law* 10(1): 129–63.

Kelly, William W. 1986. "Rationalization and Nostalgia: Cultural Dynamics of New Middle-Class Japan." *American Ethnologist* 13(4): 603–18

Kelly, William W. 1990. "Regional Japan: The Price of Prosperity and the Benefits of Dependency." *Daedalus* 119(3): 209–27.

Kelly, William W. 1991. "Directions in the Anthropology of Contemporary Japan." *Annual Review of Anthropology* 20:395–431.

Kitanaka, Junko. 2012. *Depression in Japan: Psychiatric Cures for a Society in Distress.* Princeton: Princeton University Press.

Kitaoji, Hironobu. 1971. "The Structure of the Japanese Family." *American Anthropologist* 73(5): 1036–57.

Kitazawa, Yumiko. 2012. "Jidai de yomitoku dorama no hōsoku" [The Principles for Understanding TV Dramas by Era]. *Waseda shakai kagaku sōgō kenkyū bessatsu*: 155–68.

Knapp, Kiyoko Kamio. 1995. "Still Office Flowers: Japanese Women Betrayed by the Equal Employment Opportunity Law." *Harvard Women's Law Journal* 18:83–137.

Koga, Reiko. 2016. "Watashi no shiten: kazoku no arikata shinken mondai ni mo ronten hirogete" [My Perspective: Widening the Discussion of Family Norms to Child Custody Problems]. *Asahi Newspaper*, February 19, 2016.

Kondo, Dorinne K. 1990. *Crafting Selves: Power, Gender, and Discourses of Identity in a Japanese Workplace.* Chicago: University of Chicago Press.

Konishi, Emiko, and Anne Davis. 1999. "Japanese Nurses' Perceptions about Disclosure of Information at the Patients' End of Life." *Nursing and Health Sciences* 1(3): 179–87.

Kore-eda, Hirokazu. 2011. *Kiseki* [*I Wish*]. Tokyo: Gaga.

Kore-eda, Hirokazu. 2015. *Umimachi Diary* [*Our Little Sister*]. Tokyo: Toho.

Kozu, Junko. 1999. "Domestic Violence in Japan." *American Psychologist* 54(1): 50–54.

Krauss, Ellis, and Megumi Naoi. 2010. "The Domestic Politics of Japan's Regional Foreign Economic Policies." In *Trade Policy in the Asia-Pacific: The Role of Ideas, Interests, and Domestic Institutions*, edited by Vinod K. Aggarwal and Seungjoo Lee, 49–69. New York: Springer.

Krogness, Karl Jakob. 2011. "The Ideal, the Deficient, and the Illogical Family: An Initial Typology of Administrative Household Units." In Ronald and Alexy, *Home and Family in Japan*, 65–90.

Krogness, Karl Jakob. 2014. "Jus Koseki: Household Registration and Japanese Citizenship." In Chapman and Krogness, *Japan's Household Registration System and Citizenship*, 145–65.

Kumagai, Fumie. 1983. "Changing Divorce in Japan." *Journal of Family History* 8(1): 85–108.

Kumagai, Fumie. 2008. *Families in Japan: Changes, Continuities, and Regional Variations.* Lanham, MD: University Press of America.

Kumagai, Fumie. 2015. *Family Issues on Marriage, Divorce, and Older Adults in Japan: With Special Attention to Regional Variation.* Singapore: Springer.

Kurosawa, Kiyoshi. 2008. *Tōkyō sonata.* 120 minutes.

Kurotani, Sawa. 2005. *Home Away from Home: Japanese Corporate Wives in the United States.* Durham: Duke University Press.

Kuwajima, Kaoru. 2019. "My Husband Is a Good Man When He Doesn't Hit Me: Redefining Intimacy among Victims of Domestic Violence." In Alexy and Cook, *Intimate Japan*, 112–28.

Kyodo News. 2017. "As Japanese Poverty Grows, Support Groups Spring Up to Help Single Moms Deal with Harsh Economy." *Japan Times*, June 23, 2017.

La Croix, Sumner, and James Mak. 2001. "Regulatory Reform in Japan: The Road Ahead." In Blomström, Gangnes, and La Croix, *Japan's New Economy*, 215–44.

Lane, Carrie. 2011. *A Company of One: Insecurity, Independence, and the New World of White-Collar Unemployment.* Ithaca: Cornell University Press.

Laurent, Erick. 2017. "Japanese Gays, the Closet, and the Culture-Dependent Concept." In Manzenreiter and Holtus, *Happiness and the Good Life in Japan*, 106–22.

LeBlanc, Robin M. 1999. *Bicycle Citizens: The Political World of the Japanese Housewife.* Berkeley: University of California Press.

Lebra, Takie Sugiyama. 1984. *Japanese Women: Constraint and Fulfillment.* Honolulu: University of Hawai'i Press.

Lebra, Takie Sugiyama. 2004. *The Japanese Self in Cultural Logic.* Honolulu: University of Hawai'i Press.

Lee, Haiyan. 2007. *Revolution of the Heart: A Genealogy of Love in China, 1900–1950.* Stanford: Stanford University Press.

Lin, Ho Swee. 2012. "'Playing Like Men': The Extramarital Experiences of Women in Contemporary Japan." *Ethnos* 77(3): 321–43.

Luckacs, Gabriella. 2013. "Dreamwork: Cell Phone Novelists, Labor, and Politics in Contemporary Japan." *Cultural Anthropology* 28(1): 44–64.

Lunsing, Wim. 1995. "Japanese Gay Magazines and Marriage Advertisements." *Journal of Gay and Lesbian Social Services* 3(3): 71–88.

Maccoby, Elenor E., and Robert H. Mnookin. 1992. *Dividing the Child: Social and Legal Dilemmas of Custody.* Cambridge: Harvard University Press.

Mackie, Vera. 2009. "Family Law and Its Others." In *Japanese Family Law in Comparative Perspective*, edited by Harry N. Scheiber and Laurent Mayali, 139–63. Berkeley: Robbins Collection Publications.

Mackie, Vera. 2014. "Birth Registration and the Right to Have Rights: The Changing Family and the Unchanging Koseki." In Chapman and Krogness, *Japan's Household Registration System and Citizenship*, 203–20.

Maclachlan, Patricia L. 2006. "Storming the Castle: The Battle for Postal Reform in Japan." *Social Science Japan Journal* 9(1): 1–18.

Malik, Samina, and Kathy Courtney. 2011. "Higher Education and Women's Empowerment in Pakistan." *Gender and Education* 23(1): 29–45.

Manabe, Kazufumi, and Harumi Befu. 1993. "Japanese Cultural Identity." *Japanstudien* 4(1): 89–102.

Manting, Dorien, and Anne Marthe Bouman. 2006. "Short- and Long-Term Economic Consequences of the Dissolution of Marital and Consensual Unions: The Example of the Netherlands." *European Sociological Review* 22(4): 413–29.

Manzenreiter, Wolfram and Barbara Holtus, eds. 2017. *Happiness and the Good Life in Japan.* Abingdon, UK: Routledge.

Maree, Claire. 2004. "Same-Sex Partnerships in Japan: Bypasses and Other Alternatives." *Women's Studies* 33(4): 541–49.

Maruyama, Yasunari. 2007. *Sankin kōtai [The "Alternate Attendance" System].* Tokyo: Yoshikawa Kōbunkan.

Mason, Mary Ann. 1996. *From Father's Property to Children's Rights: The History of Child Custody in the United States.* New York: Columbia University Press.

Masquelier, Adeline. 2009. "Lessons from *Rubí*: Love, Poverty, and the Educational Value of Dramas in Niger." In Cole and Thomas, *Love in Africa*, 204–28.

Mass, Amy Iwasaki. 1986. "*Amae*: Indulgence and Nurturance in Japanese American Families." PhD dissertation, University of California Los Angeles.

Masujima, Rokuichiro. 1903. "The Japanese Civil Code Regarding the Law of the Family." *American Law Review* 37(4): 530–44.

Matanle, Peter, Leo McCann, and Darren Ashmore. 2008. "Men under Pressure: Representations of the Salaryman and His Organization in Japanese Manga." *Organization* 15(5): 639–64.

Mathews, Gordon. 2017. "Happiness in Neoliberal Japan." In Manzenreiter and Holthus, *Happiness and the Good Life in Japan*, 227–42.

Matsumoto, Yasuyo, Shingo Yamabe, Toru Sugishima, and Dan Geronazzo. 2011. "Perception of Oral Contraceptives among Women of Reproductive Age in Japan: A Comparison with the USA and France." *Journal of Obstetrics and Gynaecology Research* 37(7): 887–92.

Matsushima, Yukiko. 1997. "What Has Made Family Law Reform Go Astray?" In *The International Survey of Family Law*, edited by Andrew Bainham, 193–206. The Hague: Martinus Nijhoff Publishers.

Matsushima, Yukiko. 2000. *Contemporary Japanese Family Law.* Tokyo: Minjiho kenkyukai.

Maynard, Senko K. 1997. *Japanese Communication: Language and Thought in Context.* Honolulu: University of Hawai'i Press.

McKinnon, Susan, and Fenella Cannell, eds. 2013. *Vital Relations: Modernity and the Persistent Life of Kinship.* Santa Fe: School for Advanced Research Press.

McLelland, Mark. 2000. "Is There a Japanese 'Gay Identity'?" *Culture, Health and Sexuality* 2(4): 459–72.

McLelland, Mark. 2005. "Salarymen Doing Queer: Gay Men and the Heterosexual Public Sphere." In McLelland and Dasgupta, *Genders, Transgenders, and Sexualities in Japan*, 96–110.

McLelland, Mark. 2012. *Love, Sex, and Democracy in Japan during the American Occupation.* New York: Palgrave McMillan.

McLelland, Mark, and Romit Dasgupta, eds. 2005. *Genders, Transgenders, and Sexualities in Japan.* Abingdon, UK: Routledge.

McManus, Patricia A., and Thomas DiPrete. 2001. "Losers and Winners: The Financial Consequences of Separation and Divorce for Men." *American Sociological Review* 66(2): 246–68.

McTeirnan, John, dir. 1988. *Die Hard.* Century City: 20th Century Fox.

Mendoza, Victor. 2016. *Metroimperial Intimacies: Fantasy, Racial-Sexual Governance, and the Philippines in US Imperialism, 1899–1913.* Durham: Duke University Press.

Miles, Elizabeth. 2019. "Manhood and the Burdens of Intimacy." In Alexy and Cook, *Intimate Japan*, 148–63.

Miller, Robbi Louise. 2003. "The Quiet Revolution: Japanese Women Working around the Law." *Harvard Women's Law Journal* 26:163–215.

Minamikata, Satoshi. 2005. "Resolution of Disputes over Parental Rights and Duties in a Marital Dissolution Case in Japan: A Nonlitigious Approach in *Chōtei* (Family Court Mediation)." *Family Law Quarterly* 39(2): 489–506.

Ministry of Health, Labour, and Welfare (MHLW). 2011. *Heisei 23-nendo zenkoku boshi setai-tō chōsa kekka no gaiyō* [*2011 National Survey of Mother-Child Households*]. http://www.mhlw .go.jp/seisakunitsuite/bunya/kodomo/kodomo_kosodate/boshi-katei/boshi-setai_h23.

Ministry of Health, Labour, and Welfare (MHLW). 2017. *Vital Statistics of Japan*. Tokyo: Ministry of Health, Labour and Welfare.

Miyasaka, Junko. 2015. "Rikon ni okeru yōiku-hi no genjō to mondaiten: kan'i santei hōshiki no kentō" [Current Conditions and Problems of Child Support after Divorce: A Consideration of Simplified Calculation Methods]. *Shōwa joshidaigaku josei bunka kenkyūjo kiyō* 42:47–59.

Miyazaki, Ayumi. 2004. "Japanese Junior High School Girls' and Boys' First-Person Pronoun Use and Their Social World." In Okamoto and Shibamoto Smith, *Japanese Language, Gender, and Ideology*, 240–55.

Miyazaki, Hirokazu. 2010. "The Temporality of No Hope." In *Ethnographies of Neoliberalism*, edited by Carol J. Greenhouse, 238–50. Philadelphia: University of Pennsylvania Press.

Miyazaki, Hirokazu. 2013. *Arbitraging Japan: Dreams of Capitalism at the End of Finance*. Berkeley: University of California Press.

Mizumoto, Terumi. 2010. "Aratamatta ba ni okeru tanin no haigūsha no yobi kata" [What to Call Someone's Spouse in Formal Situations]. *Nihongo jendā gakkai.* https://gender.jp/gender -essay/essay201003/.

Mnookin, Robert H. 1985. *In the Interest of Children: Advocacy, Law Reform, and Public Policy.* New York: W. H. Freeman.

Moore, Katrina. 2010. "Marital Infidelity of Older Japanese Men: Interpretations and Conjectures." *Asian Anthropology* 9(1): 57–76.

Mori, Naruki, Shigenori Shiratsuka, and Hiroo Taguchi. 2001. "Policy Responses to the Post-Bubble Adjustments in Japan: A Tentative Review." *Monetary and Economic Studies* 19:53–112.

Moriguchi, Chiaki, and Hiroshi Ono. 2006. "Japanese Lifetime Employment: A Century's Perspective." In Blomström and La Croix, *Institutional Change in Japan*, 152–76.

Moriki, Yoshie. 2017. "Physical Intimacy and Happiness in Japan: Sexless Marriages and Parent-Child Co-sleeping." In Manzenreiter and Holthus, *Happiness and the Good Life in Japan*, 41–52.

Morrison, Donna Ruane, and Amy Ritualo. 2000. "Routes to Children's Economic Recovery after Divorce: Are Cohabitation and Remarriage Equivalent?" *American Sociological Review* 65(4): 560–80.

Muehlebach, Andrea. 2012. *The Moral Neoliberal: Welfare and Citizenship in Italy.* Chicago: University of Chicago Press.

Mukai, Ken, and Nobuyoshi Toshitani. 1967. "The Progress and Problems of Compiling the Civil Code in the Early Meiji Era." *Law in Japan* 1(1): 25–59.

Mulgan, Aurelia George. 2000. *The Politics of Agriculture in Japan*. Abingdon, UK: Routledge.

Murakami, Akane. 2009. "Rikon ni yotte josei no seikatsu wa dō henka suru ka?" [How Do Women's Lives Change with Divorce?] *Kikan kakei keizai kenkyū* 84:36–45.

Murakami, Akane. 2011. "Rikon ni yoru josei no shakai keizaiteki jōkyō no henka 'shōhi seikatsu ni kansuru paneru chōsa' e no kotei kōka moderu henryō kōka moderu no tekiyō" [Divorce and Women's Socioeconomic Status: Applying Fixed Effect and Variable Effect Models to Japan's "Panel Survey on Consumer Life"]. *Shakaigaku hyōron* 62(3): 319–35.

Murakami, Shosuke. 2005. *Densha otoko* [*Train Man*]. Tokyo: Toho.

Muroi, Yūtsuki, Kurada Mayumi, Katō Seishi, Kaminarimon Shikago, and Futamatsu Mayumi. 2006. "Rikon no kiki! otoko nara dō suru?" [Divorce Crisis! What Should Men Do?] *Shunna tēma* 8:9–31.

Nakamatsu, Tomoko. 1994. "Housewives and Part-Time Work in the 1970s and 1980s: Political and Social Implications." *Japanese Studies* 14(1): 87–104.

Nakamura, Tadashi. 2003. "Regendering Batterers: Domestic Violence and Men's Movements." In Roberson and Suzuki, *Men and Masculinities in Contemporary Japan*, 162–79.

Nakano, Lynne. 2011. "Working and Waiting for an 'Appropriate Person': How Single Women Support and Resist Family in Japan." In Ronald and Alexy, *Home and Family in Japan*, 229–67.

Nakatani, Ayami. 2006. "The Emergence of 'Nurturing Fathers': Discourse and Practices of Fatherhood in Contemporary Japan." In *The Changing Japanese Family*, edited by Marcus Rebick and Ayami Takenaka, 94–108. Abingdon, UK: Routledge.

Naoi, Michiko. 1996. "Shakai kaisō to kazoku saikin no bunken no revyū" [Social Stratification and Families: Review of Recent Literature]. *Kazoku shakai-gaku kenkyū* 8:7–17.

National Institute of Population and Social Security Research (NIPSSR). 2017a. *Population Projections for Japan: 2016 to 2065.* http://www.ipss.go.jp/pp-zenkoku/e/zenkoku_e2017/pp29_summary.pdf.

National Institute of Population and Social Security Research (NIPSSR). 2017b. *Population Statistics.* Available online: http://www.ipss.go.jp/p-info/e/psj2017/PSJ2017.asp.

Neary, Ian. 1997. "Burakumin in Contemporary Japan." In *Japan's Minorities: The Illusion of Homogeneity*, edited by Michael Weiner, 50–78. Abingdon, UK: Routledge.

Nemoto, Kuniaki, Ellis Krauss, and Robert Pekkanen. 2008. "Policy Dissension and Party Discipline: The July 2005 Vote on Postal Privatization in Japan." *British Journal of Political Science* 38 (3): 499–525.

Newman, Katherine S. 1986. "Symbolic Dialectics and Generations of Women: Variation in the Meaning of Post-Divorce Downward Mobility." *American Ethnologist* 13(2): 230–52.

NHK. 2005. *Kaze no Haruka* [*Haruka of the Wind*].

NHK. 2010. *Muen Shakai—"Muenshi" 32000-nin no Shōgeki* [*Society without Ties: 32,000 Deaths without Ties*]. Tokyo: Nippon Hōsō Kyōkai.

NHK. 2017. "Naze higeki wa kurikaesa reru no ka: kenshō menkai kōryū satsujin" [Why Is This Tragedy Repeated? What Triggered Murder-Suicides During Visitation with Noncustodial Parents?]. *Ohayō Nihon*, September 19, 2017.

NHK. 2018. "Rikon ni tomonau kodomo no hikiwatashi kataoya fuzai demo kanō e hōsei shingikai bukai" [Ministry Subcommittee to Consider Transferring Child Even if One Parent Isn't Present]. NHK News Web. https://www3.nhk.or.jp/news/html/20180626/k10011496021000.html [link expired; PDF on file with author].

Nicola, Fernanda. 2010. "Critical Directions in Comparative Family Law." *American Journal of Comparative Law* 58(4): 777–810.

Nielsen, Linda. 2014. "Woozles: Their Role in Custody Law Reform, Parenting Plans, and Family Court." *Psychology, Public Policy, and Law* 20(2): 164–80.

Nihon TV. 2009. *Kayō sapuraizu* [*Tuesday Surprise*]. April 23. https://www.youtube.com/watch?v=VF98nRHyUDc.

Ninomiya, Shūhei. 2005. "Kazoku-hō ni okeru jendā kadai" [Gender Issues in Family Law]. *Kokusai josei* 19(19): 85–92.

Nish, Ian, ed. 2008. *The Iwakura Mission to America and Europe: A New Assessment.* Abingdon, UK: Routledge.

Nishimuta, Yasushi. 2017. *Wagako ni aenai rikon-go ni hyōryū suru chichioya-tachi* [*I Cannot See My Child: Fathers Made Aimless by Divorce*]. Tokyo: PHP kenkyūjo.

North, Scott. 2009. "Negotiating What's 'Natural': Persistent Domestic Gender Role Inequality in Japan." *Social Science Japan Journal* 12(1): 23–44.

Nozawa, Shinji. 2008. "The Social Context of Emerging Stepfamilies in Japan: Stress and Support for Parents and Stepparents." In *The International Handbook of Stepfamilies: Policy and Practice in Legal, Research, and Clinical Environments,* edited by Jan Pryor, 79–99. Hoboken, NJ: Wiley.

Nozawa, Shinji. 2011. "Hojū hōkoku suteppufamirī o meguru kattō: senzai suru nitsu no kazoku moderu" [Supplemental Report on Conflicts Surrounding Stepfamilies: Two Potential Family Models]. *Kazoku shakai to hō* 27: 89–94.

Nozawa, Shinji. 2016. "Suteppufamirī wa 'kazoku' na no ka" [Are Stepfamilies Families?] *Kazoku ryōhō kenkyū* 33(2): 72–77.

Nozawa, Shinji. 2015a. "Remarriage and Stepfamilies." In Qush, *Routledge Handbook of Families in Asia,* 345–58.

Nozawa, Shinji, Naoko Ibaraki, and Toshiaki Hayano, eds. 2006. *Q&A suteppufamirī no kiso chishiki—kodzure saikon kazoku to shien-sha no tame ni* [*Basic Knowledge About Stepfamilies: For Remarried Parents and Their Supporters*]. Tokyo: Akashishoten.

Nozawa, Shunsuke. 2015b. "Phatic Traces: Sociality in Contemporary Japan." *Anthropological Quarterly* 88(2): 373–400.

Oda, Hiroshi. 2009. *Japanese Law.* 3rd ed. Oxford: Oxford University Press.

Ogasawara, Yuko. 1998. *Office Ladies and Salaried Men: Power, Gender, and Work in Japanese Companies.* Berkeley: University of California Press.

Ogawa, Naohiro. 2003. "Japan's Changing Fertility Mechanisms and Its Policy Responses." *Journal of Population Reserach* 20(1): 89–101.

Ohnuki-Tierney, Emiko. 1993. *Rice as Self: Japanese Identities through Time.* Princeton: Princeton University Press.

Okada, Yasuko. 2005. *Jyōshi dono! sore wa, pawahara desu* [*Mr. Boss-man, This Is Power Harassment!*]. Tokyo: Nihon keizai shinbunsha.

Okamoto, Shigeko, and Janet S. Shibamoto Smith, eds. *Japanese Language, Gender, and Ideology: Cultural Models and Real People.* Oxford: Oxford University Press.

Okano, Atsuko. 2001. *Rikon shite shiawase ni naru hito fushiawase ni naru hito* [*Divorce Makes Some People Happy but Others Miserable*]. Tokyo: Bijinesusha.

Okano, Atsuko. 2005. *Chotto matte so no rikon! Shiawase wa docchi no kawa ni?* [*Wait a Second with That Divorce! Will It Really Make You Happy?*]. Tokyo: Jitsugyōno nihonsha.

Okano, Atsuko. 2008. *Otto toiu na no tanin: fūfu no kironi tatsu anata ni* [*My Husband Is a Stranger: You Are Standing at Relationship Crossroads*]. Tokyo: Yūraku shuppansha.

Ong, Aihwa. 2006. *Neoliberalism as Exception: Mutations in Citizenship and Sovereignty.* Durham: Duke University Press.

Ono, Hiromi. 2006. "Divorce in Japan: Why It Happens, Why It Doesn't." In Blomström and La Croix, *Institutional Change in Japan,* 221–36.

Ono, Hiromi. 2010. "The Socioeconomic Status of Women and Children in Japan: Comparisons with the USA." *International Journal of Law, Policy, and the Family* 24(2): 151–76.

Ono, Hiroshi. 2009. "Lifetime Employment in Japan: Concepts and Measurements." *Journal of the Japanese and International Economies* 24:1–27.

Ootake, Midori, Hiroko Amano, and Setsu Itoh. 1980. "Fūfu no seikatsu jikan kōzō no shitsuteki kentō" [A Qualitative Examination of Time Budgets among Married Couples]. *Kaseigaku zasshi* 31(3): 214–22.

Oppler, Alfred C. 1949. "The Reform of Japan's Legal and Judicial System under Allied Occupation." *Washington Law Review and State Bar Journal* 24:290–324.

Osawa, Mari. 2005. "Japanese Government Approaches to Gender Equality since the Mid-1990s." *Asian Perspective* 29(1): 157–73.

Osawa, Michiko, Myoung Jung Kim, and Jeff Kingston. 2013. "Precarious Work in Japan." *American Behavioral Scientist* 57(3): 309–34.

Oshio, Takashi, and Kunio Urakawa. 2014. "The Association between Perceived Income Inequality and Subjective Well-Being: Evidence from a Social Survey in Japan." *Social Indicators Research* 116(3): 755–70.

Ouellete, Laurie. 2009. "Take Responsibility for Your Self: *Judge Judy* and the Neoliberal Citizen." In *Reality TV: Remaking Television Culture*, 2nd edition, edited by Susan Murray and Laurie Ouellette, 223–42. New York: New York University Press.

Ozawa-de Silva, Chikako. 2006. *Psychotherapy and Religion in Japan: The Japanese Introspection Practice of Naikan.* Abingdon, UK: Routledge.

Ozawa-de Silva, Chikako. 2018. "Stand by Me: The Fear of Solitary Death and the Need for Social Bonds in Contemporary Japan." *The Routledge Handbook of Death and the Afterlife*, edited by Candi Cann, 85–95. Abingdon, UK: Routledge.

Park, Hyunjoon, and James M. Raymo. 2013. "Divorce in Korea: Trends and Educational Differentials." *Journal of Marriage and Family* 75(1): 110–26.

Peng, Ito. 2002. "Social Care in Crisis: Gender, Demography, and Welfare State Restructuring in Japan." *Social Politics* 9(3): 411–43.

Peterson, Richard R. 1996. "A Re-Evaluation of the Economic Consequences of Divorce." *American Sociological Review* 61(3): 528–36.

Porges, Amelia, and Joy M Leong. 2006. "The Privatization of Japan Post: Ensuring Both a Viable Post and a Level Playing Field." In *Progress toward Liberalization of the Postal and Delivery Sector*, edited by Michael Crew and Paul Kleindorfer, 385–400. New York: Springer.

Pugh, Allison. 2015. *The Tumbleweed Society: Working and Caring in an Age of Insecurity.* Oxford: Oxford University Press.

Qush, Stella R., ed. 2015. *Routledge Handbook of Families in Asia.* Abingdon, UK: Routledge.

Ramseyer, Mark, and Minoru Nakazato. 1999. *Japanese Law: An Economic Approach.* Chicago: University of Chicago Press.

Raymo, James, Setsuya Fukuda, and Miho Iwasawa. 2013. "Educational Differences in Divorce in Japan." *Demographic Research* 28:177–206.

Raymo, James, and Miho Iwasawa. 2008. "Bridal Pregnancy and Spouse Pairing Patterns in Japan." *Journal of Marriage and the Family* 70(4): 847–60.

Raymo, James, Miho Iwasawa, and Larry Bumpass. 2004. "Marital Dissolution in Japan: Recent Trends and Patterns." *Demographic Research* 11(14): 395–420.

Raymo, James, Miho Iwasawa, and Larry Bumpass. 2009. "Cohabitation and Family Formation in Japan." *Demography* 46(4): 785–803.

Raymo, James, and Yanfei Zhou. 2012. "Living Arrangements and the Well-Being of Single Mothers in Japan." *Population Research Policy Review* 31:727–49.

Rebhun, Linda-Anne. 2002. *The Heart is Unknown Country: Love and the Changing Economy in Northeast Brazil.* Stanford: Stanford University Press.

Rebhun, Linda-Anne. 2007. "The Strange Marriage of Love and Interest: Economic Change and Emotional Intimacy in Northeast Brazil." In *Love and Globalization: Transformations of Intimacy in the Contemporary World*, edited by Mark B. Padilla, Jennifer S. Hirsch, Miguel Munoz-Laboy, Robert Sember, and Richard G. Parker, 107–19. Nashville, TN: Vanderbilt University Press.

Rebick, Marcus. 2001. "Japanese Labor Markets: Can We Expect Significant Change?" In Blomström, Gangnes, and La Croix, *Japan's New Economy*, 120–41.

Reddy, Gayatri. 2006. "The Bonds of Love: Companionate Marriage and the Desire for Intimacy among Hijras in Hyderabad, India." In Hirsch and Wardlow, *Modern Loves*, 174–92.

Reitman, Valerie. 2001. "Divorce, Japanese Style." *Los Angeles Times*, October 2, 2001.

Reniers, Georges. 2003. "Divorce and Remarriage in Rural Malawi." *Demographic Research* 1(1): 175–206.

Rimke, Heidi Marie. 2000. "Governing Citizens through Self-Help Literature." *Cultural Studies* 14(1): 61–78.

Roberson, James E., and Nobue Suzuki, eds. 2003. *Men and Masculinities in Contemporary Japan: Dislocating the Salaryman Doxa*. Abingdon, UK: Routledge.

Roberts, Glenda. 2002. "Pinning Hopes on Angels: Reflections from an Aging Japan's Urban Landscape." In *Family and Social Policy in Japan*, edited by R. Goodman, 54–91. Cambridge: Cambridge University Press.

Roberts, Glenda. 1994. *Staying on the Line: Blue-Collar Women in Contemporary Japan*. Honolulu: University of Hawai'i Press.

Robinson, Michael. 1987. "Stepped Up Beef Imports? Can't Stomach It, Says Japanese." Associated Press. https://www.apnews.com/8fff51f61de3400636ec9af70a2680d8.

Rofel, Lisa. 2007. *Desiring China: Experiments in Neoliberalism, Sexuality, and Public Culture*. Durham: Duke University Press.

Rohlen, Thomas P. 1974. *For Harmony and Strength: Japanese White-Collar Organization in Anthropological Perspective*. Berkeley: University of California Press.

Ronald, Richard, and Allison Alexy, eds. 2011. *Home and Family in Japan: Continuity and Transformation*. Abingdon, UK: Routledge.

Ronald, Richard, and Yosuke Hirayama. 2009. "Home Alone: The Individualization of Young, Urban Japanese Singles." *Environment and Planning A: Economy and Space* 41(12): 2836–54.

Roquet, Paul. 2016. *Ambient Media: Japanese Atmospheres of Self*. Minneapolis: University of Minnesota Press.

Rose, Nikolas. 1998. *Inventing Our Selves: Psychology, Power, and Personhood*. Cambridge: Cambridge University Press.

Rose, Nikolas, and Peter Miller. 2008. *Governing the Present: Administering Economic, Social, and Personal Life*. Cambridge: Polity Press.

Rosenberger, Nancy. 1991. "Gender and the Japanese State: Pension Benefits Creating Difference." *Anthropological Quarterly* 64(4): 178–93.

Rosenberger, Nancy, ed. 1992. *Japanese Sense of Self*. Cambridge: Cambridge University Press.

Rosenberger, Nancy. 2001. *Gambling with Virtue: Japanese Women and the Search for Self in a Changing Nation*. Honolulu: University of Hawai'i Press.

Rowe, Mark Michael. 2011. *Bonds of the Dead: Temples, Burial, and the Transformation of Contemporary Japanese Buddhism*. Chicago: University of Chicago Press.

Rubin, Lillian B. 1983. *Intimate Strangers: Men and Women Together*. New York: Harper and Row.

Ryang, Sonia. 2006. *Love in Modern Japan: Its Estrangement from Self, Sex, and Society*. Abingdon, UK: Routledge.

Sadaoka, Minobu. 2011. "Dairi kaitai de umareta kodomo no fukushi: shutsuji o shirukenri no hoshō" [Children's Well-Being in Surrogacy: Guaranteeing the Right to Know One's Origin]. *Koa eshikkusu* 7:365–74.

Saito, Hiroharu. 2016. "Bargaining in the Shadow of Children's Voices in Divorce Custody Disputes: Comparative Analysis of Japan and the US." *Cardozo Journal of Conflict Resolution* 17(3): 937–88.

Saitō, Juri. 2005. "Jukunen rikon ni miiru tsuma-tachi" [Wives Fixing Their Eyes on "Later-Life Divorce"]. *Aera* 12(5): 83–86.

Sakai, Junko. 2003. *Makeinu no tōboe* [*The Howl of the Loser Dogs*]. Tokyo: Kodansha.

Sako, Mari. 1997. "Introduction: Forces for Homogeneity and Diversity in the Japanese Industrial Relations System." In *Japanese Labour and Management in Transition: Diversity, Flexibility and Participation*, edited by Mari Sato and Hiroko Sato, 1–24. Abingdon, UK: Routledge.

Sakuda, Hirofumi. 2017. "Menkai dekita no wa 2-nenkan de 2-kai kodomo ni aenai chichioya-tachi" [Fathers Who Have Visitation with Their Children Less than Twice in Two Years]. *Aera*, March 20: 28–30.

Salamon, Sonya. 1975. "'Male Chauvinism' as a Manifestation of Love in Marriage." In *Adult Episodes in Japan*, edited by David Plath, 20–31. Leiden: Brill.

Sandberg, Shana Fruehan. 2019. "Resisting Intervention, (En)trusting My Partner: Unmarried Women's Narratives about Contraceptive Use in Tokyo." In Alexy and Cook, *Intimate Japan*, 54–72.

Santos, Goncalo, and Stevan Harrell, eds. 2016. *Transforming Patriarchy: Chinese Families in the Twenty-First Century*. Seattle: University of Washington Press.

Sawyer, Malcolm C. 1976. "Income Distribution in OECD Countries." In *OECD Economic Outlook Occasional Studies*, edited by OECD, 3–36. Paris: OECD.

Scher, Mark J., and Naoyuki Yoshino. 2004. "Policy Challenges and the Reform of Postal Savings in Japan." In *Small Savings Mobilization and Asian Economic Development: The Role of Postal Financial Services*, edited by Mark J. Scher and Naoyuki Yoshino, 121–46. Armonk, NY: M. E. Sharpe.

Schregle, Johannes. 1993. "Dismissal Protection in Japan." *International Labour Review* 132(4): 507–20.

Shahani, Nishant. 2008. "The Politics of Queer Time: Retro-Sexual Returns to the Primal Scene of American Studies." *MFS Modern Fiction Studies* 54(4): 791–814.

Shibamoto Smith, Janet. 1999. "From Hiren to Happī-Endo: Romantic Expression in the Japanese Love Story." In *Languages of Sentiment: Cultural Constructions of Emotional Substrates*, edited by Gary B. Palmer and Debra J. Occhi, 131–50. Amsterdam: John Benjamins.

Shibamoto Smith, Janet. 2004. "Language and Gender in the (Hetero)Romance: 'Reading' the Ideal Hero/ine through Lovers' Dialogue in Japanese Romance Fiction." In *Japanese Language, Gender, and Ideology: Cultural Models and Real People*, edited by Shigeko Okamoto and Janet Shibamoto Smith, 113–30. Oxford: Oxford University Press.

Shimada, Tomiko. 1993. "Nenkin Sōdanshitsu" [Answers to Pension Problems]. *Egao* (May): 39.

Shioiri, Aya. 2017. "Shinken, menkai-sū mo arasou jidai haha ni 'toshi 100-nichi' yakusoku no chichi, gyakuten haiso" [In an Era of Disputes about Custody and Visitation, Father Who Promised 100 Days a Year Loses Case]. *Asahi Newspaper*, January 27, 2017.

Shiota, Sakiko. 1992. "Gendai feminizumu to Nihon no shakai seisaku 1970–1990-nen" [Modern Feminism and Social Policy in Japan from 1970 to 1990]. *Joseigaku kenkyū* 2:29–52.

Simmons, Christina. 1979. "Companionate Marriage and the Lesbian Threat." *Frontiers: A Journal of Women Studies* 4(3): 54–59.

Simpson, Bob. 1997. "On Gifts, Payments, and Disputes: Divorce and Changing Family Structures in Contemporary Britain." *Journal of the Royal Anthropological Institute* 3(4): 731–45.

Simpson, Bob. 1998. *Changing Families: An Ethnographic Approach to Divorce and Separation.* Oxford: Berg.

Skinner, Kenneth. 1979. "Salaryman Comics in Japan: Images of Self-Perception." *Journal of Popular Culture* 13(1): 141–51.

Slater, David, and Patrick W. Galbraith. 2011. "Re-Narrating Social Class and Masculinity in Neoliberal Japan: An Examination of the Media Coverage of the 'Akihabara Incident' of 2008." *Electronic Journal of Contemporary Japanese Studies.* http://www.japanesestudies.org.uk/articles/2011/SlaterGalbraith.html.

Smappy. 2015. "Amuro Namie no musuko, Atsuhito-kun no shinken wa dochira? Ikemen de genzai gyōsei kōkō" [Who Has Custody of Amuro Namie's Son, Atsuhito?]. http://daikaibou.com/archives/2886.

Smith, Daniel Jordan. 2006. "Love and the Risk of HIV: Courtship, Marriage, Infidelity in Southeastern Nigeria." In Hirsch and Wardlow, *Modern Loves*, 135–56.

Smith, Daniel Jordan. 2008. "Intimacy, Infidelity, and Masculinity in Southeastern Nigeria." In *Intimacies: Love and Sex across Cultures*, edited by William R. Jankowiak, 224–44. New York: Columbia University Press.

Smith, Daniel Jordan. 2009. "Managing Men, Marriage, and Modern Love: Women's Perspectives on Intimacy and Male Infidelity in Southeastern Nigeria." In Cole and Thomas, *Love in Africa*, 157–80.

Smith, Robert. 1974. *Ancestor Worship in Contemporary Japan.* Stanford: Stanford University Press.

Smith, Robert. 1983. *Japanese Society: Tradition, Self, and the Social Order.* Cambridge: Cambridge University Press.

Smith, Robert. 1987. "Gender Inequality in Contemporary Japan." *Journal of Japanese Studies* 13(1): 1–25.

Smith, Robert, and Ella Lury Wiswell. 1982. *The Women of Suye Mura.* Chicago: University of Chicago Press.

Smock, Pamela J. 1993. "The Economic Costs of Marital Disruption for Young Women over the Past Two Decades." *Demography* 30(3): 353–71.

Smock, Pamela J. 1994. "Gender and the Short-Run Economic Consequences of Marital Disruption." *Social Forces* 73(1): 243–62.

Smock, Pamela J., Wendy D. Manning, and Sanjiv Gupta. 1999. "The Effect of Marriage and Divorce on Women's Economic Well-Being." *American Sociological Review* 64(6): 794–812.

Song, Jesook. 2009. *South Koreans in the Debt Crisis: The Creation of a Neoliberal Welfare Society.* Durham: Duke University Press.

Song, Jiyeoun. 2014. *Inequality in the Workplace: Labor Market Reform in Japan and Korea.* Ithaca: Cornell University Press.

Stanlaw, James. 2004. *Japanese English: Language and Culture Contact.* Hong Kong: University of Hong Kong Press.

Steiner, Kurt. 1950. "The Revision of the Civil Code of Japan: Provisions Affecting the Family." *Journal of Asian Studies* 9(2): 169–84.

Stewart, Abigail J., Anne P. Copeland, Nia Lane Chester, Janet E. Malley, and Nicole B. Barenbaum. 1997. *Separating Together: How Divorce Transforms Families.* New York: Guilford Press.

Strathern, Marilyn. 2005. *Kinship, Law and the Unexpected: Relatives Are Always a Surprise.* Cambridge: Cambridge University Press.

Sugimoto, Yoshio. 1999. "Making Sense of Nihonjinron." *Thesis Eleven* 57(1): 81–96.

Sugimoto, Yoshio. 2003. *An Introduction to Japanese Society,* 2nd ed. Cambridge: Cambridge University Press.

Sugimoto, Yoshio, and Ross E. Mouer 1980. "Reappraising Images of Japanese Society." *Social Analysis* 5/6:5–19.

Supreme Court of Japan. 2015. *Shihō tōkei nenpō 3 kaji-hen saikō saibansho jimu sōkyoku* [*Judicial Statistics Annual Report, Section 3: Households*]. Tokyo: Saikō saibansho jimu sōkyoku.

Swidler, Ann. 2001. *Talk of Love: How Culture Matters.* Chicago: University of Chicago Press.

Świtek, Beata. 2016. *Reluctant Intimacies: Japanese Eldercare in Indonesian Hands.* New York: Berghahn.

Tachibanaki, Toshiaki. 1987. "Labour Market Flexibility in Japan in Comparison with Europe and the US." *European Economic Review* 31 (3): 647–78.

Tachibanaki, Toshiaki. 2005. *Confronting Income Inequality in Japan: A Comparative Analysis of Causes, Consequences, and Reform.* Cambridge: MIT Press.

Tachibanaki, Toshiaki. 2006. "Inequality and Poverty in Japan." *Japanese Economic Review* 57(1): 1–27.

Tachibanaki, Toshiaki. 2010. *Muen shakai no shōtai—ketsuen chien shaen wa ikani hōkai shita ka* [*The Truth of a Society without Ties: Why Have Blood, Environmental, and Social Ties Collapsed?*]. Tokyo: PHP kenkyūjo.

Tahhan, Diana Adis. 2014. *The Japanese Family: Touch, Intimacy and Feeling.* Abingdon, UK: Routledge.

Takada, Shinobu. 2011. "Factors Determining the Employment of Single Mothers." *Japanese Economy* 38(2): 105–23.

Takahashi, Satsuki. 2018. "Fukushima oki ni ukabu 'mirai' to sono mirai" [The Future of "Fukushima Future"]. *Bunka junruigaku* 83(3): 441–58.

Takahashi, Shingo, Masumi Kawade, and Ryuta Ray Kato. 2009. "Spousal Tax Deduction, Social Security System and the Labor Supply of Japanese Married Women." Shiga University Center for Risk Research Working Paper Series: 1–32.

Takeda, Hiroko. 2004. *The Political Economy of Reproduction in Japan.* Abingdon, UK: Routledge.

Takeda, Hiroko. 2008. "Structural Reform of the Family and the Neoliberalization of Everyday Life in Japan." *New Political Economy* 13(2): 153–72.

Takemaru, Naoko. 2005. "Japanese Women's Perceptions of Sexism in Language." *Women and Language* 28(1): 39–48.

Takeyama, Akiko. 2016. *Staged Seduction: Selling Dreams in a Tokyo Host Club.* Stanford: Stanford University Press.

Takezawa, Junko. 2003. "Divorce Rates and Motives of Claims for Divorces in Japan." Presentation at Congress of the Japan Society of Home Economics.

Takita, Yōjirō. 2008. *Okuribito* [*Departures*]. Tokyo: Shochiku.

Tamaki, Teiko. 2014. "Live and Die in Solitude Away from the Family: Issues Relating to Unattended Death *Kodokushi* in Japan." *Housei Riron* 46(4): 203–18.

Tanaka, Hideo. 1980. "Legal Equality among Family Members in Japan: The Impact of the Japanese Constitution of 1946 on the Traditional Family System." *Southern California Law Review* 53(2): 611.

Tanase, Kazuyo. 2004. "Rikon no kodomo ni ataeru eikyō: jirei bunseki o tōshite" [The Effects of Divorce on Children: Case Analyses]. *Kyōto joshidaigaku gendai shakai kenkyū* 6:19–37.

Tanase, Kazuyo. 2010. *Rikon de kowareru kodomo-tachi shinri rinshō-ka kara no keikoku* [*Children Hurt by Divorce: Warnings from Psychologists*]. Tokyo: Kobunsha.

Tanase, Takao. 2010. "Post-Divorce Laws Governing Parent and Child in Japan." https://travel .state.gov/content/dam/childabduction/tanase_on_visitation_law_in_english.pdf.

Tanase, Takao. 2011. "Divorce and the Best Interest of the Child: Disputes Over Visitation and the Japanese Family Courts." *Pacific Rim Law and Policy Journal* 20(3): 563–88.

TBS Program Staff. 2006. *Jukunen rikon 100 no riyū* [*100 Reasons for Later-Life Divorce*]. Tokyo: Shōnensha.

Thomas, Lynne M., and Jennifer Cole. 2009. "Thinking Through Love in Africa." In Cole and Thomas, *Love in Africa*, 1–30.

Thorsten, Marie. 2009. "The Homecoming of Japanese Hostages from Iraq: Culturalism or Japan in America's Embrace?" *Asia-Pacific Journal* 22(4). http://www.japanfocus.org/-marie -thorsten/3157.

Toivonen, Tuukka, and Yuki Imoto. 2013. "Transcending Labels and Panics: The Logic of Japanese Youth Problems." *Contemporary Japan* 25(1): 61–86.

Toshitani, Nobuyoshi. 1994. "The Reform of Japanese Family Law and Changes in the Family System." *US-Japan Women's Journal* 6:66–82.

Tsubuku, Masako, and Philip Brasor. 1996. "The Value of a Family." *Japan Quarterly* 43(3): 79–87.

Tsutsui, Kiyoteru. 2018. *Rights Make Might: Global Human Rights and Minority Social Movements in Japan*. Oxford: Oxford University Press.

Tsuya, Noriko, Larry L. Bumpass, and Minja Kim Choe. 2000. "Gender, Employment, and Housework in Japan, South Korea, and the United States." *Review of Population and Social Policy* 9:195–220.

Tsuyuki, Yukihiko. 2010. *Otoko no tame no saikyō rikon-jutsu* [*The Best Divorce Strategies for Men*]. Tokyo: Metamoru shuppan.

Ueno, Chizuko. 1987. "The Position of Japanese Women Reconsidered." *Current Anthropology* 28(4) supplement: S75–S84.

Ueno, Chizuko. 2009. *Otoko ohitorisamadō* [*Men on Their Own*]. Tokyo: Hōken.

United States Department of State. 2007. "International Parental Abduction Japan." http://travel .state.gov/family/abduction/country/country_501.html. [As of 2019, this website is accessible through web.archive.org.]

Uno, Kathleen. 1991. "Women and Changes in the Household Division of Labor." *Recreating Japanese Women, 1600–1945*, edited by Gail Lee Bernstein, 17–41. Berkeley: University of California Press.

Upham, Frank K. 1987. *Law and Social Change in Postwar Japan*. Cambridge: Harvard University Press.

Ushida, Shigeru. 2016. "Fōramu: kodomo to hinkon, yōiku-hi" [Forum: Children, Poverty, and Child Support]. *Asahi Newspaper*, March 7, 2016.

Uunk, Wilfred. 2004. "The Economic Consequences of Divorce for Women in the European Union: The Impact of Welfare State Arrangements." *European Journal of Population* 20:251–85.

Vaporis, Constantine Nomikos. 2009. *Tour of Duty: Samurai, Military Service in Edo, and the Culture of Early Modern Japan*. Honolulu: University of Hawai'i Press.

Vaughn, Diane. 1990. *Uncoupling: Turning Points in Intimate Relationships*. New York: Vintage.

Vogel, Ezra F. 1971. *Japan's New Middle Class: The Salary Man and His Family in a Tokyo Suburb.* Berkeley: University of California Press.

Vogel, Ezra. 1979. *Japan as Number One: Lessons for America.* Cambridge: Harvard University Press.

Vogel, Suzanne Hall, with Steven K. Vogel. 2013. *The Japanese Family in Transition: From the Professional Housewife Ideal to the Dilemmas of Choice.* Lanham, MD: Rowman and Littlefield.

Wagatsuma, Hiroshi. 1977. "Aspects of the Contemporary Japanese Family: Once Confucian, Now Fatherless?" *Daedalus* 106(2): 181–210.

Wagatsuma, Sakae. 1950. "Democratization of the Family Relation in Japan." *Washington Law Review and State Bar Journal* 25(4): 405–29.

Waki, Mitsuo. 2009. *Zero kara hajimeru kekkon nyūmon* [*Introductory Handbook for Marriage*]. Tokyo: Bungeisha.

Wallerstein, Judith S., Julia M. Lewis, and Sandra Blakeslee. 2000. *The Unexpected Legacy of Divorce: The 25 Year Landmark Study.* New York: Hyperion.

Wardlow, Holly. 2006. *Wayward Women: Sexuality and Agency in a New Guinea Society.* Berkeley: University of California Press.

Watanabe, Junichi. 2004. *Otto toiu mono* [*A Person Called Husband*]. Tokyo: Shueisha.

Watanabe, Yozo, assisted by Max Rheinstein. 1963. "The Family and the Law: The Individualistic Premise and Modern Japanese Family Law." In *Law in Japan: The Legal Order in a Changing Society,* edited by A. T. von Mehren, 364–98. Cambridge: Harvard University Press.

West, Mark. 2011. *Lovesick Japan: Sex, Marriage, Romance, Law.* Ithaca: Cornell University Press.

Weston, Kath. 1991. *Families We Choose: Lesbians, Gays, Kinship.* New York: Columbia University Press.

White, Linda E. 2014. "Challenging the Heteronormative Family in the Koseki: Surname, Legitimacy, and Unmarried Mothers." In Chapman and Krogness, *Japan's Household Registration System and Citizenship,* 239–56.

White, Linda. 2018. *Gender and the Koseki in Contemporary Japan: Surname, Power, and Privilege.* Abingdon, UK: Routledge.

White, Merry. 1987. "The Virtue of Japanese Mothers: Cultural Definitions of Women's Lives." *Daedalus* 116(3): 149–63.

White, Merry Isaacs. 2002. *Perfectly Japanese: Making Families in an Era of Upheaval.* Berkeley: University of California Press.

Wietzman, Leonore J. 1985. *The Divorce Revolution: The Unexpected Social and Economic Consequences for Women and Children in America.* New York: Free Press.

Wilson, Ara. 2004. *The Intimate Economies of Bangkok: Tomboys, Tycoons, and Avon Ladies in the Global City.* Berkeley: University of California Press.

Yahoo News. 2009. "'Kyōdō shinken' ni sansei? Hantai?" [Do You Agree with Joint Custody? Oppose It?]. https://news.yahoo.co.jp/polls/domestic/3482/result.

Yamada, Ken. 2011. "Labor Supply Responses to the 1990s Japanese Tax Reforms." *Labour Economics* 18:539–46.

Yamada, Masahiro, and Momoko Shirakawa. 2008. *'Konkatsu' jidai* [*The Age of "Marriage Hunting"*]. Tokyo: Disukabā touentiwan.

Yamaguchi, Tomomi. 2006. "'Loser Dogs' and 'Demon Hags': Single Women in Japan and the Declining Birth Rate." *Social Science Japan Journal* 9(1): 109–14.

Yamauchi, Sayako. 2016. "Fōramu: yōiku-hi to shinken kodomo to hinkon" [Forum: Child Support and Custody, Children, and Poverty]. *Asahi Newspaper,* April 25, 2016.

Yan, Yunxiang. 2003. *Private Life under Socialism: Love, Intimacy, and Family Change in a Chinese Village, 1949–1999*. Stanford: Stanford University Press.

Yanagihara, Kuwako, and Gaku Ōtsuka. 2013. *Zettai kōkai shitakunai: yoku wakaru rikon sōdan* [*Definitely No Regrets: The Easy Guide to Divorce*]. Tokyo: Ikeda shoten.

Yang, Jie. 2015. *Unknotting the Heart: Unemployment and Therapeutic Governance in China.* Ithaca: Cornell University Press.

Yokoyama, Izumi, and Naomi Kodama. 2018. "Women's Labor Supply and Taxation: Analysis of the Current Situation Using Data." *Policy Research Institute, Ministry of Finance, Japan, Public Policy Review* 14(2): 267–300.

Yomiuri Newspaper. 1992. "Juri sareta tsuma no rikontodoke otto ga madoguchi de 'gōdatsu' moyasu" [Husband "Violently" Burns Wife's Divorce Notification Form at City Office Window]. November 10, 1992.

Yomiuri Newspaper. 1996. "Yakusho misu de rikon-todoke juri otto no fujurishinsei wasure" [Government Office Forgot a "Divorce Nonacceptance" Form Submitted by Husband]. July 27, 1996.

Yoshihama, Mieko, and Susan B. Sorenson. 1994. "Physical, Sexual, and Emotional Abuse by Male Intimates: Experiences of Women in Japan." *Violence and Victims* 9(1): 63–77.

Yoshihiko, Miki. 1996. "Jinsei an'nai: kekkon gokagetsu, betsu no josei to saikon shitai" [I've Been Married Five Months but Want to Marry Another Woman]. *Yomiuri Newspaper*, Osaka edition A17, October 16, 1996.

Young, Louise. 1998. *Japan's Total Empire: Manchuria and the Culture of Wartime Imperialism.* Berkeley: University of California Press.

Zelizer, Viviana. 2005. *The Purchase of Intimacy*. Princeton: Princeton University Press.

Zelizer, Viviana. 2010. "Caring Everywhere." In Boris and Parreñas, *Intimate Labors*, 267–79.

Zhou, Yanfei. 2008. "Boshi setai no 'ima': zōka yōin shūgyōritsu shūnyū-tō" [Single Mothers Today: Increasing Numbers, Employment Rates, and Income.] In *Boshi katei no haha e no shūgyō shien ni kansuru kenkyū*, edited by Japan Institute for Labour Policy and Training, 26–38. Tokyo: Japan Institute of Labour Policy and Training.

Zuhur, Sherifa. 2003. "Women and Empowerment in the Arab World." *Arab Studies Quarterly* 25(4): 17–38.

Index

Page numbers followed by "f" and "t" refer to figures and tables, respectively.